PRIESTHOOD BLESSINGS

A HIDDEN TREASURE
AND
A CROWNING PRIVILEGE

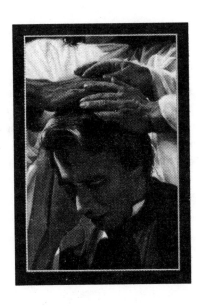

DONALD E. GOFF

Cover Artist: Liz Lemon
Courtesy of Foundation Arts, Provo, Utah
1-800-366-2781

DEDICATION

This book is dedicated to my father, Stillman Reese Goff, who as a High Priest was ordained after the order of the great Melchizedek himself. As such and as a natural patriarch, he gave me blessings inspired of heaven and also provided me with a beautiful example of a worthy and exemplary vessel whom God could and did honor with the wonderful gift of inspiration.

ISBN: 1-57636-042-3
Library of Congress Catalog Card Number: 97-68855

Typeset and Cover Design by:
SunRise Publishing, Orem, Utah

FOREWORD

So many things in the gospel are hidden treasures or gems that are unfortunately taken for granted. Yet those very things are more magnificent and beautiful than words can express. Priesthood blessings are one of these glorious things. They are a crowning privilege concealed from human view. In fact, they have by far of much greater worth and value than we are able to convey in words. Therefore, it is very difficult to do justice to this eminently wonderful subject, but it should be attempted as it can be fortifying to our faith and elevate our inner desires for righteousness.

Bruce R. McConkie explained, and it is a hidden treasure or gem, that "any person [from the least member to the greatest] who receives revelation . . . is a prophet, and can, as occasion requires and when guided by the Spirit, 'prophesy of all things.'" (*The Promised Messiah*, p.24) In other words, if we live up to our privileges, we will be prophets of God ourselves and enjoy great things and bless with much power and authority. Generally, it is in priesthood blessings that the brethren, who commune with the heavens, often act as revelators and reveal special, personal things which only God could reveal. By so doing, they have the greater enjoyments and rewards in this life. They can clearly see the big picture and touch and lift others. Enos, who himself was one of these special brethren, wrote: "And there were exceeding many prophets among us." (Enos 1:22) His son Jarom confirmed this. He said, "And there are many among us who have many revelations. . . ." (Jarom 1:4) This precious and glorious gift of gifts is available to all who have had the beautiful gift of the Holy Ghost bestowed upon them. For all who "have faith, have communion with the Holy Spirit, which maketh manifest unto the children of men, according to their faith." (Ibid.) And the greater the faith, the greater the revelations we as local members can enjoy.

And the result is, that there really are many good-hearted prophets of God in the land and all over the earth, even an "exceeding many" as in the days of Enos. In fact, "the true Church is or should be made up of prophets without number." (*The Millennial Messiah*, p.326) But as Elder McConkie also declared: "Most persons with the spirit of testimony, of inspiration, and of prophecy are prophets to themselves only, or to their families. Some are called to preside over and give inspired guidance to one organization or another," and some, as general authorities, are prophets of God to all the earth. (Ibid., p.25) But this book is about the great local men who dwell among us and are our neighbors—patriarchs and other wonderfully inspired men, and the thrilling, uplifting blessings they give.

This book is very faith-promoting. It is full of encouraging examples. And it offers insight and greater understanding of priesthood blessings and how to enjoy, recognize and speak by the spirit of revelation. It is especially written to the brethren—to those charged to give blessings in Israel and therefore be men of great inspiration on the earth. This includes all who bear the Higher Priesthood. But it is also full of encouragement for any faithful soul who dearly loves the Lord and values the sweet, endearing spiritual gifts richly poured out upon us from heaven.

As in any book or article written by anyone other than the Prophet, Seer and Revelator of the Church, this publication cannot be regarded as Church doctrine, but rather as the author's personal research into patriarchs, their special blessings and the beautiful, eternal blessings any Higher Priesthood holder can give. It is hoped that it will be helpful and beneficial to you in your discipleship. If it is, then the effort to put it together has been worth it. God bless you in the journey or adventure that awaits you in this book and in your lives, for God truly lives and dearly loves us all.

TABLE OF CONTENTS

INTRODUCTION

Spencer W. Kimball said, "These are happy days, the days of the patriarchs. . . ," local prophets of God who give us special blessings of enormous worth on earth and in heaven and for time and all eternity. (*Ensign*, October 1977, p.4) We are truly the most fortunate and the most blessed of all people on earth. For in the words of Thomas S. Monson, the beautiful blessings they give are "a rare and valuable gift"—"a precious and priceless personal treasure"—one of the greatest privileges of this or any dispensation. (*Ensign*, November 1986, pp.65-66) And as such they "verify the divinity of Christ and the truthfulness of the Church," declared James E. Faust, who also declared that "these sacred blessings also strengthen testimonies. . . ." *(1980 Devotional Speeches of the Year,* p.53) They fortify us with promises from the great God of heaven, who dearly loves us with a greater love than we will ever know in this life. And the men who give us these inspired blessings are literally prophets of God in the midst of the people.

Joseph Smith, Jr., the head of this dispensation, gave the first patriarchal blessings ever given in the latter days. "He had every right to give patriarchal blessings," declared Joseph Fielding Smith, "because, not only was he a high priest and apostle, but a patriarch, in fact, holding all the keys and all the rights and privileges of the priesthood." ("Address of President Joseph Fielding Smith," June 15, 1956, p.2) In fact, every President of the Church is a patriarch and can give patriarchal blessings. Joseph F. Smith declared, "I hold the right, the keys and the authority of the Patriarchal Priesthood in the Church," because he was the only man on earth at the time, who as President and Prophet to all the earth, held all the keys and privileges of every office in the kingdom. (*Gospel Doctrine*, p.146) For "the Presidency of the High Priesthood, after the order of Melchizedek, have a right to officiate in all the offices in the church." (D&C 107:9)

But the first man to be ordained as Patriarch to the Church in this dispensation was Joseph Smith, Sr., the Prophet's father. He was filled with the beautiful spirit of his high office, so much so that Wilford Woodruff declared that "all men who were acquainted with Father Joseph Smith know that when he laid his hands upon a man's head it seemed as if the heavens and the hearts of men were open to him." (*Journal of Discourses* 12:277) This great prophet of the Lord told Bathsheba Bigler in 1839 in her patriarchal blessing that thou "shalt have a son who shall be . . . a prophet and seer."

(Gregory Prince, *Power From on High,* p.181) This good lady later married George A. Smith and their son, John Henry Smith became an apostle of Christ, or as foretold, he became a great prophet and seer of the Lord in the Church. (*1995-96 Church Almanac,* p.48) Similarly, Nanny Longstroth Richards was promised in 1846 by the Patriarch John Smith that "Prophets, seers, and revelators shall proceed forth from thee and thy name shall be had in honorable remembrance in the house of Israel". (Lucile C. Tate, *LeGrand Richards, Beloved Apostle,* p.2) She became the mother of George F. Richards and grandmother to Stephen L. Richards and LeGrand Richards, three future apostles and prophets of the Lord Jesus Christ. (Ibid.) LeGrand once remarked, "It is amazing with what degree of accuracy Patriarchal Blessings are fulfilled depending on the faithfulness of the recipients." (*Just to Illustrate,* pp.213-214) They bear a powerful witness that Jesus is the Christ and that He loves us enough to speak to us through His servants, the prophets of the Lord who are called in each Stake of Zion.

A thirteen-year-old boy named George Albert Smith was told the following through a local stake patriarch, Zebedee Coltrin, ". . .And thou shalt become a mighty prophet in the midst of the sons of Zion. And the angels of the Lord shall administer unto you, . . . And thou shalt be wrapt in the visions of the heavens . . . for thou art destined to become a mighty man before the Lord, for thou shalt become a mighty apostle in the Church and kingdom of God upon the earth, for none of thy father's family shall have more power with God than thou shalt have, for none shall excel thee, for thy reward shall be great in the heavens. . . ." (Joseph Fielding Smith, *The Instructor,* November 1963, p.383) Note at the early age of only thirteen, he was told he would be a "mighty prophet," have "visions," "become a mighty apostle in the Church and Kingdom of God" and that "none of thy father's family shall have more power with God than thou shalt have, for none shall excel thee." Of his "father's family," his dad was John Henry Smith who became a second counselor in the First Presidency. His grandfather, George A. Smith, was a first counselor in the First Presidency. In other words, George Albert Smith was told, without realizing it, at the tender age of thirteen that he would be President of the Church and "a mighty prophet," that is, the highest of all the prophets of God in his day and time. He fulfilled this beautiful revelation. It is a matter of well-known history that he became Prophet and President of the Church from 1945 to his death in 1951.

As a twenty-six year old, Rudger Clawson was told in a patriarchal blessing by William J. Smith, a local patriarch, that his "faith shall increase and thou shalt have power to prevail with God like the brother of Jared, until thou shalt behold God face to face," for "thou shalt be a mighty minister of Jesus and herald of salvation to the nations afar off . . . and lead them like unto Moses, the great leader of Israel." (*A Ministry of Meetings,* p.200) These mighty words fit the very man who did, in fact, became a mighty leader in the kingdom of God. Note how he was compared to two different prophets. This man as an apostle and prophet served in the Quorum of the Twelve for forty-four years. This remarkable prophecy was made about fifteen years before his call to this presiding council in the Church. (*1995-96 Church Almanac,* p.48) Who but God would have known?

Patriarchal blessings are not merely beautiful, encouraging words to help us to try to live better lives, they are revelations or the authoritative words of local prophets of the living God, which is the word of God Himself to us on a very personal basis.

According to a statement of the First Presidency of the Church, "Patriarchal blessings [are] an inspired declaration of the lineage of the recipient, and also where so moved upon by the Spirit, an inspired and prophetic statement of the life mission of the recipient, together with such blessings, cautions, and admonitions as the patriarch may be prompted to give. . . . The realization of all promised blessings is conditioned upon faithfulness to the gospel of our Lord. . . ." (Bruce R. McConkie, *Mormon Doctrine,* p.558) And James E. Faust declared, "These blessings are a powerful witness of the mission of the Lord Jesus Christ in bringing exaltation to each of us." (*1980 Devotional Speeches of the Year,* p.53) I believe that with all my heart. They are so important. They seal us up to all eternity. This book is dedicated to the end that a greater understanding and appreciation for them may be portrayed and realized in a way that is edifying and encourages greater love and devotion for the cause of our Father in heaven.

My own patriarchal blessing obviously fits me to a tee. Much of my life can be seen in it. Although it is too personal to share, I can say that if there was ever a prophet, it was John K. Edmunds of the Chicago Illinois Stake back in 1967. He was such a great man he was later called to be a Regional Representative of the Twelve and later as President of the Salt Lake Temple. The beautiful blessing he gave me will never be forgotten.

I joined the Church on April 30th of 1966. When I found out that I could have a personal revelation from God through a patriarch, I was thrilled and wanted one. But I was told I had to wait for one year. I thought, if I had to wait a year, I didn't want to wait one day longer, so I began to fast and pray and plead with the Lord to let me have this special blessing on April 30th of 1967, exactly one year from my baptism. But I didn't tell anyone about it.

This special day, the anniversary of my baptism, was on a Sunday. Two great miracles took place that day. I didn't even know I needed the bishop's permission, and I didn't ask him about it. However, he left the stand during priesthood meeting and took me into his office that very morning and without explanation or even asking me a single question wrote out a recommend for a patriarchal blessing. I was surprised and dearly pleased that God had heard me and had given his special servant the inspiration to do this. I was so shy I probably would not have even asked anyone about how to get a patriarchal blessing. God arranged this for me.

Later that morning I showed Brother Edmunds my recommend. I lacked the confidence to even utter a word to him. He looked at my recommend and suggested next Thursday, and I said that would be okay. Then he looked away for a while, perhaps a minute or two. Then looking back at me with a beautiful smile on his face he said, "We will have the blessing today." An answer to my prayer! I was given what I was too shy to ask for, by revelation from a local prophet and inspired servant of the Lord.

At the appointed time that day he told me that it was sometimes frightening to be a prophet before the Lord. He explained that he had to take courage and be brave to declare the words he felt prompted to express. He began the blessing and while he spoke a question arose in my mind and heart which grew stronger and stronger and stronger. I never said a word, but felt this yearning desire to know about a special concern. Brother Edmunds then answered my question in beautiful language, which moved me greatly. He continued and finally sealed it to be binding on me for all eternity by virtue of his high office and based upon my continued obedience to God. Then two weeks later I received my written copy in the mail and the whole experience was relived. That is, I felt the question overwhelm me again and then the answer was again repeated to me with a great feeling of awe and wonder. I had received two powerful witnesses that those special words were very important, perhaps, more important than I will ever know in this life.

All this served to strengthen my testimony which has continued as I have enjoyed the beautiful blessings promised to me, and marvelled at how accurately they have been, and are being, fulfilled in my life. I can certainly see why Gordon B. Hinckley declared that patriarchal blessings are "such a precious and wonderful thing," because they truly are. (*Ensign,* October 1996, p.73) ". . .A patriarchal blessing is a very unique and remarkable privilege. . . ," according to James E. Faust. (*1980 Devotional Speeches of the Year,* p.53) Truly, "these are happy days, the days of the patriarchs. . . ." (Spencer W. Kimball, *Ensign,* October 1977, p.4) We are so fortunate to live in a day of local, as well as general, prophets to bless and encourage us. Bruce R. McConkie explained that "Those who partake of the fruits of true prophets will find them sweet, full of flavor, delicious to the taste, and desirable to the soul. . . ." (*A New Witness for the Articles of Faith,* p.15) It is hoped that this book will do some justice to these beautiful realities and of our ability to develop and nurture the glory and majesty of the gift of the Holy Ghost in our own lives.

CHAPTER ONE

BLESSINGS FOR THE FAITHFUL

"I wish to pay tribute," said James E. Faust, "to the faithful men holding this great calling and ordination [that of a patriarch]. They are often among the most humble and faithful of our brethren. These chosen men live lives that entitle them to the inspiration of heaven." (*1980 Devotional Speeches of the Year,* p.53) Revelation is a great privilege and a blessing and a precious gift that we should cherish.

As an example of the great prophetic powers established in the Church, through the Melchizedek High Priesthood, note the following. When Matthew Cowley was only six years old, Luther C. Burnham, a local stake patriarch in Mancos, Colorado, stated the following in Matthew's patriarchal blessing, "In your extreme youth you will go to the uttermost bounds of the earth to preach the gospel. You will become an interpreter among the people," which he did in a marvelous way through the gift of tongues in the South Pacific. Because Elder Cowley at age seventeen could not learn the language, the Lord, therefore, gave him the gift—a gift so beautiful that he was commissioned by the leaders of the Church as a very young Elder to translate the Standard Works into the Maori language. (*Matthew Cowley Speaks,* p.424-425) He was also told, "Thou shalt live to be a mighty man in Israel, for thou art of royal seed, the seed of Jacob through Joseph. Thou shalt become a great and mighty man in the eyes of the Lord and become an ambassador of Christ to the uttermost bounds of the earth. Your understanding shall be great and your wisdom reach the heavens. . . . The Lord will give you the mighty faith of the brother of Jared, for thou shalt know that He lives and that the gospel of Jesus Christ is true, even in your youth." (Mark E. Peterson, *Children of Promise: The Lamanites: Yesterday and Today,* pp.81-82) Matthew Cowley did go "to the uttermost bounds of the earth" as "an ambassador of Christ." He served in New Zealand and the Pacific Islands as a young Elder, then as a High Priest of God and Mission President, and later as an Apostle of the Lord Jesus Christ. He had such great faith given to him that he performed many miracles, was loved and revered and became a very great and mighty man before the Lord as foreseen by the patriarch when Matthew was only a little boy of six. (Henry A. Smith, *Matthew Cowley, Man of Faith*)

Rebecca Rose, as a seventeen-year-old, fasted and prayed and exercised her faith. And in spite of a difficult day, she received a beautiful blessing from heaven through a patriarch. She wrote that her patriarchal blessing "was a personal miracle. It seemed that the patriarch knew me so completely, even better than I knew myself. I knew he was speaking for Heavenly Father, and when he spoke, I felt the assurance that Heavenly Father did know me. He heard my prayers. He knew my name. After the patriarch had finished speaking, I felt so good about myself. Nothing has ever given me such an awesome and indescribable feeling before." (*The New Era*, June 1995, p.54) This girl had paid the price of preparation and faith and the God of Heaven was able to pour out His sweet, endearing spirit and influence upon her to the point that she knew He lived and loved her personally and she considered this special and unique occasion to be "one of the best experiences of [her] life." (Ibid.)

Thomas S. Monson said, "Remember, your patriarchal blessing is your passport to peace in this life. It is a Liahona of light to guide you unerringly to your heavenly home." (*Ensign,* September 1993, p.71) As an example, LeGrand Richards explained:

> If we do not know where we are going, then we are just like a ship in the ocean without a rudder, without anyone to steer it. We are tossed to and fro with the wind and the waves. But if we understand where we came from, why we are here, and where we are going, then we are more likely to reach the desired port. That is really the purpose of a patriarchal blessing, to be able to interpret and reveal to us, through the inspiration of the Almighty, why we are here and what is expected of us that we might fill the measure of our creation here upon the earth." (*The New Era*, February 1977, p.4)

At a different time he told of an experience his grandfather had which provided that grandfather with the extraordinary power of a revealed faith to do something truly remarkable. He wrote:

> You will recall that in the early days of the gathering of the Saints it was considered as good as an insurance policy when a company of Latter-day Saints embarked on a vessel crossing the Atlantic. I recall reading in my grandfather's diary of a time when the boat upon which he was sailing was in great jeopardy, so much so that the captain of the boat came to him and pleaded with him to intercede with the Lord in behalf of the boat and passengers. My grandfather, remembering that he had been promised that he should have power over the elements, walked out on the deck of the boat

and raised his hands to high heaven and rebuked the sea and the waves, and they were immediately calmed. And the appreciation of the captain of the boat was so great that he offered Grandfather the use of his private quarters during the balance of the journey." (G. LaMont Richards, *LeGrand Richards Speaks,* p.39)

LeGrand, himself, was blessed by his dad, a local stake patriarch at the age of eight. He was told:

LeGrand, my son . . . thou hast not come here upon earth by chance, but in fulfillment of the decrees of the Almighty to accomplish a great labor in the upbuilding of God's kingdom. . . . Thou shalt be able to fill a useful mission in the gathering of scattered Israel, the establishment of Zion, and the redemption of the dead. . . . Many shall seek thy counsels and be benefitted and blessed thereby. The power of God shall be made manifest through thee and thy ministrations. Under thy hands the sick shall be healed, the bowed down shall be cheered up and comforted, and many shall receive blessings at thy hand, both spiritual and temporal . . . friends [shall be raised up] on every hand, whose benediction and blessings shall follow thee through life; and thou shalt be exalted among thy fellows, and if thou shalt live for it, thou shalt preside in the midst of the Lord's people." (*LeGrand Richards: Beloved Apostle,* p.1)

Note that he would greatly benefit others by comforting, cheering, healing and counseling with great God-given power. And he would "accomplish a great labor" and "be exalted" among his fellows, and "preside in the midst of the Lord's people." (Ibid.) Certainly, as one of the most well beloved apostles for over twenty-four years, he did those very things and was a remarkable man of God. He was, as an eight-year-old, a child of promise who fulfilled his divine destiny as foreordained and foretold in the prophetic statements of his father. Elder Richards commented, ". . .it is a miracle to me that he should have been able to so fully indicate my mission and calling in life. It seems to be like writing history in advance." (G. LaMont Richards, *LeGrand Richards Speaks,* p.247)

Patriarchal blessings personally tell us what God expects of us. But we will never experience the blessings unless we do our part. When the original Twelve Apostles of our risen Lord in this dispensation were chosen and ordained by the Three Witnesses, some beautiful priesthood blessings were bestowed upon them through the spirit of prophecy and revelation. The following are some examples of the words spoken and recorded on the day they were given, "he shall be like unto Enoch . . . he shall be called great . . . he shall see the Savior . . . and shall behold heavenly messages . . . he shall be made perfect in faith; and that the deaf shall hear, the lame shall walk, the blind shall see, and greater things than these shall he do . . . the nations shall tremble before him. He shall hear the voice of God . . . he shall be mighty in the hands of God, and shall convince thousands . . . and be able to do wonders in the midst of this generation. . . ." (*Deseret News Weekly,* December 27, 1851, p.14) These blessings were as great and glorious, I suppose, as any ever given by anyone in this dispensation.

But a number of these men never fulfilled these blessings because of apostasy. Since prophecy is a divine declaration of our potential, and is not fortune telling, the fulfillment depends on our faith and obedience. Hence, we can easily lose those blessings by neglect or carelessness. Wilford Woodruff said:

> After the first quorum was called of God; after they had had the ministration of angels and even the power of God manifested, some yielded to temptation. . . , they stopped praying and went to merchandising. They stopped serving God, and took a decided stand against the prophet whom God had raised up to lay the foundation of this Church and kingdom. What were the consequences? It sent them to perdition. Their power fell like lightening from the heaven. Their priesthood was taken from them, and sealed upon the heads of other men. . . . With all the light they had, with all the power they had, with all the manifestations they had from God out of heaven, they turned from these things and rejected them. Those were days of sorrow to me and to those who remained faithful; for one-half of the quorum fell . . . and were cut off the Church and they today are in the spirit world, without the priesthood, without the crown, without their glory, and without celestial blessings that were promised them on condition of faithfulness. (G. Homer Durham, *Discourses of Wilford Woodruff,* pp.97-98)

But "what shall we do with these promises, there are no conditions in the blessings given to the Twelve, they were blessed to do a great work even to the coming of Christ, and several have apostatized; how shall we account for these failures? All blessings promised by the Priesthood, which had come down from the heavens, are conditional, no matter whether expressed or implied . . . ," that is, "faithfulness in the part of the receiver of blessings was requisite to ensure the blessings promised," otherwise all is lost or forfeited. (*Deseret News Weekly,* December 27, 1851, p.14)

I know of a man who was promised he would be a great high priest in the Zion of God in the last days, preside over a Temple of the Most High

God and that his name would be had in honor remembrance before the Presidency of the Church. However, his choices put him out of the Church and far away from the sweet experiences of an endearing spiritual life. He will simply never fulfill those possibilities, because he sadly sold them for a mess of pottage, that is, for nothing of any consequence.

In early March of 1930, when Howard W. Hunter was about twenty-two years old, he was blessed of heaven prophetically by George T. Wride, a local stake patriarch, who said to him among other things, "Thy strength shall be turned to Zion, and thou shalt support her institutions and become a tie and a security to the great church that shall shelter God's people." (Eleanor Knowles, *Howard W. Hunter,* p.311) Howard W. Hunter was a Bishop at thirty-two, a Stake President ten years later and an Apostle less than ten years after that. He served as an apostle of the Lord Jesus Christ, a prophet, seer and revelator for over thirty-four years and then eventually became President of the Church. (*1995-96 Church Almanac,* p.14)

The patriarch also told this great man of destiny, "Thou shalt lend thy talents to the church and shall sit in her councils and thou shalt be known for thy wisdom and thy righteous judgments." And he would be "a priest of the Most High God." He was one "whom the Lord foreknew" and had shown "strong leadership among the host of heaven" and had been ordained "to perform an important work in mortality." (Ibid., pp.227, 71) Certainly, Howard W. Hunter was faithful and true, therefore, he beautifully fulfilled the inspired blessing given him.

Victor L. Ludlow explained that, "A patriarchal blessing is sometimes compared to a 'road map of life' in that it indicates general directions, destinations, and obstacles. The details of the actual journey, however, are left to the individual. Thus it is imperative that the person remain spiritually in tune so he or she can know how to follow the course God has outlined. Also, the promises of a patriarchal blessing are almost all conditional upon continued righteousness. If one does not heed the counsel given by God through his ordained servants and is not worthy for the companionship of the Holy Spirit, one may detour from the journey that God would desire of him or her, the rewards and promises may be forfeited, and the person's divine destiny may not be met." (*Promises and Practices of the Restored Gospel,* p.352)

For example, one older lady asked her bishop why her patriarchal blessing was not fulfilled. She was promised that her future husband would become, in effect, a great and beautiful man and the president of a Temple, yet the man she chose to marry was a nonmember and had no interest in the Church. He was then seventy-two years old and still had no interest in the

Church. The Bishop told her she married the wrong man. This she acknowledged. She then admitted that she had rebelled against the Church and her parents as a teenager and married this nonmember against their advice and counsel, because she would not have anyone tell her what to do. The man she knew she should have married was at that very time a great and beautiful man, even the president of a Temple. Her rebelliousness had robbed her of her divine potential and her birthright. She had sold her blessing and her highest mission on earth for a mess of pottage. (Bernell Christensen, "After the Trial of Your Faith," tape, Covenant Communications, Inc.)

"To look upon a patriarch [or any other priesthood holder for that matter] as a fortune-teller," declared John A. Widtsoe, "is an offense to the Priesthood; the patriarch only indicates the gifts the Lord would give us, if we labor for them." (G. Homer Durham, *Evidences and Reconciliations,* p.323) In other words, "They must be earned. Otherwise they are but empty words." (Ibid.) That is, "they rise to their highest value when used as ideals, specific possibilities toward which we may strive throughout life." (Ibid.) Joseph Smith, Sr., the first Patriarch to the Church, said, "If you live for them, they shall all come upon you, and more." Brigham Young commented, "Live for the blessings you desire, and you will obtain them, if you do not suffer selfishness, pride, or the least alienation from the path of true virtue and holiness to creep into your hearts." (*Journal of Discourses* 8:55)

Brigham Young lamented by saying:

> It grieves me to see men who have believed the Gospel, forsaken the land of their nativity for the sake of life and salvation, endured all they have in coming here, and then, for a paltry sum of money, sacrifice their salvation. Such men cannot be saved in the celestial kingdom of God; they may receive their endowments, but they will do them no good; they may read over their Patriarchal blessings every day, but they will do them no good. No man or woman can receive life everlasting, only upon the principle of strict obedience to the requirements of the celestial law of heaven. . . ." (*Journal of Discourses* 3:118)

In the words of John Taylor: "It is no little boy's play that we are engaged in, it is a life-long service, and that life will last while eternity endures." (*Journal of Discourses* 17:177) Hence, there is a serious warning, if we fail to heed counsel from on High. That is, we stand on dangerous ground. As the author John L. Ward expressed it, "Those who follow lives contrary to their patriarchal blessings jeopardize their exaltation by not following God's will." (*Is There a Patriarch in the Home?*, p.63)

blessings. He would give a blessing, but it was predicated on "if you will not do this" or "if you will cease doing that." And he said, "I watched those men to whom my father gave 'iffy' blessings, and I saw that many of them did not heed the warning that my father as a patriarch had given, and the blessings were never received because they did not comply." (Clyde J. Williams, *The Teachings of Harold B. Lee,* pp.80-81)

You know, this started me thinking. I went back into the Doctrine and Covenants and began to read the "iffy" revelations that have been given to the various brethren in the Church. If you want to have an exercise in something that will startle you, read some of the warnings that were given through the Prophet Joseph Smith to Thomas B. Marsh [and others]—warnings which, had they heeded, some would not have fallen by the wayside. But because they did not heed, and they didn't clear up their lives, they fell by the wayside, and some had to be dropped from membership in the Church. (Ibid.)

John D. Lee, who was executed for his part in the Mountain Meadows massacre, was warned in his patriarchal blessing years earlier that "no power shall hinder [him from receiving great and beautiful blessings] except the shedding of innocent blood or consenting thereto. . . ." (Juanita Brooks, *John Doyle Lee: Zealot—Pioneer Builder—Scapegoat,* p.43) If he had heeded this inspired counsel, he would have spared himself the worst disaster of his life something that haunted him and brought agony to his soul, for John D. Lee participated in the illegal and unlawful murder of some civilians and innocent people were killed in the fray. The counsels of God are not to be disregarded without consequences, and sometimes those consequences are tragic. "For behold, the Lord hath said: I will not succor my people in the day of their transgression; but I will hedge up their ways that they prosper not; and their doings shall be a stumbling block before them." (Mosiah 7:29)

John W. Taylor gave the following counsel to patriarchs in a General Conference in 1902. He said:

> I wish to say a word or two to our brethren the Patriarchs. I would feel it to be a good thing when they place their hands upon the heads of this people to bless them, if they shall feel so impressed, to conclude their blessings something like this: "I seal these blessings upon your head, according to your faith and your diligence in keeping the commandments of the Lord." The Patriarchs have the gift of being prophets, seers and revelators, to reveal the mind and will of God and portray unto the faithful their future lives, and I believe it would be pleasing unto the Lord if they would

seal all blessings that they give in a manner similar to the one I have suggested, as they shall be led by the Holy Spirit. Then there can be no disappointment on the part of the family or friends of those who shall, after
receiving a patriarchal blessing, turn from the truth and fight against God;
for they shall see that these blessings are conditioned upon their keeping
the commandments of God. (*Conference Report,* April 1902, p.44)

When the covenant people of the Lord transgress, the Lord says, "For
instead of blessings, ye, by your own works, bring cursings . . . upon your
own heads, by your follies, . . . which you practice before me, saith the
Lord." (D&C 124:48) On the other hand, to the righteous are wonderful
blessings promised.

Joseph Smith, Sr., the first Presiding Patriarch in this dispensation,
declared the following in a patriarchal blessing to a righteous and solid,
good-hearted young man by the name of Lorenzo Snow:

> Thou hast a great work to perform. . . . Thou shalt become a mighty
> man. Thou shalt have . . . power to rend the vail [veil] and see Jesus
> Christ . . . there shall not be a mightier man on earth than thou, thy faith
> shall increase and grow stronger till it shall become like Peter's—thou shalt
> restore the sick; the diseased shall send to thee their aprons and handker-
> chiefs and by thy touch their owners shall be made whole. The dead shall
> rise and come forth at thy bidding. . . . Thou shalt have long life . . . yet not
> be old; age shall not come upon thee; the vigor of thy mind shall not be
> abated and the vigor of thy body shall be preserved . . . . No power shall be
> able to take thy life as long as thy life shall be useful to the children of
> men." (*The Instructor,* June 1967, p.221)

This remarkable prophecy was given to this young man at the age of
twenty-two. He had just barely joined the Church and was unknown to anyone except the Lord. Yet he proved himself the man of God that he was and
fulfilled the blessing. He did indeed do a great work and certainly there was
no mightier man on earth then he while serving as Prophet and President to
the whole Church and all the world. He healed the sick and in the ways spec-
ified in the blessing. He called forth the dead, his life was spared by a
miracle and he was restored and lived long in the earth with vigor of mind
and body. But the crowning fulfillment was seeing Christ, the Son of God
and the Redeemer of mankind. He told his granddaughter Alice Young Pond,
"'He stood right here [in the Temple], about three feet above the floor. It
looked as though He stood on a plate of solid gold.' Grandpa told me what a
glorious personage the Savior is and described His hands, feet, countenance

and beautiful White Robes, all of which were of such a glory of whiteness and brightness that he could hardly gaze upon Him." (N. B. Lundwall, *Temples of the Most High,* p.149)

Sterling W. Sill was given a remarkable patriarchal blessing at the age of twenty through James Henry Linford of Kaysville, Utah. He was told, "In preaching the gospel your tongue shall be loosed to your astonishment." (*The Nine Lives of Sterling W. Sill: An Autobiography,* pp.249-250) Both in and out of the Church, Elder Sill received recognition. He even had standing ovations for some of the beautiful and awe-inspiring addresses he had given, which at times were so wonderful that even he was astonished by them in fulfillment of the blessing. Patriarch Linford also said, "You will live to see many great and wonderful things transpire in your natural life." (Ibid., p.251) When he was born, the Wright Brothers had not yet made their first flight. There were no cars, no radios, no mechanical refrigerators, no television sets, no planes. The world was just on the verge of some of its greatest discoveries, and within his lifetime, the greatest knowledge explosion the world has ever known took place. Truly many great and wonderful things came to pass as promised. Elder Sill was also told that he would be a convincing servant of God and live long on the earth (he lived to be ninety-one years old). (Ibid., p.254) He was admonished to prepare himself for positions of honor and trust for he would become "a leader among men." (Ibid., p.252) In fulfillment of this he held many impressive positions both in the Church and in the world and at times was considered to be legendary—so remarkable were some of his accomplishments. He also later became a general authority of the Church and as such continued being a great blessing to his fellowman. (Ibid., pp.247-255)

When Alma Sonne was seven years old, Patriarch O. N. Liljenquist told him he would "live long upon the earth and be a messenger of life and salvation unto tens of thousands of the human race. . . ." (Conway B. Sonne, *A Man Named Alma: The World of Alma Sonne,* p.61) Certainly as a general authority this was truly the case. The patriarch continued that it would be his lot to be "a leader among your brethren, and a mighty man of God . . . ," and his prophetic blessing declared that "the heavens shall be opened up unto thee and you shall gaze upon the Celestial world, hear the voice of the Redeemer [and], behold his countenance. . . ." (Ibid.) Alma Sonne was noted for bestowing beautiful blessings with a beautiful feeling upon others. He was a prophet in the midst of the people—"a leader" and "a mighty man of God." His future goodness was foretold by the patriarch.

Another example of the great blessing power of patriarchs was in 1903 when John Ashman, a local stake patriarch, declared in a patriarchal blessing to a thirty-two year old stake president, Alonzo Hinckley, "Your spirit is a noble spirit of the House of Abraham, and Prince of the tribe of Ephraim. If you continue faithful in this calling, wherein you are called to labor, you will accomplish much good in your day and generation. You already have done a great work. And if you continue to labor with the zeal with which you have started, you will be numbered with the Twelve Apostles of the Church of Jesus Christ of Latter-day Saints." (Bryant S. Hinckley, *The Faith of Our Pioneer Fathers,* pp.234-235) Elder Hinckley had a hard time accepting this promise so he never mentioned it. He felt it could never happen. However thirty years later, he was ordained an apostle. (Ibid.)

George A. Seamon, Alonzo Hinckley's first counselor in the Millard Stake Presidency at the time, who recorded and witnessed this inspired declaration, wrote, "As I recall, it was at the first Stake conference, after we, with the late Thomas C. Callister, were set apart to preside over the Millard Stake of Zion. I remember the earnestness of the aged Patriarch when he asked if he might confer upon you the blessing which was in his heart to give you. I acted as scribe, and felt the inspiration that prompted the words of the blessing. I have waited patiently for their fulfillment, knowing that you have unceasingly followed the admonition given therein, and by your labors merited those blessings and even greater ones." (Ibid., p.235) This letter was written in 1935 after Alonzo Hinckley was ordained to be an apostle of the Lord Jesus Christ.

One great individual remarked that she, as a young girl, was told by a patriarch that she would "come to be known in the Church of Jesus Christ of Latter-day Saints," and that her "name would be respected." (*Conference Report,* October 1929, p.85) She was Mary Anderson who became a general president of the Primary. She declared in general conference that all the "blessings which have been pronounced upon my head have been literally fulfilled." (Ibid.)

When Gordon B. Hinckley was eleven years old he was blessed by Patriarch Thomas E. Callister, who said he would "become a mighty and valiant leader in the midst of Israel," which he most certainly is, as an apostle and member of the Twelve for about twenty years and finally holding the most important position on earth as the Prophet of the Living God to all the earth. (Sheri L. Dew, *Go Forward with Faith: The Biography of Gordon B. Hinckley,* p.60 and *1995-96 Church Almanac,* p.15) The patriarch continued, "The Holy Priesthood shall be thine to enjoy and thou shalt minister in the midst of Israel as only those who are called of God. Thou shalt ever be a messenger of peace; the nations of the earth shall hear thy voice and be brought to a knowledge of the truth by the wonderful testimony which thou shalt bear." (Ibid., p.60) This kind of blessing to an eleven year old boy was obviously meant for a future general authority of the Church who would benefit "nations" with his "wonderful testimony" which I have enjoyed and felt many times as he bore it in general conference.

A family friend, Graham Dodd, who passed away a few years ago had a beautiful patriarchal blessing. He was told he would not only shelter and benefit his own family, but others would need and be blessed by him, which included my own daughter. He was also told as an Elder, among other things, that he would advance in the priesthood, preside as a quorum leader, hold high and important offices and be a president both in the church and in civic organizations. And every sentence came true. He advanced from elder to seventy and then to what Rudger Clawson, an earlier apostle of Christ, called "the great and glorious office of a high priest." (*Conference Report,* October 1917, p.28) He was an Elder's Quorum President, and as a High Priest, he held what Joseph F. Smith called "the office of presidency in the Melchizedek Priesthood" and "in the Church." (*Conference Report,* October 1904, pp.3-4 and October 1899, p.73) He served as a presiding high priest or a counselor in a Bishopric, which is the presidency over the Aaronic Priesthood as well as all members of the Ward, and President of the National Kidney Foundation of Utah, President of the Kirton and McConkie Law Firm and President of another group. He lived a full, rich, involved life and was nothing less than a great and good man. Many of the wonderful things he did were in secret and God shall reward him openly for them. But God knew his heart and how it would manifest in loving, personable ways and contribute to the lives of others. Hence, the Lord's servant, one of the inspired patriarchs, could act in his prophetic office and declare some of the specifics of his useful and productive life before they took place.

Spencer W. Kimball declared, "The patriarch is a prophet entitled to the revelations of the Lord. . . . He . . . may also pour out blessings that are prophetic to the individual for his life." (*Teachings of Spencer W. Kimball,* p.504) And I believe with Theodore M. Burton, a former Seventy, that "if one prepares himself by prayer and fasting prior to receiving such a blessing, the patriarch may receive greater inspiration. . . . as he reaches through the veil in his search for light and knowledge." (*God's Greatest Gift,* p.122) In other words, the more worthy, receptive, prayerful and faithful we are, the greater the likelihood the Lord will reveal unforeseen promises to the man of God to help, comfort and inspire us. "Such individual blessings," declared

James E. Faust, "are part of the continuous revelation that we claim as members of The Church of Jesus Christ of Latter-day Saints." (*Ensign,* November 1995, p.62) It is a great witness to the divinity of the Church. However, "In order to receive the fulfillment of our patriarchal blessings," Elder Faust continued, "we should treasure in our hearts the precious words they contain, ponder them, and so live that we will obtain the blessings in mortality and a crown of righteousness in the hereafter." (Ibid., p.63) And with such a testimony of Christ and His great love for us, we can feel more assured, more encouraged, comforted and dearly loved of heaven, and more prepared to fight the battles of life because of it. The great blessings are a unique and remarkable privilege that should be cherished and honored.

CHAPTER TWO

PATRIARCHS AND THE POWER TO CONDITIONALLY SEAL WONDERFUL BLESSINGS ON EARTH AND IN HEAVEN FOR TIME AND ALL ETERNITY

All patriarchs are living prophets of God and hold the same authority as each other within their assigned districts. But the Patriarch to the Church holds a hereditary right to office not held by the local brethren. "The order of this priesthood [this special calling of being the Presiding Patriarch] was confirmed to be handed down from father to son, and rightly belongs to the literal descendants of the chosen seed, to whom the promises were made." (D&C 107:40) It may not always go from father to firstborn son, but it should generally follow the line of those who held this exalted office.

The first to hold this heredi-tary office, that of Patriarch to the Church, in this dispensation, was Joseph Smith, Sr. In order to graphically show the blood rela-tionships of the Patriarchs of the Church, this graph was created.

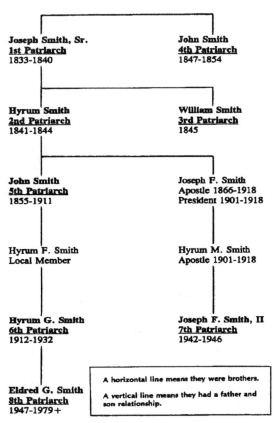

Joseph Smith, Sr.
1st Patriarch
1833-1840

John Smith
4th Patriarch
1847-1854

Hyrum Smith
2nd Patriarch
1841-1844

William Smith
3rd Patriarch
1845

John Smith
5th Patriarch
1855-1911

Joseph F. Smith
Apostle 1866-1918
President 1901-1918

Hyrum F. Smith
Local Member

Hyrum M. Smith
Apostle 1901-1918

Hyrum G. Smith
6th Patriarch
1912-1932

Joseph F. Smith, II
7th Patriarch
1942-1946

Eldred G. Smith
8th Patriarch
1947-1979+

A horizontal line means they were brothers.

A vertical line means they had a father and son relationship.

From time immemorial or the beginning of time, whenever the Gospel in its fullness has been upon the earth, there has been a Presiding Patriarch of the chosen lineage to bless all the people of the Lord. May it again be so. Eldred G. Smith was the last Presiding Patriarch of the Church. (*1995-96 Church Almanac,* pp.44, 50-51, 54, 57-58) He was given emeritus status in the October General Conference of 1979. Since this time, there had been no official Presiding Patriarch. However, as of this writing, Eldred G. Smith still gives patriarchal blessings to all who seek them, as a general patriarch, to any worthy, properly recommended member who applies from any part of the world. The Church continues to maintain an office and a secretary for him. It is hoped that one day, the Church will again have an active, rather than retired, Patriarch to the Church of the chosen lineage, who will be sustained as a prophet, seer and revelator and will be allowed to do anything that all the other general authorities can do. That is, enjoy the full dignity of this special and unique office.

Joseph Fielding Smith, Jr. made it clear that the office of Patriarch to the Church should continue with the descendants of Hyrum Smith to the end of time, or "continue . . . forever in the Church upon the earth among mortal men," even "to the uttermost." (*Doctrines of Salvation,* p.164) Since it was appointed by the finger of God to go "from father to son" and since Eldred G. Smith was the last Patriarch to the Church of the chosen seed, it would appear that his posterity would have the first and highest right to this office, because it is hereditary. But even though they are "lawful heirs, according to the flesh," Bruce R. McConkie explained that "lineage alone does not guarantee the receipt of whatever birthright privileges may be involved in particular cases. Worthiness, ability, and other requisites are also involved." (D&C 86:8-10 and *Mormon Doctrine,* p.88) Therefore it does not always go from father to son. I suppose the Lord could choose anyone from Hyrum Smith's lineage, but the highest birthright may actually belong to the descendants of Eldred G. Smith.

The great patriarchs of ancient times functioned not only as prophets and seers, who gave inspired counsel and prophetic promises in priesthood blessings, but were presiding officers as great as the Presidents of the Church are today. This is not true for this dispensation, however. Some people have become confused about what the office of Patriarch to the Church is, because Hyrum Smith held two offices. He was Presiding Patriarch and also Assistant (or Second) President under the Prophet Joseph Smith, which put him above the first and second counselors in the First Presidency and all the members of the Council of the Twelve. (*1995-96 Church Almanac,* p.44)

John Taylor made it very clear how a Patriarch to the Church in our dispensation is different from the ancient ones. He wrote, "But does not the patriarch stand in the same relationship to the church as Adam did for his family; and as Abraham and Jacob did to theirs?" "No," he continued, ". . .Adam was the natural father of his posterity, who were his family and over who he presided as patriarch, prophet, priest, and king. Both Abraham and Jacob stood in the same relationship to their families. But not so with Father Joseph Smith, Hyrum Smith, or William Smith." They "could not stand in the same capacity," but "were ordained and set apart for the purpose of conferring patriarchal blessings, to hold the keys of this priesthood, and unlock the door, that had long been closed upon the human family: that blessings might again be conferred according to the ancient order. . . ." (G. Homer Durham, *Gospel Kingdom,* p.148)

The Presiding Patriarch's office and calling, all by itself, in this dispensation is not to hold an administrative office unless it is to preside over and counsel the local stake patriarchs. However, as in the past, the Office of Patriarch could be combined with other offices, such as, a member of the First Quorum of the Seventy or an assistant or regular Counselor in the First Presidency. But, all by itself, this office is mainly one of being a father to Israel to personally bless and inspire members of the Church through special priesthood blessings. Local patriarchs are to do the same thing in their own jurisdictions. It is one of the most beautiful assignments ever given to any man.

Heber J. Grant declared with great feeling, "God bless the Patriarchs," for they regularly act as prophets in giving inspired blessings. Then he explained his experience with some local stake patriarchs. He said, "I thank the Lord for Patriarch Perkins, a noble man in St. George, who gave me a patriarchal blessing as a little child, foretelling my life in one small page of longhand writing, which has been fulfilled to the very letter. I thank God for John Rowberry, who gave me a blessing to the effect that I should be taken from Tooele and be made one of the leading officials of this Church: and who promised Francis M. Lyman that his name should be chronicled among the Apostles of the Lord Jesus Christ in these last days. God bless our Patriarchs and inspire them in their splendid work." (*Conference Report,* April 1930, p.25) Demonstrating the great inspiration that comes to these faithful brethren, President Grant was taken from being president of the Tooele Stake of Zion to be an apostle of the Lord at the age of twenty-five in fulfillment of the patriarch's true and faithful words. Two years earlier Francis M. Lyman was called to the apostleship of Christ at the age of forty. (*1995-96 Church Almanac,* pp.43,53)

Patriarchs are remarkable prophets who see into the future what our possibilities are and what God has in store for us if we are faithful to Him. As such, Harold B. Lee said, "There is no officer in the Church who requires as great care in selection as the patriarch." (from a talk given to stake patriarchs, April 7, 1956 quoted in "Handbook for Stake Patriarchs," p.3) ". . .We take it for granted," wrote Joseph Fielding Smith, "that you will agree with us . . . that because a man has filled with credit a presiding office and has attained a good age, is no reason why he should or should not make a good patriarch. . . . We suggest, [that they] should be men who have developed within them the spirit of the patriarchs; in fact, this should be their leading characteristic, and they should be men of wisdom, possessed of the gift and spirit of blessing as well." (James R. Clark, *Messages of the First Presidency* 4:58) Of course, the man the Lord has chosen and prepared for this calling is the right man, and patriarchs are to be called by revelation according to the Lord. (D&C 107:39) These brethren must exercise a precious gift—the gift of prophecy—the gift of being a prophet to speak for the Lord and conditionally give accurate prophetic promises in the name of the Lord.

John W. Taylor expressed it this way, ". . .the Lord acknowledges a Patriarch as a man who is endowed with a very high office in the Church and kingdom of God, and who has a special endowment given unto him for a special purpose. If there is any man in this Church who has a special calling for life it is a Patriarch." (*Conference Report,* October 1900, p.30) This is a great position to hold. In 1976, Eldred G. Smith, the Patriarch to the Church, had given more than 16,000 blessings since his ordination to this exalted office. He said, "To give a patriarchal blessing is as much a spiritual experience as it is to receive one," and he felt richly blessed and privileged and loved his work. (*Church News,* May 29, 1976, p.6) It is because, in the words of John Wells, a former second counselor in the Presiding Bishopric, ". . . the promptings of his Spirit . . . bring gladness and happiness to our souls . . . ." (*Conference Report,* April 1923, p.122) The spirit of revelation and prophecy are "sweet and peaceful promptings" and bring a wonderful feeling with them. (Hyrum G. Smith, Ibid., October 1928, p.82) However rich and rewarding the calling can be, it can also be scary, for it is to function as a prophet of God.

Those ordained to this office "are noble, exemplary and worthy men. . . ," declared Hyrum G. Smith. But he continued, ". . .I recommend that you . . . pray for them as you would pray for your own household. Pray for them that they may enjoy the spirit of their office and calling in the Church." (*Conference Report,* April 1924, p.88) This because the more they bear their prophetic responsibilities well, the greater will the Saints be blessed and encouraged by the outpouring of the great and special gifts of God in their lives. To be a patriarch is a "heavy and lonely responsibility," declared James E. Faust. Continuing he said, "It is a sacred and spiritual revelatory calling . . ." that can be thrilling and momentous, but frightening as well. (Ibid.)

B. H. Roberts explained that it is not to be assumed that the "prophets, apostles, presidencies, and other leaders—are without fault or infallible, rather they are treated as men of like passions with their fellow men." (*Comprehensive History of the Church* 1:vii) Elder Roberts continued that despite this they bore a rich, spiritual treasure or legacy even a portion of the glory of God which is the High and Holy Priesthood. "But while the officers and members of the church possess this spiritual 'treasure,' they carried it in earthen vessels; and that earthiness, with their human limitations, was plainly manifested on many occasions and in various ways, both in personal conduct and in collective deportment. But back of all that, and it should never be lost sight of, is the supreme fact—and it was a controlling element in all their proceedings—that they occupied such relations with God that they were, on occasion, moved upon to speak and act as God would speak and act. And when they spoke and acted as prompted by the inspiration of God, then what they said and what they did was the word and will of God, and the power of God unto salvation." (Ibid. 1:viii)

No wonder then, the First Presidency would "urge all patriarchs to [the] most earnest solicitation of divine guidance and admonition," because mistakes can be made without great care, which is why this calling can be frightening to bear and why we should pray for these men. (*Mormon Doctrine,* p.558) Ezra Taft Benson said, "This is one of the most difficult offices to fill in the Church. . . ." (*Teachings of Ezra Taft Benson*) Also the First Presidency reported, "We have reason to believe that sufficient discriminating judgment is not being exercised in the selection of men ordained patriarchs, and that as a consequence it sometimes happens that some brethren are recommended to represent this high and important office in the holy priesthood who are not in every respect suitable. . . ." (*Messages of the First Presidency* 4:57-58)

John W. Taylor, an earlier apostle of the Lord, spoke to six patriarchs who were meeting at a Davis Stake priesthood meeting and said, "I want to address a few words to these six brethren who hold the office of patriarch. I want to tell them that the Lord is displeased with the way they are discharging the high calling of their offices." He went on to say, "You have become as rusty clocks; you must repent and get the spirit of your calling, as the Lord is displeased with your attitude." (Ogden Kraut, interview with Douglas Todd, Jr., November 1969, *The Gift of Tongues,* p.76) These brethren then met with their Stake Presidency and had a remarkable meeting in which the spirit of the Lord was so strong and each expressed great remorse and their desire to manifest the right spirit and do as the Lord wished and give blessings of greater inspiration and faith. (Ibid., p.77)

It should be remembered that both the gift of healing and the gift of prophecy are strong in Israel, but sometimes we fail to measure up to our high and glorious privileges. President Brigham Young said:

> How often have we sealed blessings of health and life upon our children and companions in the name of Jesus Christ and by the authority of the Holy Priesthood of the Son of God, and yet our faith and prayers did not succeed in accomplishing the desires of our hearts. Why is this? In many instances our anxiety is so great that we do not pause to know the spirit of revelation and its operations upon the human mind. We have anxiety instead of faith. When a man prophesies by the power of the Holy Ghost, his words will be fulfilled as sure as the Lord lives; but if he has anxiety in his heart, it swerves him from the thread of the Holy Gospel, from the true thread of revelation, so that he is liable to err, and he prophesies, but it does not come to pass, he lays his hands upon the sick, but they are not healed. It is in consequence of not being completely moulded [molded] to the will of God. Do we not realize that we should constantly strive to live in the counsel and light of God day by day, and hour by hour? If we do this we shall certainly make sure to ourselves a celestial inheritance. (*Journal of Discourses* 12:125)

Wilford J. Reichmann of St. George in 1974 had already been a stake president and held other important calls, but he felt "that being a patriarch is the most difficult calling he ever had in the church. 'It scares you near to death," he said, as he spoke of the great need and responsibility to be constantly in tune with the spirit. But he had many interesting and rewarding experiences as a patriarch including refusing to give a blessing to a young lady, because he didn't have a good feeling about it. Later he discovered she was a nonmember who had deceived a bishop into giving her a recommend for a patriarchal blessing before he received her supposed general membership records. (*Church News,* November 30, 1974, p.10) Revelation is very real in the Church, but the sweet, endearing gift of revelation can be misinterpreted.

Patriarchs are counseled by the brethren to be conservative generally and avoid extravagant expressions, but if the Lord speaks, they have the authority and inspiration to say it in the name of the Lord. ("Address of Joseph Fielding Smith," June 15, 1956 at BYU, pp.5-6) But as expressed by Heber J. Grant, "There is no need of believing in an evangelist [a patriarch] unless he has the evangelical inspiration of his office." (*Messages of the First Presidency* 5:152) Then he went on to tell of how remarkably inspired two patriarchs had been in his own life and concluded, "Why do we believe in evangelists? Because they have the inspiration of God, the inspiration of their office and they are able to foretell the lives of the men and women upon whom they place their hands." (Ibid., p.153)

However, as a young man he was sorely tried by the words of one patriarch. He was deeply troubled over the fact that he was promised that he would be called into the ministry in his youth. But he wasn't and he was getting older and more despondent and troubled. Then finally:

> While walking down Main Street one day, "I had stopped and spoken out loud," he wrote, "though there was nobody to hear me. For a number of years there had been a spirit telling me that the patriarch had lied to me, that he had promised me a mission in my youth, that I had never been on a mission, that I was now nearly twenty-four years of age, and yet I had not been upon a mission." He had never told anyone, not even his mother, that this had troubled him, that it had sorely tried his faith. At this point, he recalled, he stopped, turned around and said out loud, 'Mr. Devil, shut up. I don't care if every patriarch in the Church had made a mistake in a blessing, and told a lie, I believe with all my heart and soul that the gospel is true and I will not allow my faith to be upset because of a mistake of a patriarch.'" (Francis M. Gibbons, *Heber J. Grant: Man of Steel, Prophet of God*, pp.35-36)

Never again was Heber J. Grant to be bothered by this negative, questioning spirit. And within a few weeks he was called to serve as the president of the Tooele Stake. It was then he realized that his blessing had promised that he would be called to the ministry in his youth, not that he would be called on a mission. The fulfillment of this unusual prediction was made even more dramatic when it became known that Heber was the youngest stake president in the entire church. (Ibid.)

President Grant had expressed the right attitude. Patriarchs are not perfect. No one is. Mistakes can be made, but by in large, they are remarkable prophets of God in the midst of the people. Spencer W. Kimball, as President of the Church, said, "I have great confidence in the patriarchs and in their blessings. When the patriarch is a faithful Latter-day Saint and remains close to the Lord and is a student of the scriptures, the promises which he makes under his special authority and calling will be fulfilled, if the recipient of the blessing is faithful and true." (*Ensign,* November 1977, p.4)

However, as with all callings before the Lord, from the Deacons to the great Presiding High Priest over the whole church, faith must be exercised. Hyrum G. Smith, one of the Presiding Patriarchs, said, "Sometimes I tremble with fear, because I feel the responsibility of officiating in this sacred calling [of a prophet before the Lord]. Nevertheless I feel to trust in the Lord. . . . I am astonished at the testimonies of the Latter-day Saints as they come back, declaring that those promises have been fulfilled . . . and I am grateful to be permitted to officiate in this sacred work." (*Conference Report,* April 1921, pp.185-186) Joseph F. Smith, the son of Hyrum M. Smith, a member of the Twelve, while Presiding Patriarch, declared in General Conference that "almost daily one of the greatest joys [that] comes to me—as it does to every patriarch . . . is the testimonies of persons who have received patriarchal blessings." (*Conference Report,* October 1944, p.112) It is a special calling, but also frightening sometimes.

Thomas S. Monson, of the First Presidency, tells of a patriarch who was troubled and had come to him worried about the promises he had made. He said:

> One afternoon Percy K. Fetzer, a righteous patriarch, came to my office by appointment. He was weeping as we visited together. He explained that he had just returned from the land of Poland, where he had been privileged to give patriarchal blessings to our worthy members there. After a long pause, the patriarch revealed that he had been impressed to promise to members of a German-speaking family by the name of Konietz declarations that could not be fulfilled. He had promised missions. He had promised temple blessings. These were beyond the reach of those whom he had blessed. He whispered how he had tried to withhold the promises he knew were unobtainable. It had been no use. The inspiration had come, the promises had been spoken, the blessings had been provided.
>
> "What shall I do? What can I say?" he repeated to me.
>
> I replied, "Brother Fetzer, these blessings have not come from you; they have been given of God. Let us kneel and pray to Him for their fulfillment."
>
> Within several years of that prayer, an unanticipated pact was signed between the Federal Republic of Germany and the Polish nation, which provided that German nationals trapped in Poland at war's end could now enter Germany. The Konietz family, whose members had received these

special patriarchal blessings, went to live in West Germany. I had the privilege of ordaining the father a bishop in the Dortmund Stake of the Church. The family then made that long-awaited trek to the temple in Switzerland. They dressed in clothing of spotless white. They knelt at a sacred altar to await that ordinance which binds father, mother, brothers, and sisters not only for time, but for all eternity. He who pronounced that sacred sealing ceremony was the temple president. More than this, however, he was the same servant of the Lord, Percy K. Fetzer, who as a patriarch years before had provided those precious promises in the patriarchal blessings he had bestowed. (Thomas S. Monson, *Live the Good Life,* pp.39-40)

Having the right spirit within ones heart is a serious matter for a patriarch. One patriarch wrote how he entered into a joint lawsuit and pursued it with great energy and vigor, but began to have doubts and to question if he should be involved—not because an injustice had not been suffered, but spiritually he felt something was wrong. He eventually gave it up and his feelings of misery and emptiness left him altogether. He felt so unburdened and free. The very next day a young lady called to schedule a patriarchal blessing. It was then that he realized that no one had requested a blessing during this whole affair of about ten weeks. And he wrote to a friend, ". . .a personal testimony came into my heart and mind that the spirit of suing and the spirit of blessing are opposites. Blessing is the spirit of love and agency. Suing is the spirit of force and compulsion. I saw that I personally, as a stake patriarch, could not bless if my life was dominated by feelings of suing" or revenge. (Dallin H. Oaks, *The Lord's Way,* p.180) No one had requested a blessing during this period because the Lord, who loves his children so very much, protected them from receiving anything less than all the words, cautions and encouragements He wanted them to receive.

Theodore M. Burton, a former Seventy said, "Patriarchs who realize the divine nature of patriarchal blessings seek earnest and continual guidance from the Holy Ghost in making their prophetic utterances." (*God's Greatest Gift,* p.122) Their success depends on being in tune, and being in tune depends on preparation. Spiritually this means sincere prayer, with real intent, the purifying of ones heart, being open and experienced with revelation, cultivating the prophetic gift, dearly loving God and revering everything right and good and beautiful in life. Not an impossible feat, but a rewarding and delightful labor of the heart.

Urvin Gee, a patriarch for thirty-eight years and nearly ninety-three years old said being a patriarch "is the most satisfying assignment I know, and I must always be in tune with the Spirit of the Lord." (*Church News,*

March 16, 1974, p.13) He recalled the first blessing he ever gave. He didn't know how to proceed so he repeated an introductory sentence he had decided upon prior to the blessing, then before his closed eyes, "I felt that I was looking at a large placard on which was printed part of the blessing. I read it and new words would appear. This happened a number of times. When no more words appeared I closed with an appropriate sentence, which I had previously decided upon." (Ibid.) He continued to explain that the Lord taught him that day not to expect so much help in the future. That is, he was expected to do his part and take more and more responsibility for following the promptings of the Spirit in the promises given in these blessings in the name of the Lord.

Hence, he learned, developed and nurtured this ability. He said, "I am simply the mouthpiece of our Heavenly Father in giving patriarchal blessings." (Ibid.) "If I had my choice of all the positions in the church, I would choose to be just what I am, a patriarch." (Ibid.) Spiritual experiences continued to fill his life with sweet enjoyments and memorable opportunities to feel the Lord's divine presence.

James Womack, had no hands and lost much of his vision in World War II, but God called him to be a patriarch to bless the people with his good heart, special spiritual abilities and love. When he was first called, he prayed that the impressions of the Spirit would be so obvious that no mistakes would be made, but "they were so strong I had to go back in a few weeks and pray that the Holy Ghost would lift them, because I couldn't forget them. The scenes, the thoughts, the ideas of those blessings I gave stayed stamped on my mind as if I had witnessed them." (*Ensign,* July 1979, p.13) Hence, he learned to listen better and exercise the prophetic gift at a less intense level in order to function properly in everyday activities.

W. Leigh Fullmer was ninety-one in 1990 and had been a patriarch for twenty-one years. He explained that this high and beautiful calling is "so sacred, it's difficult to talk about sometimes." He got choked up about it and considered himself to have "been richly blessed" because of it. His calling made him feel a special need "to be worthy of the Spirit" to prophesy and speak for God. (*Church News,* July 14, 1990, p.4) Joseph Smith said, "When a man speaks by the Spirit of God he speaks from the abundance of his heart [and] his mind is filled with intelligence. . . ." (Lucy Mack Smith, *History of Joseph Smith by His Mother,* pp.193-194) It is a beautiful, rich and elevating experience to give such blessings—one of the greatest privileges on earth.

Harold B. Lee related the testimony of a Sister Mortimer, who was the wife of a stake president in New York, who witnessed the ordination of a family friend to be the stake patriarch. She wrote:

I went into the room where Brother DeWitt Paul was to be ordained a patriarch of the Church. There were Brother and Sister Paul, some new bishoprics and their wives, and the stake presidency of the New York Stake. A chair was set in the center of the bishop's office in the Manhattan Ward building. It is not a large room—very full with eighteen to twenty people in it. It is situated in the basement floor of the building. It has no windows, the only ventilation for the room coming from a ventilator fan. The door is the only opening in the room. The chapel is on the floor above.

Brother Paul sat in the chair in the center of the room with his back towards the door. The door was closed. You, Elder Lee, stood behind Brother Paul and gave him the ordination and blessing.

Just as Elder Lee lifted his hands to place them on Brother Paul's head, a shaft of bright light came onto the back and top of Elder Lee's head. It was like bright sunshine suddenly coming through a square window—eight to ten inches square—and shining down on a forty-five degree angle on the back and top of his head. It was as if a shade had suddenly been drawn to let in the bright sun. I saw the light just before I bowed my head. I thought what a coincidence that that shaft of light should shine on Elder Lee just at this particular instant—as he was putting his hands on Brother Paul's head.

Just as quickly as I thought this I realized that there were no windows, therefore this was not sunlight. I knew in the same instant that it was a stream of light from Heaven that needed no physical window to come through. I open my eyes and looked up to see and again the shaft of light was visible. Finally, my eyes could no longer see the light, but I knew it was still there for Brother Paul was receiving information and advice that could only come from the Lord, and then I knew the source from which Brother Paul could declare lineage and project blessings that would come to the individuals he would bless in the years that lie ahead. (L. Brent Goates, *Harold B. Lee: Prophet and Seer,* p.334)

David B. Haight of the Twelve told how, when he was a Regional Representative, he traveled to California to a stake with Harold B. Lee in which a patriarch was to be called. The stake president gave Elder Lee a number of suggestions. Then they attended the Priesthood Leadership Meeting and "Brother Lee, noting a man sitting on the back row, asked the stake president who he was." In a disapproving tone, the stake president responded. Yet that was the man the Lord had prepared and chosen, picked out of a congregation by pure inspiration—"a humble man who proved to be an inspired patriarch." (Lucile C. Tate, *David B. Haight: The Life Story of A Disciple,* pp.299-300) Neal A. Maxwell described how Harold B. Lee, a prophet and an apostle of the Lord Jesus Christ, in calling a new patriarch for a different stake said to the man and his wife, "'Brother Facer, the Lord would like to call you as a patriarch.'" Brother Facer began to weep, and Sister Facer asked, 'Why don't you tell him, Moyle?' After Brother Facer regained his composure sufficiently, he said, 'Brother Lee, the Lord told me two weeks ago I was going to be called as a patriarch!' Brother Lee then turned to me and said, 'See, Neal, why general authorities must operate under the direction of the Spirit?'" (L. Brent Goates, *He Changed My Life: Personal Experiences of Harold B. Lee,* pp.238-239) To call the wrong man is to get in the Lord's way and hinder the Lord's work. Thomas S. Monson said, "From my own experience I testify that patriarchs are called of God by prophecy." (*Ensign,* November 1986, p.65) He also said, "I have never called a man to this sacred office but what I have felt the Lord's guiding influence in the decision." (Ibid.) Because the Lord wants to have unusual men who He can speak through to encourage and lift up His beloved children, He calls special men to this great and unusual office.

LeGrand Richards related the following faith-promoting experience, which a local patriarch shared with him:

> He told about a blessing he gave to a woman who came to him from one of the missions. Among other things, he told her that her progenitors had made a great contribution to the bringing forth of the gospel in these latter days. And after the blessing was given she said, "I'm afraid you made a mistake this time. I am a convert to the Church; I am the first one out of my family to join the Church." "Well," the Patriarch said, "I don't know anything about it. All I know is that I felt prompted to say that to you." And when he told me the story, she had just been in the Genealogical Department and had found that some of her relatives—her grandparents or her great grandparents—had made great sacrifices in the early days of the Church, and a part of the family had drifted up into the East. She did not know that she was descended from any of the pioneers who had made such great sacrifices. The patriarch did not know it of himself. All he knew was by the inspiration of the Holy Ghost. (*Miscellaneous Speeches,* May 27, 1953, p.8)

Hence, sometimes patriarchs must exercise great courage to speak the word of the living God as it comes to them and let the consequences, whatever they are, follow. Most often it builds and strengthens testimonies and faith because time is always on the side of truth. That is, eventually the inspiration is vindicated. And the patriarch shines as the Lord's special servant who told the truth. "You are not the source of the promises," said Spencer W. Kimball, "you have no blessing for anyone; you are but the tube through which the blessings flow—the wire through which the promises are carried." (*Teachings of Spencer W. Kimball,* p.505) Patriarchs function like radios tuned into the broadcast of the Almighty to tell a precious soul what the Lord wants said.

James E. Faust explained:

> The patriarch has no blessing of his own to give. We heard Elder LeGrand Richards tell of a patriarch who once said to a woman, "I have a wonderful blessing for you." But when the Patriarch laid his hands on the head of the recipient, his mind went completely blank. He apologized. "I was mistaken. I do not have a blessing for you." [The patriarch found out that he did not have a blessing for anyone. The blessings are from God alone and he had offended the Lord by saying he rather than God had a blessing for the individual.] The woman came back the next day, and after the patriarch had prayerfully importuned the Lord, a blessing came that mentioned many concerns known only to this good sister. All blessings come from God. Our Heavenly Father knows their capabilities and potential. Our patriarchal blessings indicate what He expects of us and what our potential can be. (*Ensign,* November 1995, p.63)

As declared by Hyrum G. Smith, "when these blessings are given and properly recorded, they are just as eternal and binding upon us through our faithfulness as were the blessings which were given by Adam, Abraham, Jacob or any of the former patriarchs in times which have passed." (*Conference Report,* April 1924, p.89)

To the Presiding Patriarch belongs "the keys of the patriarchal blessings upon the heads of all my people, that whoever he blesses shall be blessed, and whoever he curses shall be cursed; that whatsoever he shall bind on earth shall be bound in heaven; and whatsoever he shall loose on earth shall be loosed in heaven." (D&C 124:92-93) The local patriarchs "possess the same powers in blessing . . . as the general patriarch of the church in his wider sphere," that is, they possess "the same privileges and authority within their districts as belong to the Presiding Patriarch throughout the Church." (B. H. Roberts, *Outlines of Ecclesiastical History,* p.370 and James E. Talmage, *The Articles of Faith,* p.208) Therefore, whosoever the local patriarchs bless shall be blessed and whosoever they seal on earth in their blessings shall be sealed on a conditional basis in the heavens. This does not give them the right to perform a Temple sealing, only the right to authoritatively seal the promise or potential to receive this in time or in eternity.

This grand privilege is part of the general and conditional sealing powers which is part of the High Priesthood which is after the order of the Son of the living God. In fact, every ordinance of record whether baptism or ordination is sealed as a blessing upon us for time and all eternity on a conditional basis depending on our continued love and faithfulness to the cause of truth.

In terms of blessing and cursing, the Lord warned the inhabitants of the earth who would rebel and disobey by saying, "Behold, this is mine authority, and the authority of my servants . . . . to them is power given to seal both on earth and in heaven, the unbelieving and rebellious; Yea, verily, to seal them up unto the day when the wrath of God shall be poured out upon the wicked without measure." (D&C 1:6,8-9) In other words, beware of the Lord's servants for they represent the Most High God—he who is mighty to save and to destroy according to inspired and righteous judgement.

The first Patriarch to the Church, Joseph Smith, Sr., exercised this mighty gift to bless and curse as illustrated in the following story as told by a faithful observer:

In the year 1838, when on my way out of Missouri, near Palmyra, in company with Father Joseph Smith, the father of the Prophet, and Carlos Smith, his brother, we encountered a heavy snow storm. We halted at a farm house to buy corn and to stay all night. Father Smith asked the owner if we could camp there and buy feed for our animals. He asked: "Are you Mormons?" Father Smith answered: "Yes, we are." He became very angry and said: "Damn you, you can't stay on my property," and with many insulting words and threats we were driven out into the street. Here we stopped and gathered together in the falling snow. Slowly Father Smith removed his hat and with uplifted hands he prayed: "In the name of the Lord whom we serve, let this man's name be cut off from under heaven." We all said, Amen.

When I came to travel this same road two years later, this incident was brought fresh to my mind. For behold there was nothing to mark the spot but the ruins of his home burned to ashes; his orchard broken down; his farm an absolute picture of desolation; his wife and three lovely children were burned to death in their home and he at this time was in close confinement for the insane. I saw the power of the priesthood manifested, for at the next farm we were received and given all the comfort and assistance we needed and Father Smith left his blessing on this household as we departed. Here my eyes beheld the fulfillment of his words to the letter as there I looked upon a picture of prosperity and happiness. All this passed and the two neighbors were ignorant of the curse or the blessing placed upon them as we passed on. (Autobiographical Journal of Alfred Douglas Young, 1808-1842, pp.21-23 as found in *Manifestations of Faith* by Joseph Heinerman, pp.132-133)

The conditional power to bless and curse is very real as well as the high gift of the living God to bind on earth and in heaven. However, certain conditions impact upon the full use of this authority to seal. One is a proper record. The Prophet Joseph explained that the nature of the general sealing powers of the priesthood for all blessings and ordinances of record require that a record be made. It is so serious and important that "whatsoever you record on earth shall be recorded in heaven, and whatsoever you do not record on earth shall not be recorded in heaven. . . ." (D&C 128:8) "Hence, whatsoever those men did in authority, in the name of the Lord, and did it truly and faithfully, and kept a proper and faithful record of the same, it became a law on earth and in heaven, and could not be annulled, according to the decrees of the great Jehovah." (D&C 128:9) The only way a patriarchal blessing can be a law on earth and in heaven is: (1) it is done by "authority," (2) it is done "truly and faithfully" by the inspiration of heaven, and (3) "a proper and faithful record of the same" is made. (Ibid.)

This is why a copy must be made of a patriarchal blessing that it may be recorded or be bound eternally in the heavens. For an inspired blessing "shall be scripture, shall be the will of the Lord, shall be the mind of the Lord, shall be the word of the Lord, shall be the voice of the Lord, and the power of God unto salvation." (D&C 68:4) No wonder Brigham Young could say to some newly ordained patriarchs that "the Patriarchal office gives you the Highest Power to Bless" in Israel, for these men who seal blessings upon our heads, through our faithfulness, are recognized by God as having the full divine right to bind on earth and in heaven on a conditional basis. (Susan Staker, *Waiting for the World's End: The Diaries of Wilford Woodruff,* p.305)

Eldred G. Smith explained that:

> The blessing pronounced, with all it contains, should serve as a comfort and guide through life according to faithfulness and is sealed forever upon the conditions of faithfulness to the laws of God, which includes the laws of nature." (*Conference Report,* April 1952, pp.38-39)

Therefore, "if we are worthy, neither death nor the devil can deprive us of the blessings pronounced." (James E. Faust, *Ensign,* November 1995, p.63) We will enjoy them in time and in eternity forever. John A. Widtsoe wrote, "In summary, a patriarchal blessing . . . confers [a mighty blessing even the full weight of God's intervening providence of additional] power upon us, if we will use it, to win the fulfillment of these promises, as we journey through life. . . ." (*Evidences and Reconciliations,* p.325) That is, it confers extra help or additional heavenly assistance to succeed and enjoy effective lives for good and for God.

Patriarchs are high priests, after the order of the Son of God, and Joseph Smith explained that "the order of the High-priesthood [the great and eternal office of high priest] is that they have power given them to [conditionally] seal up the Saints unto eternal life. And said it was the privilege of every Elder present to be ordained to the High priesthood [this greater priesthood office]." (Donald Q. Cannon and Lyndon W. Cook, *Far West Record,* pp.20-21) The historical and scriptural records confirm this about this great priesthood office. "And of as many as the Father shall bear record [in other words, by revelation], to you [to the high priests after the order of the Son of God] shall be given power to [conditionally] seal them up to eternal life." (D&C 68:12 and Lyndon W. Cook, *Revelations of the Prophet Joseph Smith,* p.145) And in the words of George Q. Cannon, "There is no power that can deprive that individual of the fruits of that blessing which has been thus sealed upon him by authority of the Holy Priesthood." (*Journal of Discourses* 26:249) It is as eternal as our Father and God is eternal for it is the power and authority He has imparted. That is, ". . .Whatsoever ye shall bind on earth shall be bound in heaven: and whatsoever ye shall loosed on earth shall be loosed in heaven." (Matthew 18:18)

After this, high priests began sealing people conditionally up to the glory and honor of God, that is, to eternal life. Generally, only Temple Sealers and Patriarchs are regularly authorized to use this awesome, impacting authority. For example, most patriarchal blessings seal people up and the Temple marriage ceremony includes conferring on couples everything pertaining to exaltation, dominions, principalities and eternal life, through faithfulness to the covenants of this holy "order of the priesthood [meaning the new and everlasting covenant of marriage.]" (D&C 131:2)

These beautiful ordinances, no matter how great and eternal they are, are not to be confused with the fullness of the priesthood, some times called the second anointing or the "unconditional" sealing up to eternal life which makes one's calling and election sure. They are different ordinances. Bruce R. McConkie explained that "making one's calling and election sure comes after and grows out of celestial marriage." He said, "The one [a temple marriage] is a conditional promise of eternal life, the other [the fullness of the priesthood] is an unconditional promise." (*Doctrinal New Testament Commentary* 3:343,332)

Another example of a "conditional" sealing is in the following excerpt of a patriarchal blessing given to Vilate Kimball, the wife of Heber C. Kimball.

This conditional sealing was given before either of them experienced the "unconditional" gift of the fullness of the Priesthood a year or two later. The following patriarchal blessing was given by Hyrum Smith, the Presiding Patriarch in Nauvoo in 1842:

> Beloved Sister: I lay my hands upon your head in the name of Jesus, and seal you unto eternal life—sealed here on earth and sealed in heaven, and your name written in the Lamb's Book of life never to be blotted out.
>
> The same is mentioned and manifested to comfort your heart, and to be a comfort unto you henceforth all your days. It is even a promise according to the mind of the Spirit, and the Spirit shall bear record of the truth; the same is called the Second Comforter, not his presence, but his promise. The same is as immutable as an oath by Himself, because there is none greater, and there is no greater promise nor no greater blessing that can be given, and no greater riches, it being the riches of eternity, which are the greatest riches of all riches. (Hyrum Andrus, *Principles of Perfection*, p.352)

What a beautiful and exquisite blessing of comfort and eternal power. But, in the words of Joseph Fielding Smith, if people break their covenants, "then the Spirit withdraws the seal and the guilty party or parties, stand as if there had been no sealing or blessing given. All covenants are sealed based upon faithfulness. Should a person endeavor to receive the sealing [or a patriarchal] blessing by fraud, then the blessing is not sealed, notwithstanding the integrity and authority of the person officiating. Instead of a blessing they will receive a cursing, the heaviest of all. Therefore, a person who may deceive the bishop or any other officer [including a patriarch], will stand condemned before the Lord, for he [God] cannot be deceived and justice will be meted out to all." (*Doctrines of Salvation* 2:98-99 and D&C 41:1) However, in most cases, these blessings can be renewed through sincere repentance, that is, "subsequent worthiness will put the seal in force" again, such that, they are again binding forever and throughout all eternity. (Bruce R. McConkie, *Mormon Doctrine*, pp.361-362) This is because if we conform, heart and soul, to the requirements of heaven, "there is no power anywhere in existence that can invalidate the force, the efficacy, or . . . fulfillment of that promise when it is pronounced . . . by the authority of the Holy Priesthood. . . ," declared George Q. Cannon. (*Journal of Discourses* 26:249) He went on to say:

> When a man has this authority [the Priesthood after the order of the Son of God] and goes forth and confines himself to its legitimate exercise

and keeps within the bounds of his authority, God is with him; God confirms that which he does; God places His seal and His blessing and approval upon his acts; and though all the earth should endeavor to undo them and to say they are of no effect, they will stand, nevertheless, and in the Courts of heaven will be recorded and confirmed. There is no power among men that can disannul these acts, that can revoke or invalidate them in any manner. . . . That which is done in the name of the Holy Priesthood will stand . . . both in time and in eternity. (Ibid.)

The power of these blessings are awesome and eternal. One beautiful example is Miriam Spain Peterson, who was a Catholic nun for twenty-five years and was converted to the higher truth and glory of the restoration including the great privilege of recognizing true prophets and patriarchs of the living God in the last days. She was told in her patriarchal blessing that when the right one, the right man to marry came along "the Spirit of our Heavenly Father would bear witness that this was to be my companion and I would know it by having a happy, peaceful feeling." When she did meet this man who the Lord had chosen for her, she not only had this sweetness, but "I distinctly heard a voice say, 'This is the one!' Simultaneously I experienced a beautiful, indescribable feeling!" He had also had the miracle of revelation and a little over two months later they were married for time and all eternity in the Salt Lake Temple. (Hartman and Connie Rector, *No More Strangers* 3:151, 158) The glorious power to seal such great blessings upon others is a part of the glory of the Melchizedek Priesthood which the patriarchs of Israel enjoy in large measure.

Matthias F. Cowley and Orson F. Whitney wrote:

Inherent in the priesthood is the principle of representation. So plenary [unlimited and great] and far-reaching are its powers, that when those holding this authority are in the line of their duty, and possess the spirit of their calling, their official acts and utterances are as valid and as binding as if the Lord himself were present, and doing and saying what his servants do and say for him. (Forace Green, *Cowley & Whitney on Doctrine*, p.413)

This is great authority if there ever was to represent the greatest power in existence, even the Godhead. "Patriarchs," explained James E. Faust, "are privileged to impart [these great] blessings directly rather than just solicit blessings . . . for the patriarchs are entitled to speak authoritatively for the Lord." (*1980 Devotional Speeches of the Year*, p.53) Patriarchs have sealed upon them the wonderful privilege of prophecy and revelation. They hold a great calling and ordination, and can bless and seal, but they are human beings and need our faith and prayers like anyone else to magnify their high and sacred callings. (Ibid.)

Joseph F. Smith explained that "a patriarch should be the acme of fatherhood to the church in exercising the spirit of his calling and priesthood." (Stan Larsen, *The Ministry of Meetings,* p.463) "Acme" as in "acme of fatherhood" means, according to the dictionary, "one that represents perfection of the thing expressed" or "the highest point or stage" one can attain to. (*Webster's Ninth New Collegiate Dictionary,* p.52) In this case, being loving, understanding and venerable—a leader, model and example and source of strength as well as a creator or architect of nobility. (Ibid., pp.451-452 and *The Synonym Finder,* p.398) In other words, a patriarch should be truly great in every sense of the word. President Smith said, "Patriarchs should impress those who come to them that they have the spirit and power to bless, and the people would then feel that a patriarchal blessing is beyond price." (*The Ministry of Meetings,* p.463) It is an heavy responsibility.

Wilford Woodruff implored the Lord to "Remember in loving kindness thy servants, the Patriarchs. May they be full of blessings for thy people of Israel. May they bear with them the seeds of comfort and consolation, of encouragement and blessing. Fill them with the Holy Spirit of promise, and be graciously pleased to fulfil their words of prophecy, that thy name may be extolled by the people of thy Church and their faith in thee . . . may be increasingly strengthened." (*Discourses of Wilford Woodruff,* p.342)

To be a patriarch is to be a prophet in Israel. They have the enormous power to bless. But they must live worthy of this remarkable gift—a gift that is both extraordinary and wonderful. And we must live worthy to receive the full weight of the wonderful rewards promised of the living God to us.

CHAPTER THREE

THE GREAT HIGH PRIESTHOOD OFFICE HELD BY THE PATRIARCHS

Joseph Fielding Smith said, "The first authority of Priesthood in the earth was Patriarchal. Adam was a patriarch, so were those who succeeding him. Being patriarchs, of course they were, as stated by Alma, high priests of the Holy Order. This Patriarchal (or Evangelical) order of Priesthood continued through the generations from Adam to Noah, and from Noah to Moses." (*The Way to Perfection*, p.72) No doubt "these men received some lesser office in the Priesthood before the authority of the evangelist was conferred upon them by father Adam." (Ibid., p.73) But as the scriptures confirm they "were all high priests . . . ." and "held presiding office." (D&C 107:53 and *The Way to Perfection*, p.73)

Joseph Smith explained that when Peter, James and John came to restore the Melchizedek Priesthood in the last days, they confirmed upon Joseph Smith and Oliver Cowdery "the High Priesthood after the Holy Order of the Son of the Living God." (Dean C. Jessee, *The Papers of Joseph Smith* 1:3) This is actually referring to the office of High Priest or the High Priesthood. "Hood," as a suffix, denotes a state or condition of holding something in common—the office of High Priest in this case. (*New Webster's Dictionary and Thesaurus of the English Language*, p.465) In another dictionary it lists the word "high priesthood" as a synonym for "high priest." (*The American Heritage College Dictionary*, p.641) "Melchizedek Priesthood" refers to all those who hold the greater priesthood. The term "Higher Priesthood" also refers to the Melchizedek Priesthood, but High Priesthood refers to High Priests. The "offices of elder and bishop are necessary appendages [lesser or subordinate adjuncts or offices] belonging unto [or under the direction of] the high priesthood." (D&C 84:29 and *New Webster's Dictionary and Thesaurus of the English Language*, p.96)

Hence, "an Elder is not a High Priest," explained George Q. Cannon, "until he is ordained to the High Priesthood," which is to be made a High

Priest. (*Juvenile Instructor,* October 15, 1891, 26:622) He continued: "He [an Elder] cannot legally act in that office by being merely set apart; he must be ordained, and the High Priesthood [the higher and greater office of High Priest] must be bestowed upon him." (Ibid.) The term "High Priesthood" was commonly and routinely used in the early history of the Church for the office of High Priest. Later and little by little, the term became synonymous with the Melchizedek Priesthood or Higher Priesthood as we generally use it today.

But to be aware of the original meaning of the title "High Priesthood" can help reveal some very great and wonderful treasures. For example, the Doctrine and Covenants says, "Wherefore, from deacon to teacher, and from teacher to priest, and from priest to elder, severally as they are appointed, according to the covenants and commandments of the church. Then comes the High Priesthood [the office of High Priest], which is the greatest of all." (D&C 107:63-67) William W. Phelps made it obvious that this means the office of high priest by basically quoting this passage, but using the title of "high priest" instead of the term "High Priesthood" in the official Church periodical of those times. (*The Evening and the Morning Star* 1:74) Commenting on the High Priesthood being "the greatest of all," Hyrum M. Smith of the Twelve also concluded that men "are advanced to Elders, in the Melchizedek Priesthood, and finally to High Priests, which is the greatest of all." (*Doctrine and Covenants Commentary,* p.64)

However, even though Elders hold a "lesser" office, the Elders have much in common with the High Priests. They might in truth be looked upon as assistants to the High Priests, for it is their duty and privilege, in the absence of High Priests, to preside," declared Thomas C. Romney. (D&C 107:17, 10-11 and *World Religions in the Light of Mormonism,* p.193) This is just like a priest "is to take the lead of meetings when there is no elder present. . ." and a teacher "is to take the lead of meetings in the absence of the elder or priest—And is to be assisted always, in all his duties in the church, by the deacons, if occasion requires." (D&C 20:49, 56-57) Thus the grades or levels of authority and responsibility go from the High Priests in a descending order down to the deacons.

Bruce R. McConkie used the following scripture to prove that the office of Deacon is "the lowest in the priesthood hierarchy," that is, the "school of the prophets," which was also called "the school of mine apostles," was to consist of all "those who are called to the ministry of the church, beginning at the high priests, even down to the deacons." (*Mormon Doctrine,* p.183; *Doctrinal New Testament Commentary* 3:82 and D&C 95:17; 88:127) This scripture can also be used to show that High Priests are the highest in the priesthood hierarchy. This office, which is the greatest of all," according to the Lord, is also the exalted office of the patriarchs and the apostles as well. John Taylor explained that these ancient men "held the High Priesthood [that is, the great and exalted office of High Priest], and were consequently prophets of the Lord . . . ." (*Mediation and Atonement,* p.389) Because as declared by Joseph Smith, "no man is a minister of Jesus Christ without being a prophet." (*History of the Church* 3:389) And High Priests are to be "better" than all others and to "excel" all others in spiritual things, because the greater the calling the greater the responsibility. (*Teachings of the Prophet Joseph Smith,* p.21 and Joseph F. Smith, *Conference Report,* April 1908, pp.5-6)

John Taylor spoke "of the High Priesthood, or the place and calling of a High Priest" in a talk, and described the purpose of the High Priesthood, the uncommon office of High Priest as being "to prepare men to preside, to be fathers of the people." (*Journal of Discourses* 19:242) Alma, the prophet, made it clear in chapter thirteen of the Book of Mormon that those ordained to "the holy order, or this high priesthood" were "high priests of God," even "high priests forever." (Alma 13:9-10) Parley P. Pratt, described the day when Elders were first ordained to the office of High Priest in this dispensation, and said, "Several were then selected by revelation, through President Smith, and ordained to the High Priesthood after the order of the Son of God; which is after the order of Melchizedek," that is, they were made High Priests of the Melchizedek order. (Parley P. Pratt, Jr., *Autobiography of Parley P. Pratt,* p.53) When John Smith, the son of Hyrum Smith, was made Patriarch to the Church, he was only twenty-two years old. He was an Elder at the time and needed to be ordained a High Priest to be given this great honor. Brigham Young declared in his ordination blessing, I "ordain thee to the High Priesthood of Almighty God . . ." making him a High Priest, and then conferred upon him the patriarchal office and keys that his father and grandfather held. (Irene M. Bates and E. Gary Smith, *Lost Legacy,* p.125)

Joseph Fielding Smith explained that Joseph Smith and Oliver Cowdery "were not ordained to the special calling, or office, as apostles." (*Doctrines of Salvation* 3:147) They were "decreed" or called apostles by virtue of being special witnesses of heavenly visions, but they were not actually ordained as such. (D&C 27:12 and *Mormon Doctrine,* p.40) It was Joseph himself who explained what he and Oliver were really given on that day, that is, "the High Priesthood [the office of High Priest, 'which is the greatest of all.'] after the Holy Order of the Son of the Living God." (*The Papers of*

Joseph Smith 1:3 and D&C 107:63-64) Joseph F. Smith explained that "it is the duty of him who holds the High Priesthood, which is after the order of the Son of God, to preside over all the offices of the Priesthood and over all the members of the Church, when he is chosen and set apart to preside . . . three High Priests, who are chosen from the body of High Priests . . . to preside over the Church" and everyone. (*Collected Discourses* 3:95)

Hyrum G. Smith, the Presiding Patriarch in 1930 said in general conference, "I pray for the great body of High Priests throughout the Church. It was a thrilling sight when I saw them arise in this conference." (*Conference Report,* April 1930, p.174) Alonzo A. Hinckley, a stake president at the time, also bore witness, "I never experienced such a day in my life. . . . I never felt a spirit more thrilling than on that occasion. As I stood with that great body of high priests . . . , my soul went out in gratitude." (Ibid., p.178) Patriarch Smith continued, "God bless the High Priests of the Church, that they too may know that they possess that power [the power of the Son of God], for the Lord himself was a great High Priest. The Lord Jesus Christ declared it, and these men bear His power in the earth today and are his witnesses; and I share that with them [the glorious office of high priest], in which I glorify the Lord," for it is a great privilege. (Ibid., p.174)

High Priests of the Mighty God "have reached the most advanced ground to be had in the Church"—the highest pinnacle in terms of priesthood office, according to an *Improvement Era* article in 1910. (September 1910, p.1031) And Milton V. Backman among others have concluded "that the office of High Priest was the highest office in the Melchizedek Priesthood . . . ," that is, the greatest and the most important of all in the Church. (*The Heavens Resound,* p.241)

Thus they hold a "high and exalted status." (*The Mortal Messiah* 1:144-145) The word "high," as in "High Priest," means "at a relatively large distance above," "noble," "elevated," "lofty," "exalted," "eminent," "grand," "towering," "prominent," "ranking," "remarkable" and "outstanding." (*New Webster's Dictionary and Thesaurus of the English Language,* p.457 and *Roget's International Thesaurus* 206.19, 912.19, 916.11) "High" also means "exceptional," "noteworthy," "leading," "uppermost," "principle," "of great importance," "ruling," "powerful," "dominant," "chief," "highest," or most "advanced," and "extending far upward." (*The American Heritage College Dictionary,* pp.450, 640 and J.I. Rodale, *The Synonym Finder,* p.506) Thus being a High Priest literally means being the "highest" or "greatest" priest in the Church after the order of Melchizedek. And they are called to be remarkable men before the Lord as well.

The Lord has made it clear that "a high priest of the Melchizedek Priesthood has authority to officiate in all the lesser offices. . . ," which includes "the offices of an elder, priest (of the Levitical order), teacher, deacon, and member." (D&C 107:17, 10) B. H. Roberts commenting on the above scripture, wrote, "While the statements here made about the higher offices of the Church administering in the lower offices—a High Priest officiating in the office of Elder, Priest, Teacher or Deacon—are limited to High Priests, yet the principle holds good. . ." for all higher offices. (*The Seventy's Course in Theology,* p.25) Because, in the words of Joseph F. Smith, the higher offices, such as high priest and apostle, are "able to minister in all the lesser offices of these two priesthoods, because the greater always comprehends the lesser." (*Collected Discourses* 3:5)

Rudger Clawson, an earlier apostle of Christ, hailing the inauguration of a new Church program of priesthood training in his day, said, "Think what it means, brethren and sisters, to the Church of Jesus Christ of Latter-day Saints, when an elder in Israel shall have . . . training in the priesthood before he is permitted and found worthy to receive the high-priesthood," that is, the office of High Priest. (*Conference Report,* October 1909, p.68) He then spoke of training for deacons, teachers, priests and elders, "and he will receive his training as a Seventy, and even if he goes beyond and higher up, he will still be instructed and taught his duty in the Church, as a High Priest. . . ," even the highest of all the great offices of the priesthood. (Ibid.)

In a book published by the Church, Lowell L. Bennion explained that "advancement in the priesthood is based on training and experience. Authority and offices in the priesthood are not given to men all at once, but step by step, one office following another, with sufficient lapse of time between offices for them to gain experience in Church service and to prove their ability and worthiness to bear responsibilities." (*The Religion of the Latter-day Saints,* p.171) Wallace F. Bennett wrote, "The pattern of the two priesthoods is a simple one. Each is subdivided into three grades or offices, with different power or responsibilities attached to each grade. Generally the bearer of the priesthood begins with the lowest office of the lower priesthood and rises through succeeding offices." (*Why I Am A Mormon,* p.89) He continued on the highest of the three offices in the Melchizedek Priesthood and wrote, "Men who are high priests, as your author is, are eligible to hold any office in the Church for which they may be selected." (Ibid., p.90)

For "it was revealed that bishops and presiding men in the Church [the prophets, seers and revelators, etc.] should hold the office of a High Priest," declared Anthon H. Lund. (*Conference Report,* October 1908, p.117) John

Taylor explained, "The high priesthood [the great and exalted office of high priest], as you are aware, differs from the priesthood of the seventies in this respect—the high priests are to preside. It is a part of their office and calling to do that." (*Gospel Kingdom,* p.183) To preside, according to the dictionary, is "to be in a position of control or authority," which in the Church means to hold the keys of power for the eternal welfare and good of others to bless, encourage, inspire and love them into living better lives in Christ. (*New Webster's Dictionary and Thesaurus of the English Language,* p.792)

Thomas C. Romney, a prominent mission president, in 1946 in a book forwarded by John A. Widtsoe, wrote, "The calling of a High Priest is largely that of an administrative officer. High Priests are called to preside over the Church; to be Apostles and assistants to the Apostles; to preside over stakes and wards; to serve as high councilors in the various stakes of Zion and to fill the office of patriarch, whose duty it is to bless the people." (*World Religions in the Light of Mormonism,* p.193) Lowell L. Bennion said, ". . .men who are called to such positions in the Church as bishoprics, stake high councils and presidencies, apostles, patriarchs, and president of the Church are either already high priests, or are ordained high priests before they assume these positions." (*An Introduction to the Gospel,* p.225) And the *Encyclopedia of Mormonism* declares that "men called to presiding positions in the Church such as bishoprics, high councils, and stake presidents, as well as Patriarchs and apostles, are high priests." (Hoyt W. Brewster, Jr. 3:1035)

No wonder then the Assistants to the Twelve, who served as general authorities from 1941 to 1976, "shall be High Priests." (J. Reuben Clark, *Conference Report,* April 1941, p.95 and *1995-96 Church Almanac,* p.63) "They are high priests," wrote Bruce R. McConkie, "not apostles, and serve pursuant to the revelation which says: 'Other offices of the church, who belong not unto the Twelve, neither to the Seventy . . . notwithstanding they may hold as high and responsible offices in the church.' (D&C 107:98)." (*Mormon Doctrine,* p.56) Notice that other authorities (High Priests) can hold as high and responsible (equal or equivalent) offices in the Church as the Apostles and Prophets of the Quorum of the Twelve.

In 1961 the First Council of the Seventy, who were Seventies only, were ordained High Priests "in order to better assist the Twelve in overseeing the growing number of wards and stakes." (William G. Hartley, *Encyclopedia of Mormonism* 3:1042) President David O. McKay in general conference explained that to preside, ordain high priests, bishops, stake presidents, etc. "requires the High Priesthood"—the ordained office of High Priest, therefore, these Seventies "are now given the authority of high priests to set in order all things pertaining to the stake and the wards, under the direction of the Twelve Apostles." (*Conference Report,* October 1961, p.90) In 1995, the position of an Area Authority was announced. "These will be high priests chosen from among past and present experienced Church leaders." (*Ensign,* May 1995, p.1) Recently, these high priests were included into the quorums of the Seventy and join other high priests and general authorities as "especial witnesses" of the Lord Jesus Christ. (D&C 107:25) All of this because to the great and elevated office of High Priest "belongs the right of general and local presidency in the church." (*Comprehensive History of the Church* 2:370)

In addition to the right to hold presiding keys or be rulers in the Church of God, James E. Talmage declared that "High Priests are ordained with power to officiate, when set apart or otherwise authoritatively directed, in all the ordinances and blessings of the Church." (*Articles of Faith,* p.207) This means they can give patriarchal blessings, because they can officiate "in all the ordinances." And no wonder then a stake president, as a high priest in Israel, who have "power to officiate . . . in all the ordinances and blessings of the church" can ordain a patriarch.

Joseph Fielding Smith taught that "the offices in the Melchizedek Priesthood are as follows: elder, seventy, and high priest." (*Doctrines of Salvation* 3:105) He explained that "patriarchs" are merely "high priests with [a] special ordination" to more powerfully bless the people. (Ibid. 3:157) In other words, they hold with others "the High Priesthood [the great and elevated office of a High Priest], which is the greatest of all" or highest of all with a special assignment or appointment to bless. Orson F. Whitney explained that "the Melchizedek Priesthood comprises, in an ascending scale, the offices of elder, seventy, and high priest [the high priest being the highest and greatest]. There are also the callings of patriarch, apostle, and president, who must all be high priests after this order." (*Gospel Themes,* p.83 and *Cowley & Whitney on Doctrine,* p.421) This special office is a most "high and exalted status" before the Lord that should be acknowledged and treasured for what it really is—a great gem whose worth cannot be estimated. (*The Mortal Messiah* 1:144-145) For not only are "all the ancient patriarchs . . . high priests," but this same glorious privilege and blessing has been restored. All of the "evangelists, or patriarchs [of today], are high priests," explained Joseph Fielding Smith, and they enjoy a "special ordination as patriarchs . . . , and from among the high priests [those who hold this great office] come the presiding officers of the Church and in the stakes and wards of the Church." (*Doctrines of Salvation* 3:104-105)

The word patriarch comes to the English from the Latin and the French and essentially means father." (Daniel H. Ludlow, *A Companion to Your Study of the Doctrine and Covenants* 2:197) Eldred G. Smith, while Patriarch to the Church, said: "The words father and patriarch, then, are synonymous." (*The Instructor*, February 1962, p.42) No wonder, then, Joseph F. Smith would say of the patriarchs that "they are fathers . . . and to be fathers indeed of the people, leading them into all truth." (*Conference Report*, October 1904, p.4) "The title father is sacred and eternal. It is significant that of all the titles of respect and honor and admiration that are given to Deity, he [God] has asked us to address him as Father." (*Duties and Blessings of the Priesthood, Part B*, p.95)

Rudger Clawson declared that stake presidents "whose authority is very great and far-reaching in its character . . . ," also preside as fathers in Israel. (Rudger Clawson, *Conference Report*, April 1908, p.31) And High Councilors, according to Joseph F. Smith, are "fathers indeed to the people and judges . . . assisting the presidencies of the various stakes . . . ." (Ibid., October 1904, p.2) But all who bear the office of High Priest, Joseph F. Smith explained, "are indeed the fathers of the people at large." (Ibid., April 1907, p.5) The next year, Joseph F. Smith again encouraged the High Priests in General Conference to magnify their great and holy callings, "that they may be, indeed, fathers among the people, exercising the functions that belong to their calling. . . ." (Ibid., April 1908, p.5) Years earlier, John Taylor encouraged the High Priests to magnify their great office "and act as fathers in Israel, looking after the welfare of the people and exerting a salutary influence over the Saints of the Most High God." (*Journal of Discourses* 23:219) For as President Joseph F. Smith explained, "there is no body of Priesthood in the Church who should excel . . . those who are called to bear the office of High Priest . . . ," on a local level or on any level. That is, so great and remarkable is this unusual and uncommon office that all ordained patriarchs must hold it to function in all the glory of their high and exalted callings. (Ibid., April 1908, p.5)

Joseph Smith, Sr., the prophet's father, was identified as "the oldest man of the blood of Joseph or of the seed of Abraham. . . ." (Joseph Fielding Smith, *Teachings of the Prophet Joseph Smith*, p.151) "He was ordained a Priest of the Most High God [that is, a High Priest after the order of the Son of God on June 3, 1831], and became the first Presiding Patriarch in the Church [on December 18, 1833 at the age of 62]. . . ." (B. H. Roberts, *New Witness for God* 2:326 and *1995-96 Church Almanac*, p.50) However, even though this is not an administrative office, but an office of blessing, Joseph

Fielding Smith explained it is "one of the greatest positions of honor and trust ever conferred upon man" to prophesy, counsel, comfort and seal gifts and privileges of great power upon modern Israel. (*Doctrines of Salvation* 3:169) And every patriarch does this. Joseph F. Smith said, ". . . all the patriarchs, and all others who have been ordained to the office of high priest [hold] . . . the office of presidency in the Melchizedek Priesthood. . . ." (*Conference Report,* October 1904, p.3) However, not "every man who holds the office of high priest is a president. Only he who is called, appointed, and set apart to preside among the high priests holds the presiding authority and office." (Ibid.) Thus, even though Joseph Smith, Sr. was ordained a mighty Priest of the Most High God that which is "the greatest of all" in the Church, even "the office of presidency," he was not given an administrative or leadership office, as Patriarch to the Church, but one of blessing as "a Father to Israel." (*Doctrines of Salvation* 3:169) However, Joseph Smith, Sr. was also an Assistant Counselor in the First Presidency from 1837 to his death in 1840 and therefore held more than one office. (*1995-96 Church Almanac,* p.50)

Alma, one of the greatest prophets who ever lived on the Western Hemisphere in ancient times, declared that those "ordained unto the high priesthood of the holy order of God" were "High Priests of God." (Alma 13:10, 6) Bruce R. McConkie taught that "Book of Mormon prophets gave the title *priest* to officers known in this dispensation as *high priests*. That is, they were priests of the Melchizedek Priesthood, or . . . 'priests after his holy order. . . .'" (*Mormon Doctrine,* p.599) He also explained that "Alma tells us that those who are faithful high priests in this life were in fact 'called and prepared from the foundation of the world according to the foreknowledge of God, on account of their exceeding faith and good works' while they yet dwelt in his presence. (Alma 13:3)." (*A New Witness for the Articles of Faith,* p.34)

Commenting on this same chapter in Alma, Orson F. Whitney declared in general conference that, "They [the leaders of the Church] came into the world with the ordination of God upon their heads; and there are others who have been ordained in like manner [as the Lord's anointed and the general authorities], High Priests after the Order of Melchizedek, though it may never be theirs to sit among the leaders of Israel. But they are numbered with those whose mission it is to follow the Lamb wheresoever He goeth, and they are here to help prepare the way before the glorious coming of the Son of God." (*Conference Report,* October 1905, p.93) Wilford Woodruff prayed: "Bless abundantly, O Lord, the high priests in all the varied duties and positions to which thou hast called them. As standing ministers of thy word in the multiplying Stakes of Zion wilt thou endow them richly with the spirit of their exalted callings. As Presidents, Counselors, Bishops, members of High Councils, and in every other office which their Priesthood gives them the right to fill, may they be righteous . . . loving fathers . . . and . . . judges. . . ." (*Discourses of Wilford Woodruff*, p.343)

Since High Priests are to excel and be exceptional, remarkable and inspired men, they are also to be great prophets in Israel. Joseph Smith said, ". . . I did not profess to be a prophet any more than every man ought to who professes to be a preacher of righteousness. . . ." (*History of the Church* 5:231-232) George Q. Cannon explained that Joseph Smith's message to mankind was "that every man might be a prophet of God . . . if he would live for it . . . and that would make him a prophet, it would fill him with the spirit of God. . . ." (*Journal of Discourses* 23:137) "In a sense," said Harold B. Lee, "the word prophet might apply to all faithful Church members. . . . Each of us has the right to revelation. . . ." and "anyone who enjoys the gift . . . is a prophet. . . ." In fact, "prophecy in the Church and kingdom of God is not confined to one man. This is a nation of prophets." (*Teachings of Harold B. Lee*, pp.418-419) In other words, High Priests should be inspired men of God filled with divine gifts to bless. Since, "it is the High Priest's duty to be better qualified" than others, they should be filled with inspiration as much as any patriarch in the Church. (*Teachings of the Prophet Joseph Smith*, p.21) For "theirs [the special privilege of this office] is the power to officiate in all ordinances and blessings of the Church," and "the authority of the Priesthood should cause a gushing forth from the foundation of the heart, a bubbling forth of streams of blessing, of consolation, of comfort and of rejoicing. . . ." (*The Priesthood and You*, p.333 and *Journal of Discourses* 26:100)

Franklin D. Richards declared that the Twelve Apostles are "upheld as prophets, seers and revelators. . . ." (*Collected Discourses* 3:28) They are given this special endowment. And "prophets and seers, how great they are!," said Bruce R. McConkie. "They stand in the place and stead of the Lord Jesus in administering salvation to fallen man. Their vision is endless and their understanding reaches to heaven." (*The Millennial Messiah*, pp.68-69) It is their "privilege to receive revelation to see visions, to entertain angels, and to see the face of God." (Ibid.) And according to Elder Richards, "it should be just so with these men who are High Priests in Israel." (*Collected Discourses* 3:28) They "should [also] so live before God as to be prophets, seers and revelators to their people." (Ibid.) This is a very significant statement, because "a seer is greater than a prophet . . . and a gift which is greater can no man have . . . ," because it provide a "means that man, through faith, might work mighty miracles; therefore he becometh a great benefit. . . ." (Mosiah 8:15-16,18)

Because the Melchizedek Priesthood holds "the keys of all the spiritual blessings of the church . . . to have the heavens opened unto them, to commune with the general assembly and church of the Firstborn, and to enjoy the communion and presence of God the Father . . . ," Bruce R. McConkie said, "Ordination to any office in the Melchizedek Priesthood is an open invitation to see the face of" God. (D&C 107:18-19 and *A New Witness for the Articles of Faith,* p.496) In other words, every Elder of the Church is invited into the sacred realms of being a special witness of Christ and a prophet of God. Elder McConkie asks:

> Does it seem unseemly to seek such a spiritual reward as seeing the face of the Lord? Is it presumptuous, improper, beyond the bounds of propriety? Hear this divine counsel to the saints: "Care for the soul, and for the life of the soul. And seek the face of the Lord always, that in patience ye may possess your souls, and ye shall have eternal life." (D&C 101:37-38) We seek eternal life, which is life in the Divine Presence. To receive this greatest of all the gifts of God, we must be worthy to dwell in that Celestial Presence. Ought we not—nay, must we not—then become worthy, here and now, and thus qualify for the divine association that we hope to enjoy forever in the realms ahead? (Ibid., p.492)

We are all called to a prophetic calling—an exalted ordination. We are "appointed to be the greatest" of all men. (D&C 50:26) We have a glorious challenge before us to be faithful and true. We are messengers of the covenant—children of the prophets. We can and should be men of great inspiration. We can be spiritual giants or spiritual pygmies. We can be better than we are and sustain our own local "prophets, meaning the quorum presidents, bishops, and stake presidents who direct the work of the kingdom in the stakes of Zion." (Robert L. Millet and Joseph Fielding McConkie, *Our Destiny: The Call and Election of the House of Israel,* p.112) And may we be great and mighty prophets in our own right.

Rudger Clawson said, "The brethren who hold the priesthood and are faithful, are all prophets, but it would not be consistent to say Prophet Shurtliff [the stake president], Prophet Jones, Prophet Middleton, Prophet Flyfare. The term is too sacred." (*A Ministry of Meetings,* p.618) It would be better to say President Shutliff or Elder Flyfare. James E. Talmage in an article entitled "The Honor and Dignity of Priesthood" said, "Though a man be ordained to the exalted and honorable office of Patriarch, he is still an Elder, and the special designation 'Patriarch' is not to be used in every-day converse." (*The Improvement Era*, March 1914, p.410) He should be called Brother or Elder even though he is a prophet and a patriarch in the Church and Kingdom of God.

Of course, as Bruce R. McConkie declared, "There is only one presiding prophet on earth at any one time, and he is the President of the Church. All other prophets [whether high priests, seventies or elders] are subject to him and his direction. There is not now on earth and there shall not be—as long as the earth shall stand . . . a prophet who is not subject to and whose acts are not governed by the presiding prophet."—the President over the whole Church. (*The Millennial Messiah*, p.326) But, "every man should be a prophet for his family and for those over whom he is called to preside in the Church and kingdom of God on earth." (Ibid.) And these "prophets are members of the Church of Jesus Christ of Latter-day Saints. They are stake presidents and bishops and quorum presidents who are appointed to guide and direct the destinies of their stakes and wards and quorums." (Ibid.)

Hence, Eldred G. Smith, while serving as Patriarch to the Church and a Prophet of God, said, "I had a Mission President write me a letter once and say, 'What can we do about people in my mission who want Patriarchal Blessings or who want a blessing?' I wrote back to the Mission President and said, 'You're the Patriarch [that is, the father in Israel] or head of that Mission; you give them the blessing.'" (Salt Lake Institute of Religion Lecture, January 17, 1964, p.3) That is, give them a priesthood blessing of comfort, inspiration and prophecy and manifest the Lord's great love for his children.

"High Priests [above all others] have the responsibility for administering the spiritual powers and blessings of the Church (see D&C 107:10)." (*Duties and Blessings of the Priesthood, Part A*, p.69) Apostles, Patriarchs and Presidents are all High Priests and can enjoy the full privileges and blessings of this office. Since High Priests are to be the highest and the greatest priests of Melchizedek in the Church, no wonder, ". . . the great and glorious office of a High Priest" is the exalted office held by all the patriarchs of the Lord. It gives them their remarkable power to bless and "invite all to come unto Christ" according to their special and unique calling. (Rudger Clawson, *Conference Report*, October 1917, p.28 and D&C 20:59) The call to be a patriarch "may come to any worthy, spiritually mature high priest,"who loves the Lord and has the spiritual gift to bless beautifully and wonderfully like the ancient prophets. (Ariel S. Ballif, *Encyclopedia of Mormonism* 3:1064)

John Taylor explained how great the office of high priest is by saying, "if they are appointed to any particular office in the Church [high or low], they have a right to administer in that office," whether as an apostle or local member. (*The Gospel Kingdom*, p.197) This is the office of the prophets and the great men of ancient days. It is as eternal and everlasting as God himself.

Rudger Clawson, one of the apostles, wrote, "The priesthood is a precious gift from God, which is sealed upon us with an oath and covenant and is the power by which we will be exalted in the kingdom of God." Therefore, "if a man is ordained a high priest, he is a high priest forever, if faithful, both in the world and in the next. . . ." (*A Ministry of Meetings*, p.408) That is, as Bruce R. McConkie declared, "those who hold the ordained office of high priest continue as such in time and in eternity. . . ." (*A New Witness for the Articles of Faith*, p.351)

A very spiritual and gifted patriarch and high priest, Charles R. Woodbury, explained that when he was very sick and in great pain, the Lord sent an old friend to him with a message from on high. His friend was also an ordained patriarch of the Lord on the earth. Brother Woodbury asked him what he was doing in the spirit world and the answer was:

> "I'm working with the Priesthood some, but my main work is giving Patriarchal Blessings." "Why do you give Patriarchal Blessings in the Spirit World?" He said, "In mortal life we give blessings to people to be an inspiration and guide to them, so that they will know the blessings that are in store for them. Many people on earth lived good, pure, honest lives, but were guilty of the sin of omission, and those are the ones I'm giving blessings to there, so that when their loved ones do their work in the Temple for them, and they atone for the sin of omission, that they will be privileged to enjoy those blessings."
>
> I said, "I'm glad to know that. When I have given blessings to boys and girls whose father was a Patriarch, it was revealed to me that he was giving blessings in the Spirit World, but I didn't know what for." ("Faith-Promoting Experiences of Patriarch Charles R. Woodbury," BYU Archives, p.1)

To be ordained is to be ordained forever as long as we are faithful and true enough to retain that special portion of the glory that God has bestowed upon us. But High Priests, according to the Lord, hold the office "which is the greatest of all" the offices in the Church. (D&C 107:64) In fact, it is probably greater than we will ever know in this life. For, according to the Doctrine and Covenants Index, the Topical Guide to the Standard Works and Bruce R. McConkie, High Priests of the Lord are actually "Priests of the Most High" God and this office is associated with the greatest men of all eternity—those that obtain "all that the Father hath." Hence, there is something of tremendous importance here—a hidden pearl of great price. (D&C 76:57 {see first footnote}; D&C Index, p.153; Topical Guide, p.210; Rulon T. Burton, *We Believe*, p.D-111 and D&C 84:38)

LeGrand Richards emphasized that "this authority [of the Priesthood] is the greatest thing we possess next to life itself," which is quite a statement. (*Just to Illustrate*, p.27) He continued:

> Just to illustrate—When our son, Alden, was ordained a deacon in Atlanta, Georgia, he came into my office and said, "Father, I have more authority than the President of the United States, haven't I?" It took my breath away, and after composing my thoughts, I replied, "Well, yes, you have. The President of the United States gets his authority from the people. When his term of office ends, his authority ends with it. But your authority comes from the Lord, and if you will live for it, it will be your forever and forever." (Ibid.)

In conclusion, to be a High Priest is also to hold that which "is the greatest thing next to life itself." (Ibid.) It is a beautiful, hidden treasure concealed from human view. It is the priesthood office which is the highest, the greatest and the most advanced of all in the Church—the eternal and everlasting office of presidency, rule and general administration in the kingdom of God. Lorenzo Snow prayed, "Endow Thou Thy servants, the High Priests, with all the gifts and qualifications of their holy calling," because it is so great it means to be a prophet and inspired man in Israel. (*Temples of the Most High God*, p.109) Therefore, to hold and magnify this special office is one of the highest compliments one can be given in this life. But most importantly, it is a monumental test of our commitment to Christ to manifest the profound inner goodness, love, warmth and beauty required of a man ordained to the same glorious office as the prophets and patriarchs held in ancient Israel. May we treasure and cherish this gift of gifts, love and glorify God and obtain its beautiful, eternal blessings. For more on this enormously important and extraordinary office and its priceless privileges and challenges, see the book *Priests of the Most High God* by this author.

CHAPTER FOUR

THE LINEAL DECLARATION OF THE HOUSE OF ISRAEL

The literal seed of Abraham, through the chosen lineage, are the lawful heirs to all the remarkable promises given anciently to Abraham, Isaac and Jacob. This includes many beautiful and special promises of greatness and glory. The following are scriptures that describe some of them.

"I will multiply thy seed as the stars of the heaven, and as the sand which is upon the sea shore; and they seed shall possess the gate of his enemies; And in thy seed shall all the nations of the earth be blessed," (Genesis 22:17-18); and "I will bless thee above measure, and make thy name great among all nations. . . ." (Abraham 2:9) Paul describes the incredible fact that Abraham was made "the heir of the world. . . ." (Romans 4:13)

The Lord told Abraham he'd bless all mankind through his seed, because they would hold the great power of God unto salvation. Moses also prophesied mighty blessings upon all the house of Israel, if they would love and obey the Lord. He told them that:

(1) God would "make thee [Israel as a people] high above all nations which he hath made." (Deuteronomy 26:19)

(2) ". . .Thou shalt reign [or rule] over . . . nations, but they shall not reign [or rule] over thee." (Deuteronomy 15:6); ". . .And ye shall possess greater nations and mightier than yourselves." (Deuteronomy 11:23)

(3) Showing economic superiority, Moses promised, in the name of the Lord, that they should "lend unto many nations, but thou shalt not borrow." (Deuteronomy 15:5)

(4) ". . .And the people of the earth shall be afraid of thee." (Deuteronomy 28:10)

(5) "And the Lord shall make thee the head, and not the tail; and thou shalt be above only. . . ." (Deuteronomy 28:13)

(6) And showing military superiority, he said: "One [shall] chase a thousand, and two put ten thousand to flight. . . ." (Deuteronomy 32:30) And "there shall no man be able to stand before you. . . ." (Deuteronomy 11:25)

Israel never obtained these exceptional promises, except in small, short-lived instances of fading glory, but they will obtain them in the last days. They will put on the beautiful garments of righteousness as never before and be the glory and astonishment of all the earth. However, collectively together in ancient times, the chosen seed failed to "bless all nations," therefore, it was fulfilled that "the Lord shall scatter thee among all people from one end of the earth even unto the other. . . ." (Deuteronomy 28:64) And the Prophet Hosea said: "Ephraim [the birthright holder—the greatest and best of all in the pre-existence] . . . shall be wanderers among the nations. . ." to bless all nations with their inherent goodness. (Hosea 9:16-17)

These great and enormous blessings of Abraham were passed down through Isaac and Jacob to Joseph's two sons Ephraim and Manasseh. Ephraim obtained the birthright blessing to be "greater" than his older brother, but Manasseh was also to be "great," and both "shall be blessed above thy brethren [the other tribes of Israel], and above thy father's house . . . wherefore thy brethren shall bow down unto thee from generation to generation. . . . For thou shalt be a light unto my people . . . to bring salvation unto them, when they are altogether bowed down under sin." (Genesis 48:19 and JST Genesis 48:9-11)

To Ephraim and Manasseh, Jacob (or Israel) prophesied, "The blessings of thy father [Joseph] have prevailed above the blessings of my progenitors unto the utmost bound of the everlasting hills: they shall be upon the head of Joseph, and on the crown of the head of him that was separate from his brethren." (Genesis 49:26) In other words, greater blessings, great lands, even the whole Western Hemisphere or the everlasting hills were promised to Ephraim and Manasseh. They were also to have "the blessings of heaven above, blessings of the deep that lieth under, blessings of the breasts, and of the womb," or a large and numerous posterity as well as the riches of eternity and the treasures of great material wealth. (Genesis 49:25) In fact, their blessings are greater than all the other tribes combined.

Anciently, Joseph of Egypt, the father of Ephraim and Manasseh, prophesied of his future seed that a choice seer would be raised up unto them and would bring forth the word of God to them. And his seed would have both the words of the loins of Judah (the Bible) and the written words of the prophets of Ephraim and Manasseh (the Book of Mormon). (Ezekiel 37) This choice seer's name was to be Joseph and his father's name would also be Joseph. He would be "great in the sight of God, unto the bringing to pass much restoration unto the house of Israel, and unto the seed of thy brethren." (2 Nephi 3:15,24)

Joseph Smith, Jr., the son of Joseph Smith, Sr., the first Presiding Patriarch, was that great man prophesied of in ancient days, and what God did with him as his special servant is the greatest event that has ever happened on this earth since the resurrection of the Son of God. Joseph Smith, Jr. brought forth the words of the ancient prophets of the Western Hemisphere, restored the glory of the Holy Priesthood and the Church in the last days, all for the salvation of all mankind both the living and the dead. This means the exciting news that the redemption of Israel and her greatest blessings are near, even at the doors. The greatest blessings ever known on earth are about to burst forth in all their glory. This will be a glorious day for the covenant people of the Lord. Zion will be established and flourish, righteousness will abound, beautiful miracles will be wrought and every knee will bow to Christ, because the sons of Joseph will magnify their callings.

Moses, the great prophet and law giver of ancient times, blessed each tribe of Israel. To Joseph and his sons, Ephraim and Manasseh, he said, "Blessed of the Lord be his land, for the precious things of heaven . . . the precious fruits . . . the chief things of the ancient mountains . . . the precious things of the earth and [the] fulness thereof, and for the good will of [God]. . . . His [Joseph's power, excellence and] glory . . . shall push the people together. . . ." (Deuteronomy 33:13-16) The seed of Joseph were to do great things and bless all mankind but most especially the House of Israel. In the last days the Lord describes the glory manifest in the exalted appearance of the Ten Tribes coming back from the land of the north to the tribe of Ephraim. "And they shall bring forth their rich treasures unto the children of Ephraim, my servants. And the boundaries of the everlasting hills shall tremble at their presence. And there shall they fall down and be crowned with glory . . . by . . . the children of Ephraim . . . and . . . be filled with songs of everlasting joy. Behold, this is the blessing of the everlasting God upon the tribes of Israel, and the richer blessing upon Ephraim and his fellows." (D&C 133:26-34)

The ancient tribe of Ephraim, the great and chosen of God, the valiant of the grand councils of God, was scattered among all nations as prophesied, to lift them to higher levels as a blessing to every nation to prepare them for greater things. Erastus Snow, one of the early apostles of this last dispensation, stated, "And when the books shall be opened and the lineage of all men is known, it will be found that they [the royal house and children of Ephraim] have been the first and foremost in everything noble among men in the various nations." (*Journal of Discourses* 23:186)

On "Ephraim," Brigham Young said, "No hardship will discourage these men; they will penetrate the deepest wilds and overcome almost insurmountable difficulties to develop the treasures of the earth, to further their indomitable spirit of adventure." (Ibid. 10:188) Hyrum G. Smith, one of the Presiding Patriarchs of the Church, said, "those who are leaders in Israel, no matter from where they came, no matter what nation they have come, are of Ephraim; while the blood of Manasseh is found in the tribes and nations of the Indians of North and South America. They are great, they are wonderfully blessed, but Ephraim seems to prevail in the greater blessings, greater in responsibility and in faithfulness. . . . It is my testimony that 'today' is the day of Ephraim." (*Conference Report,* April 1924, p.123) Joseph Fielding Smith explained that the God of heaven "set Ephraim, according to the promises of his birthright, at the head. Ephraim receives the 'richer blessings,' these being those of presidency or direction. The keys are with Ephraim. . . . All the other tribes of Jacob, including the Lamanites, are to be crowned with glory in Zion by the hands of Ephraim. . . ." On the subject of the great temple of the New Jerusalem, "it is Ephraim . . . who will stand at the head and direct the work." (*Doctrines of Salvation* 2:250-251)

Joseph's dream of supremacy came true that "the sun and the moon and the eleven stars made obeisance to [him]. (Genesis 37:7) He saved the family of Israel anciently with the power and glory of ancient Egypt at his command. The sons of Joseph will again stand as God's mouthpiece on earth and save all the tribes of Israel from destruction, but with the immense power and glory of God in their hands.

Melvin J. Ballard said in 1924:

> I was thrilled not long ago when I read an article appearing in one of our national magazines. The author was discussing the question: "Are the Jews the Chosen People of God?" He denied them the right to claim for themselves and their posterity all the blessings pronounced upon all the sons of Jacob, but limited their blessings to their own particular line—the tribe of Judah. After tracing the history of the Jews and the several tribes of Israel the author concludes: "If we could find in the earth somewhere today the descendants of Joseph, we would find the chosen people of God," because the blessings of Joseph were so much greater than the blessings of his brethren that you will recall they despised him and were jealous of his blessings, and sold him into Egypt; but the Lord was with him and raised him up and made him mighty to become the deliverer of his father's household. I say, when I read that statement my soul thrilled with a new sensation of gratitude to God that I live to see the day when Joseph's children are being gathered again, and realize that the Latter-day Saints are of Joseph, children of his favored son, Ephraim, gathered "one of a city and two of a

family," a few from the midst of the nations of the earth, whither they have been scattered, and brought to the land of Zion. The Lord has selected and picked them. They were chosen spirits before they were born. He knew them in the spirit world. He held them in reserve to come forth at the right time. (*Conference Report,* October 1924, p.28)

Mark E. Peterson shared the following results of a survey of patriarchal blessings, which blessings contain a divine pronouncement of each persons lineal connection to the house of Israel. He said, "Patriarchal blessings clearly point out that it is the tribe of Joseph that is carrying forward the last dispensation. . . . Patriarchal blessings give the lineage of Church members receiving the blessings, and they are predominantly of Joseph." (*Joseph of Egypt*, pp.15-17) The following are the results of a survey. It is not a complete and total assessment of all blessings ever given, but it still indicates what is typical.

IN NORTH AMERICA: Native Americans are declared nearly all to be of the tribe of Manasseh.

IN LATIN AMERICA: Mexico, one patriarch: 75% were Manasseh and almost 25% were of Ephraim, only 2 or 3 out of hundreds were of other Tribes.

IN SOUTH AMERICA: Peru, one patriarch, 247 blessings surveyed, 122 were of Ephraim, 130 of Manasseh, 90 of Joseph, 2 of Ashur, 2 of Benjamin and 1 of Levi. Another patriarch in Peru had given over 900 blessings, 90% were of Manasseh, 9% were of Ephraim and 15 of other Tribes. Argentina, 100 blessings surveyed, 66 were of Ephraim, 33 were from Manasseh and 1 of another Tribe. Chile, 60 were of Ephraim and 40 from Manasseh. Uruguay, 21 from Ephraim, 76 were of Manasseh and 3 of other Tribes.

IN GREAT BRITAIN: three different patriarchs: about 1400 blessings surveyed and all were of Ephraim except 5 who were of other Tribes.

IN EUROPE: France, from two patriarchs, 394 blessings were surveyed, 373 were discovered to be of Ephraim, about 17 from Manasseh and about 4 from Judah. In Italy, out of 150 blessings, all were of Ephraim.

IN THE SOUTH SEAS: New Zealand, all Europeans were of Ephraim, all Polynesians were from Manasseh and a few from Joseph. Tonga, 75% were of Manasseh, 25% of Ephraim and only 4% were related to any other Tribe.

IN THE ORIENT: Hong Kong, 326 blessings were surveyed, 323 were of Ephraim and 3 from Manasseh. Taiwan, 210 blessings surveyed and all were of Ephraim. The Philippines, all blessings given so far were of

Ephraim. Japan, out of 2,641 blessings, 1,326 were of Joseph, 444 were from Ephraim and 871 were of Manasseh.

IN TOTAL: from the areas where there are numbers instead of percents, that is, in Great Britain, France, Italy, Uruguay, Chile, Argentina, Peru, Mexico, Tonga, Japan Taiwan and Hong Kong, the following percents were tabulated: 42% Manasseh, 30% Joseph, 27% Ephraim and 1% other Tribes.

Mark E. Peterson concluded: "The sifting of the blood of Joseph and his sons Ephraim and Manasseh to all parts of the world is nothing short of miraculous. And it is likewise obviously an act of Providence that the Latter-day Saints being brought into the Church in all parts of the world are over-whelmingly of the blood of Joseph." (Ibid.)

Joseph's glorious birthright work is to save all mankind who will respond to the call of the Everlasting God. He was promised all the glory and magnificence of the whole Western Hemisphere, even the great land of the Americas. Ephraim and Manasseh were to be given "a chosen land of the Lord" and "choice above all other lands, which the Lord God had preserved. . . ." (Ether 13:2, 2:7) And Nephi, an ancient Native American prophet of God, prophesied "that the Lord God will raise up a mighty nation among the Gentiles, yea, even upon the face of this land . . . [and] the Lord God will proceed to do a marvelous work among the Gentiles, which shall be of great worth unto our seed . . . [and] unto all the house of Israel. . . ." (1 Nephi 22:7-9)

This was done that a platform, a solid foundation of liberty and freedom as well as a financial springboard of immense wealth would be established to support and nurture the gospel of Jesus Christ as the cradle of the Great God of heaven to help all mankind. Hence, Ephraim is empowered with resources to further the work of the living God in all the earth. The conferral of this birthright on Joseph conferred the richest, most valuable material inheritance ever to pass from father to son. The magnitude of this is staggering and beyond comprehension until you know the mind of God and His great love for all His children.

Would it surprise you that the United States, this land "choice above all other lands," in 1970 had seventy-five percent of all the worlds natural resources. ("Anglo-American Miracle," October/November 1970, p.1) This important land of the high birthright of Israel in 1970 had six percent of all the world's population on only seven percent of the earth, and yet these very people controlled more than fifty percent of all the wealth and riches of the whole earth, and enjoyed the highest standard of living the world has ever known. (Ezra Taft Benson, *Speeches of the Year*, April 21, 1970, p.3) For example, the gross income of General Motors at one time was greater than the income of all but four of the members of the United Nations. The State of Illinois annually produced more than the entire continent of Africa at one time. And if either California or New York were separately chartered as nations, either one of them would be the sixth richest nation on earth. ("Anglo-American Miracle," October/November 1970, p.2)

If that isn't impressive enough, carefully consider the following. Comparisons often help us see straight, because we very often feel we are poor in America. Consider four questions:

(1) Do you own two sets of shoes?
(2) Can you choose what you will eat twice a day and how much?
(3) Do you have access to your own transportation?
(4) Do you have more than one set of underwear?

If you can say "yes" to three or more of the above questions, then you are living out the wildest fantasy of most of the people who ever lived on this earth. (reference unknown) For example, the average man on this earth will simply:

(1) never own a car or TV,
(2) never know a real vacation,
(3) will live in a shack at best,
(4) will never/ever have a telephone or subscribe to a magazine or own a refrigerator,
(5) He will, in short, experience malnutrition and all the diseases that go with it. He has very little, but at least he has food to eat.

Another group, the hopelessly poor, almost one fourth of humanity, live constantly on the brink of starvation and children die like flies around them. ("Good News for the Average Man," May 1980, p.39)

"The Lord has blessed us as a people with a prosperity unequaled in times past," declared Spencer W. Kimball. (*Ensign*, June 1976, p.4) In the great land of America, we are rich and wealthy beyond the rest of the world. We have the highest standard of living the world has ever known. We are blessed above all people. We have nothing to complain about. President Kimball continued:

> The resources that have been placed in our power are good, and neces-
> sary to our work here on the earth. But I am afraid that many of us have

been surfeited [so filled up and satiated] with flocks and herds and acres and barns and wealth and have begun to worship them as false gods, and they have power over us. Do we have more of these good things than our faith can stand? Many people spend most of their time working in the service of a self-image that includes sufficient money, stocks, bonds, investment portfolios, property, credit cards, furnishings, automobiles, and the like to guarantee carnal security throughout, it is hoped, a long and happy life. Forgotten is the fact that our assignment is to use these many resources in our families and quorums to build up the kingdom of God—to further the missionary effort and the genealogical and temple work; to raise our children up as fruitful servants unto the Lord; to bless others in every way, that they may also be fruitful. Instead, we expend these blessings on our own desires. . . . (Ibid.)

We must be wide awake and realize the great purpose of the tremendous wealth we enjoy or we will be punished and suffer for our selfishness and pride.

The descendants of Joseph, mixed among the Anglo-Saxons, the Orientals, the European gentiles, the black Americans and the Lamanite blood of Israel in this land and nation, enjoy, without knowing it, much of the enormous financial blessings promised to Israel in the last days. This nation is so important to all the earth and to the eternal purposes of God, that the Lord told the prophet Ether "that whoso should possess this land of promise, from that time henceforth and forever, should serve him, the true and only God, or they should be swept off when the fulness of his wrath should come upon them. . . . For behold, this is a land which is choice above all other lands; wherefore he that doth possess it shall serve God or shall be swept off; for it is the everlasting decree of God." (Ether 2:8,10) We cannot get around it. Two great and mighty nations, the Jaredites and Nephites, have already been destroyed before the United States ever became a nation. This stands as a sobering warning to anyone who loves this land and what it represents. Because it is God's land and we must use our financial resources to do His work.

In fact, this land is so choice and so rich that "the United States is the most generous nation under heaven," probably the most generous nation that has ever existed. (John Mowbray, *Scouting*, October 1979, pp.41-42) This great land has given over 25 billion dollars worth of food assistance by 1979 and 80% of all the aid given to anyone anywhere in the earth is given by the United States. (Ibid.) However, much of the money is given away with strings attached.

But only one thing can guarantee our continued prosperity and that is righteousness. More than a century ago, Alexis de Tocqueville, a world-famous French historian and statesman, who spent ten years studying the United States, expressed his own soul stirring explanation of the greatness of this choice, land of Israel. He wrote,

> I sought for the greatness and genius of America in her commodious harbors and her ample rivers, and it was not there; in her fertile fields and boundless prairies, and it was not there; in her rich mines and her vast world commerce, and it was not there. Not until I went to the churches of America and heard her pulpits aflame with righteousness did I understand the secret of her genius and power. America is great because she is good, and if America ever ceases to be good, America will cease to be great. (Ezra Taft Benson, *God, Family, Country*, p.360)

Sadly, the flames of righteousness are flickering. There are many good and wholesome people in this land, but there is much that is appalling as well. In proverbs we read that "righteousness exalteth a nation: but sin is a reproach to any people." (Proverbs 14:34) And if that reproach becomes ripe or ugly enough we will all terribly suffer for it. (Helaman 13:13-14)

Pertaining to the Saints, President Brigham Young said:

> There is one principle I would like to have the Latter-day Saints perfectly understand—that is, of blessings and cursings. For instance, we read that war, pestilence, plagues, famine, etc., will be visited upon the inhabitants of the earth; but if distress through the judgements of God comes upon this people, it will be because the majority of the people turn away from the Lord. Let the majority of the people turn away from the Holy Commandments which the Lord has delivered to us, and cease to hold the balance of power in the Church, and we may expect the judgements of God to come upon us; but while six-tenths or three-fourths of this people will keep the commandments of God, the curse and judgements of the Almighty will never come upon them, though we will have trials of various kinds, and the elements to contend with, natural and spiritual elements. While this people strive to serve God according to the best of their abilities, they will fare better, have more to eat and to wear, have better houses to live in, better associations, and enjoy themselves better than the wicked ever do or ever will do. (*Journal of Discourses* 10:335-336)

Orson Pratt prophesied that if we truly unite ourselves with God and obey all His commandments, heart and soul, "the Lord will make us the richest of all people that have been upon the face of the earth, . . . and make us mighty; and when we go forth He will make the nations to tremble before us, because His power and glory will be with us when we are doing His will and are united in one." (*Journal of Discourses* 2:104)

But, the greatest blessings of Jacob are not financial and never were. They are everlasting and eternal. They transcend, beyond words, the financial concerns. They pertain to the glory and power of God and the glorious rewards and beautiful treasures of eternity. Eldred G. Smith, the last Patriarch to the Church, said, "The blessings of Israel are leadership blessings [the Celestial glory is a kingdom of leadership], and leadership blessings are the blessings of the priesthood." ("Patriarchal Blessings," January 17, 1964, p.3) In other words, the greater and more elevated blessings of Israel pertain to the everlasting priesthood of God—the most glorious and wonderful gifts ever enjoyed on earth. The Lord told Abraham, "Thou shalt be a blessing unto thy seed after thee, that in their hands they shall bear this ministry and Priesthood unto all nations; And I will bless them through thy name. . . . And I will bless them that bless thee, and curse them that curse thee; and in thee (that is, in thy Priesthood) and in thy seed (that is, thy Priesthood), for I give unto thee a promise that this right shall continue in thee, and in thy seed after thee (that is to say, the literal seed, or the seed of the body) shall all the families of the earth be blessed, even with the blessings of the Gospel, which are the blessings of salvation, even of life eternal." (Abraham 2:9-11) Since the priesthood created the universe for man, the ultimate blessings of Israel is exaltation. For the priesthood and its ordinances lead to the exaltation of the gods and nothing could be greater.

John Taylor commenting said, "Oh, if we could comprehend the glory, the intelligence, the power, the majesty and dominion of our Heavenly Father! If we could contemplate the exaltation, the glory, the happiness which awaits the righteous, the pure and the virtuous, of those who fear God, even the Saints of the Most High! If we could comprehend the great blessings that God has in store for those people that fear him and observe his laws and keep his commandments, we should feel very different from what we do." (*Journal of Discourses* 22:315-316) This is the staggering heritage of Manasseh and Ephraim, and their responsibility to share it with all people.

Melvin J. Ballard, one of the earlier apostles, said, of all the tribes of Israel, from Ephraim, the highest and the greatest, "shall come the majority of the candidates for Celestial Glory." ("Three Degrees of Glory," address delivered September 22, 1922, p.26) It is a great compliment to be of Ephraim, but only the righteous can maintain this high and exalted status before heaven. "For they are not all Israel, which are of [the lineage of] Israel," declared the Apostle Paul. (Romans 9:6) "For, verily I [God] say that the rebellious are not of the blood of Ephraim, wherefore they shall be plucked out," and lose the honor and glory of God that could have been theirs. (D&C 64:36) But the adopted righteous of Israel "shall come from the east and west, and shall sit down with Abraham, and Isaac, and Jacob, in the kingdom of heaven. But the children of the kingdom [the literal descendants of Israel who fail to measure up] shall be cast out . . . ," for only the righteous are blessed. (Matthew 8:11-12)

Joseph Fielding Smith wrote:

> Every person who embraces the gospel becomes of the house of Israel. In other words, they become members of the chosen lineage, or Abraham's children through Isaac and Jacob unto whom the promises were made. The great majority of those who become members of the Church are literal descendants of Abraham through Ephraim, son of Joseph. Those who are not literal descendants of Abraham and Israel must become such, and when they are baptized and confirmed they are grafted into the tree and are entitled to all the rights and privileges as heirs." (*Doctrines of Salvation* 3:246)

Hence, Spencer W. Kimball declared, "We are all of Israel! We are of Abraham and Isaac and Jacob and Joseph through Ephraim and Manasseh. We are all of us remnants of Jacob." (*Teachings of Spencer W. Kimball*, pp.600-601) It really doesn't matter which way one becomes of Israel. The important thing is that one becomes such and continues in that status, because the family of Israel is the family of the great ones who obtain the highest degree of glory in eternity. Nephi tells us that "as many of the Gentiles as will repent are the covenant people of the Lord; and as many of the Jews [or other tribes of Israel] as will not repent shall be cast off; for the Lord covenanteth with none save it be with them that repent and believe in his Son, who is the Holy One of Israel." (2 Nephi 30:2) James E. Faust declared, "No one need assume that he or she will be denied any blessing by reason of not being of the blood lineage of Israel." (*Ensign*, November 1995, p.64)

When asked whether the Latter-day Saints are literal descendants of Israel or Israelites by adoption, Bruce R. McConkie answered as follows: "We are literally of the seed of Abraham. Let's just drill it into ourselves! We are literally of the seed of Abraham. We are natural heirs according to the flesh. We are not adopted nor anything else. I don't know how there could be language more express than these revelations, 'natural heirs according to the flesh,' 'lawful heirs,' 'the literal seed of the body.' You see He [the Lord] just goes out of his way to make it literal. The literal seed of your body had the right to the priesthood and the gospel, and that is us. Now, granted that somebody can be adopted in but they are so few and far between up to now, that we can just about forget about them." (Robert J. Matthews, *Thy People Shall Be My People and Thy God My God*, p.14)

However, as Joseph Fielding Smith declared, "Nearly all of the Latter-day Saints are of Gentile ancestry as well as being of the house of Israel." (*Answers to Gospel Questions* 4:38) In other words, it is true that the great majority of members of the Church are literally of the house of Israel, but they are also of gentile blood as well. To find an individual who is a pure blood Israelite would be very improbable, so we are all adopted to some extent and thus have become heirs to the vast priesthood privileges of the chosen seed. Therefore, as both adopted lawful heirs, and literal lawful heirs, to the immense blessings of Israel, President Ezra Taft Benson taught the following concerning us and our children:

> It is my conviction that the finest group of . . . people that this world has ever known anything about have been born under the covenant into the homes of Latter-day Saint parents. I have a feeling that in many cases at least, these choice spirits have been held back to come forth in this day and age when the gospel is upon the earth in its fulness, and that they have great responsibilities in establishing the kingdom. (*Improvement Era*, June 1951, p.422)
>
> Our young people are not just ordinary people. They are not just run-of-the-mill. They are choice spirits. (*Title of Liberty*, p.197)
>
> Your heritage is one of the very greatest in all the world. You need never envy one born heir to millions in worldly wealth, nor even one whose birth entitles him to rule an empire. Your birthright surpasses all these, and blessed are you because of your lineage.
>
> Your life has come down from generation to generation through the patriarchs and the prophets of ancient Israel, through the noblest and most faithful of the descendants of the dark days of their dispersion, from kings and rulers, great nobles and warriors and law-givers of many nations, from many God-fearing men and women of honest lives—some of them outstanding leaders in service to their race and age. You need never apologize for your earthly fathers and mothers, for in your veins runs the best blood in the land. ("The Greatest Leadership," BYU Student Leadership Conference, Sun Valley, Idaho, September 1959.) (*The Teachings of Ezra Taft Benson*, pp.554-555)

Being of Ephraim, those who bear the priesthood keys of eternity under Christ, many of the children born in this dispensation are unusually choice. Brigham Young remarked that "some of the brightest spirits who dwell in the bosom of the Father are making their appearance among this people. . . ." (*Journal of Discourses* 11:132) And he said, "They are in some instances called willful and ungovernable; but these wild boys, properly guided and directed, will make the greatest men who ever lived upon this earth. . . ." (*Journal of Discourses* 11:118)

But who were these people who should be given such great privileges and possibilities? They were the worthy and obedient in the pre-earth life who had earned the honor and commendation of heaven. And this is the only principle upon which blessings can come to anyone. In the pre-existence, as on the earth, not all are alike or equal in all things. Orson F. Whitney, one of the apostles, declared, "There are degrees of greatness in heaven as upon earth, choice spirits and choicer." (*Gospel Themes*, p.148) He also declared, "Some of those 'intelligences' were more deserving than others; some nobler and greater than others; and because of their superior merit and larger capacity, they were made 'rulers' over the rest," that is, servants of all mankind. (Ibid., p.145)

The children of Israel, and especially the descendants of Joseph, were chosen before they were born to bless the world, bear the burdens and the glory of the priesthood and minister in the most sacred of all things as inspired and loving souls who serve God with all their hearts. They were great people before they came here on earth. They were valiant and good, loyal and true. Hence, they were chosen to help and lift stumbling humankind to higher levels of life. In Deuteronomy it says, "When the most High divided to the nations their inheritance [in the pre-existence], when he separated the sons of Adam, he set the bounds of the people [he organized them] according to the number of the children of Israel [the most deserving of all the hosts of heaven]." (32:8)

Bruce R. McConkie commenting on this said:

> What then is believing blood? It is the blood that flows in the veins of those who are the literal seed of Abraham—not that the blood itself believes, but that those born in that lineage have both the right and a special spiritual capacity to recognize, receive, and believe the truth. The term is simply a beautiful, a poetic way of referring to the seed of Abraham to whom the promises were made. It identifies those who developed in the pre-existence the talent to recognize the truth and to desire righteousness" so much so that they live it and thrive on it and accomplish great things in

their own lives and for others. (*A New Witness for the Articles of Faith*, pp.38-39)

Being lawful heirs they have claims on the blessings of the gospel above all others. They have a right to greater protection and guidance, even that which brings the sweet peace and wonders of eternity into their lives. George Q. Cannon explained concerning those of Israel who embrace the fullness of the gospel:

> You may strip them, as I have seen them stripped, of earthly posses-sions, and turned loose in a wilderness without a place of security and not knowing where they would find a resting place, and yet they were as happy a people as I ever saw in my life. Destitute of many things that men and women consider essential to earthly comfort, yet they had that which is above price, and which riches cannot bestow, namely, the peace of heaven, the peace of God resting down upon them. . . . They may not have rich sur-roundings, an abundance of this world's goods, elegant houses, nor elegant furniture for their houses; but when they have this spirit they are happy and they are full of peace and joy. (*Journal of Discourses* 24:220)

To be of the chosen people, to be of high birth, and bear the birthright of nobility is a brilliant and shining honor, but it is also an important calling to serve, to be the salt of the earth and to let our light so shine that people are impressed with the beautiful work of God in the last days. One man, W. J. Cameron, wisely observed:

> A man may rise and demand, "By what right does God choose one race or people above another?" I like that form of the question. It is much better than asking by what right God degrades one people beneath another, although that is implied. God's grading is always up through its ministry. If he exalts a great man, an apostle of liberty or science or faith, it is that He might raise a degraded people to a better condition. The divine selection is not [alone] a prize, a compliment paid to the man or the race—it is a burden imposed. To appoint a Chosen people is not a pandering to the racial vanity of a "superior people," it is a yoke bound upon the necks of those who are chosen for a special service. (quoted in *Our Destiny: The Call and Election of the House of Israel*, p.22 written by Robert L. Millet and Joseph Fielding McConkie)

The focus of modern Israel must be to fulfill their divine purpose and bless all people with the glory and honor of God as taught in the gospel of

Jesus Christ and as foretold by the prophets of old. "The practice of giving patriarchal blessings is [also] a constant reminder of the honor and glory of family: that one is not alone and that every person stands on the shoulders of those who have gone before." (William J. Mortimer, *Encyclopedia of Mormonism* 3:1066) That is, we belong one to another and we have common ancestors. And those ancestors were great souls of the chosen lineage. We must do what we can for them. Their temple work needs to be completed. Being of Israel also means that we were of the nobility of heaven, choice spirits, chosen to serve and to bless. It is a great honor and a beautiful compliment, but also a heavy responsibility. It is important that we know about it. Therefore, "a vital part of every patriarchal blessing is the declaration of lineage [to reveal the lineal channel or identity of our blessings]. . . . The patriarch should be responsive to the whisperings of the Spirit as he identifies lineage and the special promises and blessings attendant thereto. . . . The declaration of lineage is to come by the promptings of the Holy Ghost. This inspiration can come to the patriarch regardless of the race or nationality of the person receiving the blessing." (Information and Suggestions for Patriarchs, p.4; quoted by permission.) (quoted by Daniel H. Ludlow, *Ensign*, January 1991, p.52)

Eldred G. Smith said, "I have had many faith-promoting experiences in declaring lineage," because the Lord sustains and blesses the local and general patriarchs by the gift and power of special, individual revelation. (*Conference Report,* April 1966, p.65) An interesting story was told by Theodore M. Burton at a Faculty Luncheon at Brigham Young University on January 28, 1977:

Charles Hyde, former counselor to President Lee in the Pioneer Stake, and Patriarch, in about 1945 gave a patriarchal blessing to a young man with an English name.

When he came to the part where he was to declare lineage, he went blank. He paused for a few minutes, hoping to catch the thread which never came. He backed up and started over. When he arrived at the same point, his mind went blank a second time. He began again, this time somewhat embarrassed, but still hoping that he could pick up the blessing at the right point. He began to perspire with embarrassment. The third time he began again, and he could not discover the lineage. By now he was perspiring so profusely with embarrassment that he could feel the drops of sweat running down his collar.

Finally, he told the young man that he was not of the House of Israel. Then he assigned him, by adoption, to the tribe of Ephraim and the rest of the patriarchal blessing began to flow again.

Later, Patriarch Hyde, in talking to the young man, asked him why a man with an English name would not have the blood of Ephraim in him. He learned that the boy's father was from Turkey, and upon learning that English men could not pronounce his name, he simply took a name off a sign and used it as his own. He was a [full blooded] gentile [lawfully adopted] within the House of Israel, in a sense. (F. S. Gonzalez, "The Patriarchal Order of the Priesthood," p.8)

The gift to discern divine lineage is also illustrated in the following as told by Eldred G. Smith:

I remember, on one occasion some time back, when Brother Wallace Toronto (whom many of you know) came to me with a couple who had come from Czechoslovakia. He knew them in Czechoslovakia and they had come over to Canada and then down into the States after he had left there. He brought them into my office to receive a Patriarchal Blessing. Wallace Toronto and I went to high school together, so we started reminiscing a little bit, and in the midst of our reminiscing and discussions, I turned to the lady who was to receive the blessing and I said to her, "Would you be surprised if there were Jewish blood in your ancestry?" She turned to me and said, "How did you know that?" And Wallace Toronto's face dropped and he said to me, "Why, Eldred, I've known these people for years. I'd never suspected that there was any Jewish blood in their line." I said, "Well, there is in hers, but there isn't in her husbands." And they verified that as far as they knew, that was right. Now this is the way it comes.

Wallace Toronto said to me, "Now, Eldred, How did you know this?" I said, "Wallace, if you had asked me out on the street, I couldn't have told you," but there, under that circumstance, that was the impression that came to me, and that was the responsibility that was mine in giving them the blessing. And it came to me while we were just reminiscing, before I had even started to give the blessing."

I remember another occasion when a young man came to me for a blessing and I pronounced him of Judah. A few days after, Brother Kimball told me he was at a sacrament and testimony meeting, where a young man got up and bore testimony that he had come to me for a blessing. He had never seen me before, we didn't know each other, but he said that I had pronounced him of Judah and he was of Judah and he knew it, and that was a testimony to him. (*Speeches of the Year*, November 8, 1966, p.8)

Joseph Fielding Smith explained that "a patriarch giving a blessing has the right of inspiration to declare the literal descent of the person receiving the blessing; he does not have the authority to assign that individual to any tribe," unless the individual is adopted then he must assign him by revelation to the tribe through which his or her blessings will flow in order to fill up his or her life with the good things of heaven. (*Doctrines of Salvation* 3:171) But "we are all mixtures. There is no such thing," declared Eldred G. Smith, "as far as I have been able to determine, as any one of us being just one lineage and no other mixture in our genealogy at all. . . . So it is the right of the Patriarch to declare which line through which the blessings will come." ("Patriarchal Blessings," an address given January 17, 1964 at the Institute of Religion in Salt Lake) Hence, brother and sisters could be declared of different tribes. But the important thing to remember, no matter what race, color or tribe we are from, as was told to Abraham, "as many as receive this Gospel shall be called after thy name, and shall be accounted thy seed, and shall rise up and bless thee, as their father." (Abraham 2:10)

Patriarchs in a very real sense either seal or reconfirm upon us all the promised blessings of Abraham, Isaac and Jacob and designate the tribe or lineage through which we will be blessed of the Great God of heaven. So enormously great is this blessing that the blessings of Abraham, Isaac and Jacob are again reconferred more fully and in addition are sealed upon us on a higher level in the Temple marriage covenant. These Abrahamic blessings constituted the greatest blessings ever known on earth or in eternity and comprise the promise of eternal life through continued obedience. They include the fact that Abraham was made the lawful heir of the whole earth including all that the Father hath through the redemption of the Holy One of Israel, such that, his (Abraham's) extraordinary blessings involve the blessings and privileges of leadership, financial resources, priesthood powers and glory, spiritual gifts, but most importantly the riches, wonders and treasures of eternity. Thus the Abrahamic covenant confers upon us the mighty responsibility and privilege to greatly love the Lord and His teachings so much that we live them and shine for our Lord and His other children, and then God can pour out upon us in rich abundance his greatest treasures.

Now, "the Lord has expressed this many times," Joseph F. Smith explained, "in the word that He gave to His servant Joseph Smith the Prophet; He designed that His people should become the richest of all people. And this not only means the richest of all people in heavenly gifts—in spiritual blessings and riches, but it also means that the people of God shall be the richest of all people with regard to temporal matters." (*Conference Report,* April 1898, p.9) Orson Pratt said, ". . . wealth will be poured into the laps of the Latter-day Saints till they scarcely know what to do with it."

(*Journal of Discourses* 21:136) He continued, ". . . there are not people on the face of the whole globe, not even excepting London, Paris, New York, or any of the great mercantile cities of the globe—there are no people now upon the face of the earth, so rich as the Latter-day Saints will be. . . ." (Ibid.) But all of this is predicated upon strict and heartfelt obedience and love for the Church and Kingdom of God. John Taylor declared, "I will tell you in the name of Israel's God that if you keep his commandments you will be the richest of all people, for God will pour wealth upon you; but if you do not, you will have to struggle a good deal more than you have done for the Spirit and blessings of God will be withdrawn from us, just in proportion as we withdraw ourselves from God." (*Journal of Discourses* 21:61) John Taylor prophesied:

> . . .We shall rear splendid edifices, magnificent temples and beautiful cities that shall become the pride, praise and glory of the whole earth. . . . This people will excel in literature, in science and the arts and in manufactures. In fact, there will be a concentration of wisdom, not only of the combined wisdom of the world as it now exists, but men will be inspired in regard to all these matters in a manner and to an extent that they never have been before. . . . [We shall have] the most magnificent buildings, the most pleasant and beautiful gardens, the richest and most costly clothing, and be the most healthy and the most intellectual people that will reside upon the earth. . . . In fact, if there is anything great, noble, dignified, exalted, anything pure, or holy, or virtuous, or lovely, anything that is calculated to exalt or ennoble the human mind, to dignify and elevate the people, it will be found among the people of the Saints of the Most High God. . . . [In Jackson County, Missouri, we will] build the most magnificent temple that ever was formed on the earth and the most splendid city that was ever erected . . . all under the guidance and direction of the Lord. . . . The people will be so perfected and purified, ennobled, exalted, and dignified in their feelings and so truly humble and most worthy, virtuous and intelligent that they will be fit, when caught up, to associate with that Zion that shall come down from God out of heaven. (*Journal of Discourses* 10:146-147)

However, the Church and the world must suffer through many problems first. But as Marion G. Romney, a former member of the First Presidency, encouraged us, we need to keep the vision of these positive things continually before our minds during hard times. He said, "This I do because upon a knowledge of them, and an assurance of their reality and a witness that each of us may have part therein, rests the efficacy of Christ's admonition, 'be not troubled.'. . ." (*Conference Report,* October 1966, pp.51-52) We must embrace the positive and be obedient and faithful.

By going after the fullness of the rich inner treasures of Israel, the glory and magnificence of the covenant people, Zion can put on her beautiful garments, the glorious clothing of the righteous, be protected, and shine and glow for God. Then "with the power of God in great glory," we will be much closer to the time when every knee shall bow and every tongue confess that Jesus is the Christ. (1 Nephi 14:14) For "I am not ashamed to say that he [Joseph Smith] was a prophet of God," declared Wilford Woodruff, "and he laid the foundation of the greatest work and dispensation that has ever been established on the earth." (*Discourses of Wilford Woodruff*, p.41-42) In fact, the Church will one day be so impressive that she will shine with light and be "clear as the moon, and fair as the sun, and terrible as an army with banners" and a glorious standard to all people. (D&C 5:14) "And the day shall come when the nations of the earth shall tremble because of her and shall fear because of her terrible ones." (D&C 64:43) This is the one special dispensation that God will be beautifully crown with success, and it is the final, glorious triumph and victory of our God and His Christ through His distinguished sons of Israel in the last days, those of high birth, the birthright holders, the royal blood of Ephraim and Manasseh, the truly righteous of the covenant, the adopted and literal descendants of Abraham, the exalted and chosen of the Lord.

CHAPTER FIVE

ELEVATING PROPHETIC EXPERIENCES

"The patriarchal blessing is, in essence, a prophetic blessing and utterance," declared James E. Faust. (*Ensign*, November 1995, p.63) In 1837, Wilford Woodruff, at the age of thirty, was blessed by Joseph Smith, Sr., the Presiding Patriarch. He was told that he had "a great work to do in the earth." This he did. He became the Prophet and President of the whole Church. "Thine eyes shall be opened to look within the veil and behold the things of eternity," which he did as he enjoy beautiful visions from time to time. "Yea the Lord of glory shall appear unto thee," which He did. "Thou shalt put thy hands upon his feet and feel his wounds with thy hands that thou mayest be a special witness of his name." He was also told he would "be a great man in the earth." He was chosen of heaven and ordained an apostle and special witness of the Lord Jesus Christ in 1839 and served valiantly as such, all his life until his death in 1898, almost sixty years later. He became the President of the Church as stated and certainly therefore "a great man in the earth." (*Waiting for the World's End: The Diaries of Wilford Woodruff*, pp.17-18 and *1995-96 Church Almanac*, p.42) In addition, he was told that "if thou wilt claim it by faith thou mayest bring all thy relatives into the kingdom of God for they are of the blood of Ephraim," which this great and good man was miraculously able to accomplish through the intervention of God. And the fulfillment of this remarkable prophecy concerning his family comforted Elder Woodruff all his life. (Ibid.)

It is interesting to realize what great and enormous powers are given to the patriarchs as prophets of God to foretell the future. N. Eldon Tanner as a very young man was told by his grandfather, who was an ordained patriarch, that he would be involved in directing the mighty priesthood powers of the eternal God throughout the vast empires and continents of the earth. Quite a promise! But this special statement was fulfilled. Some forty years later Elder Tanner was called into the First Presidency to preside over all the priesthood of God in all the earth. (G. Homer Durham, *N. Eldon Tanner: His Life and Service*, p.227)

Arthur Winter was told in two patriarchal blessings that he would "travel from nation to nation . . . ," but not until he was called into the Presiding Bishopric did he finally go "from nation to nation" to preach and bless, and not until then did he understand how this mysterious promise from the Lord could be fulfilled in his life. (*Conference Report,* October 1930, p.15) Delbert L. Stapley explained that he did not have the slightest expectation of the honor God would give him in due time, but he was told in his patriarchal blessing that he would be called to positions of responsibility and trust and would travel much for the gospel's sake. When he was called into the Quorum of the Twelve Apostles all of this became understandable for it was fully fulfilled in that position. He remarked, "I'm grateful to the faithful patriarchs of the Church who enjoy the spirit of their calling, and for the ability they have to lay out before us our pattern of life, and I know if we keep in the way of God's commandments, we will realize that pattern of life." (*Conference Report,* October 1950, pp.98-99)

Samuel O. Bennion told the following experience he had while serving as the mission president of the Central States Mission:

> I have witnessed some remarkable manifestations of the Spirit and power of God in my calling as a mission president. I want to say to the young men who happened to be in this conference that when you are sent to a mission or to a conference you must bear in mind that God rules and reigns and he knows you; that you did not go into the mission field by chance, but under the inspiration and power of God you were called by men who stand at the head of the Church. Some months ago four young men came into the Central States mission. We had received but very few elders for months past, on account of the influenza, and a certain portion of our mission was very much in need of elders, as we had only one or two in a great territory. I said to the secretary of the mission: "We will send these four men to such and such a place, away into the South, a thousand miles from Kansas City." He said: "I believe that is the place they ought to go. We need them there." But when I thought about it. I saw three of those boys sitting together and one apart, at one side. I could not get the vision of those boys out of my mind, and so I said to the secretary: "Elder Pratt, we will leave it until tomorrow. We can't send them out today anyway." In the morning when I met again with the young men, I was going to say we would send them all to this certain place; but in my mind again three of them sat together and one was by himself. I said to the three: "We will send you to Texas." To this young man I said: "We will keep you here, and you may labor in Kansas City." I did not know why I had come to this decision. I battled against it, because I wanted to send him away, but a month after

that time, in a priesthood meeting, he bore his testimony and mentioned the fact that when he was a boy, ten years of age, he had been promised by a patriarch, in his patriarchal blessing, that he would grow up and fill a mission, and that he would be sent to the state of Missouri. Then I found out why I was impressed to keep that young man in the state of Missouri. (*Conference Report*, June 1919, pp.127-128)

Patriarchal blessings are so incredibly powerful as demonstrated by the following experience. Robert K. Hillman was told by a stake patriarch that as long as he kept the commandments, his life would not be taken from him while he served his country in war. In the jungles of Vietnam, his backpack had just been ripped off by machine gun fire. Grenade explosions were all around him and very close. He had fallen down just inches from a trip wire. His helmet had fallen off in the fray and was stuck by a punji stick, a sharpened bamboo stake dripped with fresh snake venom. After the gun fire stopped the other soldiers expected only to recover his body but were astonished to see him alive with two more punji sticks inches from his legs, and his boot almost touching another trip wire leading to a mine. His sergeant declared him to be the luckiest man he'd ever seen. He wasn't even wounded. Death could easily have swallowed him up that day. But a powerful patriarchal promise of the Most High God had prevented his premature death. (*Ensign*, September 1995, pp.62-63)

In the early eighteen hundreds, Martin Harris, one of the three divinely chosen witnesses of the Book of Mormon, he who saw the plates, witnessed the angel and heard the voice of God declare it to be true, was given a patriarchal blessing by Joseph Smith, Sr. that proclaimed that "thy testimony shall yet convince thousands and tens of thousands; it shall shine like the sun, and though the wicked seek to overthrow it, it shall be in vain, for the Lord God shall bear it off victorious." (*Church News*, September 9, 1984, p.6) Martin Harris responding to one individual said with impressiveness, "Young man, do I believe it? Do I see the sun shining? Just as surely as the sun is shining on us and gives us light, and the moon and stars give us light by night, just as surely do I know. . . . I saw the plates; I saw the Angel; I heard the voice of God. I know the Book of Mormon is true. . . . I might as well doubt my own existence as to doubt the divine authenticity of the Book of Mormon, or the divine calling of Joseph Smith." (Keith Marston, *Missionary Pal*, p.177)

Martin's testimony in the Book of Mormon, as with his personal testimony to thousands and thousands of people, still continues to help people gain their own testimony that Jesus Christ is the Son of the living God and that God has reestablished His Church in all its glory, majesty and power as in ancient days. And because of this glorious restoration, the restoration of the High Priesthood, patriarchs bestow blessings of great power on the covenant people of the Lord, not just in the days of the ancient prophets, but in our own day and time. How fortunate we are beyond words to have such great blessings in our midst.Hopefully we can sense this beautiful reality.

Spencer W. Kimball's father was told in a patriarchal blessing in 1898, "Andrew Kimball, . . . thou shalt have the spirit of discernment to foretell future events and thy name shall be handed down with thy posterity in honorable remembrance from generation to generation." Later another patriarch said, ". . . for thou art a prophet and came upon the earth in this dispensation to be a great leader." (*Conference Report,* October 1943, p.17) Spencer W. Kimball's father, who was promised he would be a prophet, prophetically declared that his son Spencer would be a mighty man in the Church and Kingdom of God in the last days. (Ibid.) His mother's patriarchal blessing said among other things, "Sister Olive Woolley, . . . thou shalt be numbered among the mothers of Israel and shall raise up a numerous posterity to the joy of thy husband. They shall grow up to become mighty men and women in the Church and Kingdom of God. Thy sons shall be stars of the first magnitude in thy crown and shall be healthy, strong and vigorous in helping to direct the purposes of God in the last dispensation." (Ibid.) President Kimball did "direct the purposes of God" as President of the Church and was "a mighty man" in the Kingdom. And his brothers and sisters were valiant as well. For years and years as an apostle of Christ, he faithfully served as a "healthy," "strong and vigorous" man who was helpful, personable, loving and beautiful in his ways. No wonder he was popular and loved. He was a true Christian as well as a star of the "first magnitude" and a "joy" to his father.

Joseph Fielding Smith was told in his patriarchal blessing from John Smith at the age of about twenty, "Thou art numbered among the sons of Zion, of whom much is expected. . . ." It is "the will of the Lord that you should become a mighty man in Israel. . . . It shall be thy duty to sit in counsel with thy brethren and to preside among the people . . . to travel much at home and abroad by land and water, laboring in the ministry. . . . His Spirit shall direct thy mind and give thee word and sentiment that thou shalt confound the wisdom of the wicked and set at naught the councils of the unjust." (Leon R. Hartshorn, *Classic Stories from the Lives of our Prophets,* p.309) Joseph Fielding Smith did become "a mighty man in Israel"—an apostle at the age of thirty-three and president of the Church at ninety-three.

He presided, counseled, traveled and left a beautiful testimony of Christ for over sixty years all over the earth (*1995-96 Church Almanac*, p.43)

Paul H. Dunn, who as a young man was drafted into the United States military in World War II, received the following as part of his patriarchal blessing, "Now concerning the future: Thou shalt experience combat. Angels shall intercede in thy behalf and protect thee all the days of thy life and thou shalt live many years to testify to all the nations of the world that Jesus is the Christ." ("Seek and Ye Shall Find," tape, Covenant Communications, Inc., 1985) He did bear a beautiful testimony to the nations and was a popular speaker, and did a great work in the earth.

But not only do general authorities as young men receive remarkable blessings and promises, members of the Church all over the world receive special, unique blessings and beautiful promises, because God loves us all. In East Germany, two boys were given the unlikely promised that they would go on missions like other young men in the free world. This would be a dream come true, but this promise was impossible at that time. There was simply no hope of this ever happening, but in November of 1989 the impossible did happen. The wall came down between East and West Germany. And these young men went on missions according to the word of the Lord. (*Church News*, October 17, 1992, pp.6,10)

LeGrand Richards bore a strong personal testimony of the power of God in the following experience he had as a boy:

> While working in the field with my father when I was a mere lad, I received one of the greatest testimonies that ever came to me, and that through the giving of a patriarchal blessing. My father related to us three boys, who were engaged with him in filing up an old cellar, a visit he had made the night before to administer a patriarchal blessing. After he had taken his hands from the head of the brother blessed, some disappointment was expressed that Father had not promised the man, who was very sick, that he should get well and live. Father said that when he placed his hands upon the head of this brother, something seemed to say to him that he should not give him too good a blessing for this life, for his days were numbered; so he promised him the blessings of eternal life for his faithfulness. When disappointment was expressed, and the voice of inspiration came again, Father said: "If I am inspired by the Spirit of the Lord, Brother So-and-so will not live more than so many hours," and he told us the time.
>
> While we were working together, a good brother passed along the old hedge fence. Father called to him and asked if he knew how Brother So-and-so was. He said he had passed away. Father asked the hour and he told us. Then Father looked at us, because it was the exact time he had told us. (*LeGrand Richards Speaks*, p.59)

One sister at the age of nineteen, a Mary Russell, was heartbroken and pined for the privilege of seeing her family again. She was in America and they were in England. There was no likelihood they'd ever come or even want to, but she tearfully prayed for them to see the beautiful light of the gospel and move to Utah. She was to see a patriarch that day and prayed that if God could see fit to give her two promises in her patriarchal blessing she would be brave enough to endure whatever the future held for her. She pleaded that her family and friends would come to this country and that she'd be married in the Temple. The patriarch described glorious and beautiful promises. Then she almost heard her very words spoken only to God about an hour earlier, "Your loved ones from whom you have been parted—the Lord will bless and protect them, and many of them will follow you to the fold of the Good Shepherd and bask in the life-giving light of the gospel of their Redeemer. With them you will sing the songs of Zion and have much joy in their society. You shall have the privilege of going to the house of the Lord to receive a worthy helpmate and companion to be with you for time and all eternity." Tears trickled down her face as the old patriarch continued to outline blessings for her if she remained faithful. She did and everything came true, and the blessing sustained and fortified her through the normal trials of a life well lived heroically and valiantly for God. She learned to enjoy the sweet inner peace and endearing love that comes with full compliance to the divine instruction given in Proverbs 3:5-6, "Trust in the Lord with all thine heart; and lean not unto thine own understanding." (*The New Era*, August 1978, pp.47-49)

The Lord is the best psychologist and when we are worthy, He ensures that very special passages come through that have special meaning to us through the years. Gerald E. Melchin told how he had done some foolish things in his youth but no major transgressions. But the patriarch's words brought him joy for years and years to come. Part of his blessing stated, "You are truly blessed of the Lord and well preserved; notwithstanding the follies of youth, you are clean this day before the Lord." Reflecting on this, he wrote, "Even though I had never before dwelt on this thought to any extent, these words filled me with a feeling of great happiness. To think that the Lord was that mindful of me and willing to overlook and forgive the foolishness of youth and would pronounce me clean touched me very deeply. I have returned to read those words many times and have reflected that if he forgave me then, perhaps he will continue to forgive me and grant me the blessings of peace." (*Ensign*, January 1995, pp.20-21)

Jared Edge, an eighteen year old, wrote, ". . .the patriarch laid his hands upon my head and began to prophesy about my life. I could tell . . . I could feel it was all true and that it was really God that was speaking through the patriarch. I wept. I learned many things about myself that day." (*The New Era*, March 1992, p.18) Many people have special experiences with these inspired brethren.

Sarah Pea Rich wrote in her journal that she thought she was going to die and the family went to fetch Joseph Smith, Sr., the Presiding Patriarch, to come and bless her. She wrote, ". . .he came to the bedside and looked at me and he said he thought I would die. Mr. Rich quickly answered Father Smith: 'She won't die.' The old gentleman hung his head for a few moments and then looked and then said 'Let us administer to her, and I will give her a Patriarchal blessing.' He did so and the Spirit of the Lord was poured out upon him that blessed me with a long life, and said I should speedily recover, and gave me such a blessing that all in the room [were] weeping for joy, for they had all been looking for me to die. When he got through the blessing he stood a moment looking at me and then said, 'I did not have faith when I commenced blessing Sister Rich that she would get well, but the Lord poured out His spirit upon me to give her the blessing, and promised her a long life, and many blessings and said he, 'every word will be fulfilled.' And I commenced to get better right away." ("Journal of Sarah DeArmon Pea Rich," BYU Archives, pp.32-33)

Eliza R. Snow wrote how her brother Lorenzo Snow, who later became President of the Church, was:

> . . .present at a 'Blessing Meeting,' in the [Kirtland] Temple, previous to his baptism into the Church; after listening to several patriarchal blessings pronounced upon the heads of different individuals with whose history he was acquainted, and of whom he knew the Patriarch [Joseph Smith, Sr.] was entirely ignorant; he was struck with astonishment to hear the peculiarities of those persons positively and plainly referred to in their blessings. And, as he afterwards expressed, he was convinced that an influence, superior to human prescience [foresight], dictated the words of the one who officiated. (*Biography and Family Record of Lorenzo Snow*, p.9)

This helped convert this great and good man to the Church realizing that he was associating with a man like the ancient prophets and patriarchs of old. And he wanted to partake of the glory and wonder of what he was experiencing.

Eliza R. Snow received a beautiful blessing from Isaac Morley, a Stake Patriarch, in which she was told "thou shalt have the blessing to be admired and honored . . . to speak in wisdom and counsel in prudence. . . . Thy influence shall be great—thy examples shall not be excelled. . . . Thou shalt . . . be capable with thy pen to communicate. . . . Thy name shall be handed down to posterity from generation to generation: and many songs shall be heard that were dictated by thy pen and from the principles of thy mind, even until the choirs from on high and on the earth below, shall join in one universal song of praise to God and the Lamb." (Maureen Ursenbach Beecher, *The Personal Writings of Eliza Roxey Snow*, pp.89-90) Is it surprising that we still sing some of the beautiful songs composed by Eliza R. Snow in the Church today? She is still honored as one of the truly great pioneers and a former General President of the Relief Society. God knew what she'd do with her life. Truly there are inspired local men who manifest remarkable inspiration. God bless them for the marvelous gifts they share.

In 1884 at age eleven, Melvin J. Ballard received a patriarchal blessing from Zebedee Coltrin, a local stake patriarch. He was told that if he remained faithful he would "go forth in the midst of the nations of the earth proclaiming the Gospel of the Son of God; and thou shalt proclaim the Gospel unto the seed of Manasseh and shall do many mighty miracles in the midst of the Lord." (Melvin R. Ballard, *The Instructor*, November 1965, p.458) The article from which this is quoted goes on to describe the miraculous conversion of many Native Americans, who saw Elder Ballard in dreams and visions before he came to them. Great spiritual gifts and blessings were manifest among them including restoring a blind young man, who had been blind from birth, to sight. (Ibid., pp.458-459) The patriarch also prophesied that Melvin J. Ballard "would become a mighty prophet in the midst of the Zion of the Lord," that he would see angels and visions and have mighty power "for thou art destined to do a great work upon the earth, and thou shalt behold the Lord. . . ." (Ibid., p.458) Elder Ballard was called to the apostleship and became recognized as a prophet of the Lord in 1919. He did many remarkable things as a faithful special witness of Christ and was privileged to dedicate the whole South American continent for the gospel, which was a special blessing primarily for the seed and lineage of Joseph through his son Manasseh, and many other mighty works. He also saw the Lord Jesus Christ in a glorious and inspiring vision which he reported to the Council of the Twelve on the day of his ordination to the apostleship. He said:

> As I entered the room I saw, seated on a raised platform, the most glorious Being I have ever conceived of, and was taken forward to be introduced to Him. As I approached, He smiled, called my name, and stretched

out His hands towards me. If I live to be a million years old, I shall never forget that smile. He put His arms around me and kissed me, as He took me into His bosom; and He blest me until my whole being was thrilled. As He finished I fell at His feet, and there saw the marks of the nails; and as I kissed them, with deep joy swelling through my whole being, I felt that I was in Heaven, indeed. The feeling that came to my heart then was: "Oh! if I could live worthy, though it would require fourscore years, so that in the end, when I finished, I could go into His presence and receive the feeling that I then had in His presence, I would give everything that I am and ever hope to be!" (Ibid., p.460)

Elder Ballard was to become a great man and a prophet and only the spirit of the living God could reveal this at the tender age of eleven to a so-called unimportant little boy.

Orson Hyde received a very special patriarchal blessing from Joseph Smith, Sr. in 1835. He was told he would be a great missionary to the nations, be a mighty and powerful man in the earth, enjoy the richest blessing God can provide on earth and in heaven and see the vision of eternity, even of Christ, the Lord of all. And this he did on more than one occasion. And he was a great apostle and special witness to the nations. He served as president of the Quorum of the Twelve for thirty years—longer than any other man in this dispensation. He achieved his great potential brilliantly and wonderfully as foreseen by one of the prophets and patriarchs of the Lord's Church. (Howard H. Barron, *Orson Hyde: Missionary, Apostle, Colonizer,* pp.41, 71, 109, 181, 314-316)

LeGrand Richards told a story about the death of one of his sons and how it also illustrates the great inspiration and seership of the patriarchs. He said:

> Many years ago my wife and I laid away in the grave our eldest son, who was nearly sixteen years of age—the greatest sorrow that has ever come into our lives. We had four daughters before he was born. Less than a year prior to that we took him and his younger brother into the office of the Patriarch to the Church, Brother Hyrum G. Smith, and he gave them each a blessing.
>
> Now, I ask you, suppose the Patriarch had known that one of these boys would die within a year, couldn't he promise him anything? What would it have meant to the oldest son, had he walked out of the Patriarch's office with no promise and no blessing, and the younger son had all the promises and blessings, for the older boy truly loved God and kept his commandments? When that boy passed away, I wondered, if God could only

give us to understand that boy's blessing, so that Sister Richards and I might be comforted.

In the oldest boy's blessing, the one who passed away, the Patriarch said: "For it will be thy privilege to bear the Holy Priesthood and to go even among strangers and in strange lands, in defense of truth and righteousness." And to the younger boy he said: "For thou shalt bear the Holy Priesthood in defense of righteousness and truth, both home and abroad."

A few nights later I took Sister Richards for a ride. We asked the younger boy if he would like to go with us. He said, "No, I think I will stay home." The next morning he came in and, holding in his hand the two patriarchal blessings, said: "While you were out riding last night I read these blessings. You see, I am going to labor at home and abroad, but LeGrand was to go to strange lands and strange people. They are not on this earth. We know all the lands of this earth and we know all the people that are here."

To the oldest boy the Patriarch had said: "And in due time thy home shall be a fit abode for the spirits of thy loved ones," and to the younger boy he had said: "Thou shalt enjoy the comforts of a happy home and the blessings of honored fatherhood, for thou shalt see thy posterity grow up around thee, to honor thee in the same kind of way in which thou hast honored thy parents."

Now, reverse the blessings and give the younger boy's blessing to the older boy, and there would be no explanation. He said, "You see, LeGrand's home is to be the home of the spirits of his loved ones, and my home is to be here on this earth, where I will see my children grow up around me."

You can't tell me that God, the Eternal Father, didn't give that fourteen-year-old boy inspiration and revelation to understand these blessings, and our hearts have been comforted.

My faith in God and his eternal purposes is such that I never doubt but that he has made adequate provision for the fulfillment of every promise, and to complete and perfect the work that he has here commenced. In a revelation to the Prophet Joseph, he said: "For his purposes fail not; neither are there any who can stay his hands." And again: "A new commandment I give unto you, that I, the Lord your God, am bound when ye do what I say, and when ye do not what I say, ye have no promise." And when we receive a promise from the Lord through his servants, it is my faith that that promise shall be realized if we keep his commandments, if not in this life, then after this life. (G. LaMont Richards, *LeGrand Richards Speaks*, Deseret Book Company, 1972, pp.61-62, Used by permission)

The correct interpretation of a patriarchal blessing is the right and privilege of those who receive it. However, sometimes merely the passage of time clarifies what was meant. (*Conference Report*, April 1930, p.25)

Further illustration of this principle was given in the following quote from Joseph Fielding Smith. It also shows how patriarchal promises should be viewed from an eternal perspective.

Let us say a few words on these patriarchal blessings. Sometimes the individual receiving the blessings can't understand all that's in it. Maybe it's well that he can't, but in course of time the Lord unfolds to his mind [the full truth] when that blessing becomes fulfilled. There are some things the patriarch may say in a blessing that he has to say rather guardedly, because he couldn't say a direct and simple truth. I call your attention to one: when I was in Canada one time a father came to me with his son's patriarchal blessing. In it the patriarch had said: "In a short time you will be called on an important mission." That's all he said. It was only a few months later when the young man was killed. He was a good, faithful young man. The father said: "That blessing was never fulfilled." I said: "How do you know? Maybe his mission wasn't here."

In another case where the patriarch had said, in giving a blessing to another young man, "You shall be changed in the twinkling of an eye." They got the idea that he was going to live until the coming of Christ and then would be changed. Out in the field one day he was struck with lightning. The patriarch could not have said in that blessing that the time would come when you will be struck with lightning and taken to the other side where your work will continue. And in his own mind he never had any such thought, there is no doubt about that; but they have the right of prophecy and revelation to pronounce upon those who receive these blessings. The main purpose of the blessing is to be a guide to the individual who receives it, to encourage him, to direct him, to help him as he journeys through life.

My uncle, John Smith, who gave as many blessings I suppose as anybody, said one day to me in the presence of others: "When I give a patriarchal blessing, the dividing line between time and eternity disappears." If that be the case, I guess I ought to be willing to accept it. Then there may be things in these blessings that pertain to our future existence. There might be promises made to us that are not fulfilled here that will be fulfilled. For instance, suppose a patriarch says in giving a blessing to a young woman that she will be married and that she will have posterity, and yet she dies without posterity. Married for time and all eternity in the temple of the Lord, she receives there the blessings of eternal lives, which is a continuation of the seeds forever. Perhaps the patriarch, in giving her a blessing of posterity, sees beyond the veil; so I don't think we should be too hasty in condemning a patriarch when he promises posterity, and then in this life that blessing is not fulfilled. We may ourselves be at fault in judging in matters of this kind. ("Address of Joseph Fielding Smith," at BYU, June 15, 1956, pp.5-6)

Mary Brown Pulsipher received a blessing in Kirtland, Ohio in the early eighteen hundreds through Joseph Smith, Sr. She was told that she would have her friends in the church with her and "would be the means of saving and redeeming them" before the great plan of redemption for the dead was revealed that made this type of blessing possible. She was also promised that she would be blessed a hundred fold for having left all for Christ and for her faithful and endearing love for God. What that passage meant became clear over time. In 1874, years later, she reflected, "That [promise about being blessed a hundred fold] is fulfilling very fast. I have 56 grandchildren and 75 great grandchildren. So you see, there is upwards of a hundred fold now and increasing at a wonderful rate." (Mark L. McConkie, *The Father of the Prophet*, p.90)

Many special and unique promises in my own blessing have become clear and understandable only after their fulfillment. I believe this will also be the case with some of the prophecies of Isaiah, John the revelator and other of the great prophets. But a greater gift and blessing than interpretation is the ability to do our part to ensure that the promises come to pass, especially those that pertain to eternal life and exaltation, for everything else pales into insignificance before the privilege of godhood, which includes such wonderful things as the creation of stars, galaxies and worlds without end.

Harold B. Lee discussed how a righteous and good-hearted young man, before going to war, received a patriarchal blessing promising him a posterity of sons and daughters. However, he died in the war. He also told of a good sister in the Church who was worthy in every way and was promised posterity, but died of tuberculosis shortly after returning from a full-time mission. He quoted the patriarch who gave these blessings as saying, "When a patriarch pronounces an inspired blessing, such a blessing encompasses the whole of life, not just this phase we call mortality." He then said, "If we fail to understand this great truth, we will be miserable in time of need, and then sometimes our faith may be challenged. But if we have a faith that looks beyond the grave and trusts in divine Providence to bring all things in their proper perspective in due time, then we have hope, and our fears are calmed." ("From the Valley of Despair to the Mountain Peaks of Hope," p.8)

John A. Widtsoe explained:

> It should always be kept in mind that the realization of the promises made may come in this or the future life. Men have stumbled at times because promised blessings have not occurred in this life. They have failed

to remember that, in the gospel, life with all its activities continues forever and that the labors of earth may be continued in heaven." (*Evidences and Reconciliations*, p.323)

This eternal, long range perspective on patriarchal blessings makes understandable such promises as seeing the Son of God coming in the clouds of glory in one's lifetime, because this can easily be fulfilled in the spirit world, which is part of ones mortal probation, along with such ideals as assisting to build the "New Jerusalem," or preaching the gospel on other planets as spirit beings or in a translated or resurrected state as righteously assigned by the Lord. There is no particular time limit. Blessings are fulfilled both on earth and in heaven. In fact, the great blessing of marriage and family in heaven far transcends in beauty, glory and magnificence anything else on earth.

Since it is so easy to misinterpret blessings, comparing them can create additional problems and misunderstandings or "breed a sense of jealousy or competition if one feels his [own] specific promises are not as glorious as those of someone else." We really need to remember that "the greatest blessing God can give to anyone—eternal life and exaltation with him in the celestial kingdom—is universally granted to every member of the house of Israel who faithfully keeps the covenants. Who could ask for more?" (Victor L. Ludlow, *Principles and Practices of the Restored Gospel*, p.352) Indeed, could anything be greater? What could hold a candle to it or involve more magnificence, glory and wonder? Nothing ever could! All such blessings are incomparably grand and in this we are all equal inasmuch as we stay on the straight and narrow path that leads to it.

Another example of possible misinterpretation is when a patriarch uses superlatives or blesses you that you will do a great work in the earth that is remarkable. It is not to be interpreted as the world would interpret great or outstanding. God sees things entirely different. "For my thoughts are not your thoughts, neither are your ways my ways, saith the Lord. For as the heavens are higher than the earth, so are my ways higher than your ways, and my thoughts than your thoughts." (Isaiah 55:8-9)

God sees things very differently than we do. Joseph F. Smith said, "After all, to do well those things which God ordained to be the common lot of all mankind is the truest greatness." (*Gospel Doctrine*, p.285) Howard W. Hunter said:

To be a successful Primary president or den mother or Spiritual Living teacher or loving neighbor or listening friend is much of what true greatness is all about. . . .

Frequently it is the commonplace tasks that have the greatest positive effect on the lives of others, as compared with the things that the world so often relates to greatness.

It appears to me that the kind of greatness that our Father in Heaven would have us pursue is within the grasp of all who are within the gospel net. We have an unlimited number of opportunities to so the many simple and minor things that will ultimately make us great. (Clyde J. Williams, *Teachings of Howard W. Hunter*, p.72)

Therefore, in the words of President Joseph F. Smith, "To be a successful father or a successful mother is greater than to be a successful general or a successful statesman." (*Gospel Doctrine*, p.285) Because as Brother Robert Millet put it, "The family is the most important unit in time and in eternity. No work, no service, no outside agency or interests can supersede the family in eternal significance." (*When a Child Wanders*, p.148) Yet to the world being a successful parent is almost nothing, but to be a successful general or statesman is to be the envy of all men. It is to be prominent, important and great. But hopefully we will not see things in a twisted or worldly sense, but as the gods and angels of heaven would, understanding that some things are fulfilled in eternity rather than in mortality or later in life. And we must do our part to expect divine help, for it seems quite evident for the most part that God only helps those who are willing to help themselves. Hence, it is unfair to demand the fulfillment of blessings we haven't earned or don't really care about. A patriarchal blessing, Harold B. Lee, explained tells us through the "spirit of prophecy . . . what each of us can become," not necessarily what we will become. (*Stand Ye in Holy Places*, p.117)

Antoine R. Ivins, a past general authority, said:

. . .When I was a teenager, about sixty-two years ago, I went to a patriarch to have a blessing, and it was a very fine blessing. Mind you, at that time I was living in Mexico with the possibility that upon obtaining my majority, I could become a Mexican citizen. Some of the promises [like becoming a true and righteous statesman in Mexico] in that blessing would depend upon my remaining there and becoming a citizen. That I did not want to do. So when these promises have not been realized, I have never blamed the patriarch. I looked upon that blessing, brethren and sisters, as a vision of what I might do if I would seek the blessings of the Lord, live true to the covenants that I had made, and endeavor to realize those blessings.

I think that all of the blessings that are promised to us throughout the Church are dependent upon our efforts to help them come to pass. I never have felt that a patriarchal blessing was a prediction as to what must come to pass, but what might come to pass if we would help those conditions so that those things could be realized. (*The Improvement Era*, December 1961, p.936)

Eldred G. Smith said, "The blessings given by a patriarch are usually the outstanding things which might happen if we work a little harder to get them and exercise a little extra faith," that is, we must do our part. (*The Instructor*, February 1962, p.43) ". . . But there comes great comfort and consolation from having our blessings both promised and sealed upon us by authorized servants of the Lord . . . for neither death nor the destroyer will end these blessings, but the receiver will possess and enjoy them forever and ever." (*Conference Report*, April 1953, p.30)

The Lord does not interpret human suffering in the same way that we do. Because life was meant to be hard to challenge us and teach us important lessons for eternity. Christ learned from the things which he suffered and so must we. (Hebrews 5:8) It may be our lot to experience hard times as a blessing to stretch our souls and learn to find our comfort from God rather than from worldly distractions or sins. This kind of blessing may result in having a serious life threatening disease, accident or permanent crippling handicap, but it is a blessing in disguise if we take it well or endure well.

I, myself, was blessed of heaven by divine will with a thorn in the flesh for many many years, but it turned out to be good for me. I grew in understanding and insight. And if I were God, out of my overwhelming love and superior insight, I would have given myself the same problem as a young man to help me grow. It was not a curse. It was a blessing and as prophesied by the priesthood of Almighty God, it was entirely removed. And having tasted the bitter, I know how to prize, enjoy and love the sweet. Hence, a priesthood blessing may faithfully promise full recovery and a most beautiful and engaging feeling may bear witness that it is true, but that special deliverance may not come for years and years and years or even a lifetime, because God loves us way too much to spare us the growth some difficult problem may bring us.

The glory of the Godhead or prophetic power of the ancient prophets is so evident in patriarchal blessings that they inspire the Saints and bring them hope and bear testimony to the fact that God lives and that Jesus is the Christ. Joseph F. Smith, for example, was told as a young man of thirteen, by the fourth Presiding Patriarch John Smith, who was the brother of Joseph Smith, Sr., that he would hold the "fullness in due time which will reveal unto" him "all the hidden mysteries of the Redeemer's Kingdom," that his name would be had in honorable remembrance among the Saints forever and that his posterity would be great and that "none shall excel them in Israel. They shall spread upon the mountains so numerous that they cannot be numbered for multitudes." (Patriarchal Blessing of Joseph F. Smith, Brigham Young University Archives) He was given the eternal fullness and glory of the priesthood and attained to the honor of becoming the sixth President of the Church, the highest position any mortal man could ever hold on earth. As such he will be remembered by the Saints forever as one of the truly great men of the last days. Of his posterity, two sons became apostles and one of them became the tenth President of the Church, Joseph Fielding Smith, Jr. Another son served as first and second counselor in the Presiding Bishopric and a grandson—another namesake also served as Patriarch to the Church. (*1995-96 Church Almanac*, pp.42-42, 54, 57) No doubt his posterity is beginning to be difficult to number as well and have had great success with their lives in general. His blessing is still being fulfilled.

Ezra Taft Benson was told as a boy, by a local patriarch John Edward Dalley, that he would go "to the nations of the earth," which he did as an apostle of the Lord Jesus Christ, and that "his life would be preserved on land and sea" and "many would rise up and bless his name" for the good he would do, which was fulfilled in the many lives which he influenced. (Sheri L. Dew, *Ezra Taft Benson: A Biography*, pp.28-29) President Benson's name has become a name of great honor and respect the world over, but no honor could be greater than the highest sacred office on earth even the honor of being the prophet, seer and revelator of the whole Church at the end of his useful and productive life. Ezra Taft Benson was President of the Church from 1985 to 1994 or for about eight years. (*1995-96 Church Almanac*, p.44) His patriarchal blessing was obviously meant for a boy who would one day become a well-known and highly respected general authority. B. H. Roberts was told by John Smith, the fifth Presiding Patriarch to the Church, the son of Hyrum Smith, on August 24, 1877 that he was "numbered with the sons of Zion of whom much is expected. . . ." (Gray James Bergera, *The Autobiography of B. H. Roberts*, p.75) Brother Roberts was a man of promise who eventually attained to the honor of being a President of the Seventy and wrote many wonderful books to promote the work of the Lord. He was told he would "become a mighty man in Israel" and his "name shall be handed down to posterity in honorable remembrance. . . ." (Ibid.) He was certainly one of the great men of the last days who valiantly served God and really made something of his life as foretold.

Abraham O. Smoot was blessed by Patriarch Joseph Smith, Sr. on June

23, 1837 in Kirtland, Ohio. He was told, ". . .if thou keepest the commandments of God, thou shalt become great upon the earth like unto Elijah. . . ."
(Loretta D. Nixon and L. Douglas Smoot, *Abraham Owen Smoot: A
Testament of His Life,* p.9) He was ordained a patriarch and sealed blessings
on earth and in heaven for time and all eternity similar to Elijah. He was also
told, ". . .thou shalt become great with thy brethren. . . ." (Ibid.) He served as
a Stake President. His blessing continued, "Thou shalt have great wisdom,
many shall seek wisdom at thy mouth. . . ." (Ibid.) As a Church leader
appointed to counsel the Saints, he shared his special insights. The patriarch
then said, "Thou shalt have much persecution on the earth thy enemies shall
seek thy life but thou shalt be delivered out of their hands and return to Zion
when thy labours in the Lord's vineyard are ended and thy fame known
among the Saints." (Ibid.) This great and good man went on eight missions,
suffered persecution for the Lord, had a large and numerous posterity, was
sought after for his great wisdom and his fame was that he, through years of
personal sacrifice and labor, financially perpetuated the continuance of
Brigham Young Academy through dark and foreboding times which threatened its very existence.

This foundation blessed thousands and eventually became Brigham
Young University, which continues to empower students with knowledge
and testimony. No wonder one of the most important administration buildings is named after him this man who contributed so much. (Ibid.)

Hugh B. Brown wrote in his memoirs of a special experience he
enjoyed. He received a patriarchal blessing at the age of about twenty-one
also from John Smith, the son of Hyrum Smith. In it he was told:

> "Thou shalt be wise in counsel among they brethren and valiant in the
> defense of truth, virtue, and righteousness. Thou shalt travel much at home
> and abroad, laboring in the ministry, and thy voice shall be heard among
> the nations of the earth, proclaiming the words of life and salvation unto all
> who shall listen. And when necessary thou shalt prophesy, for thy guardian
> angel will often whisper in thine ear and open the eyes of thine understand-
> ing." At the time, I did not interpret this blessing to mean that I would
> become one of the General Authorities, but afterwards Patriarch Smith said
> to me, "Young man, you will someday sit among the highest councils in the
> church." (*The Memoirs of Hugh B. Brown: An Abundant Life*, p.114)

Elder Hugh B. Brown was called as an Assistant to the Twelve at the age
of sixty-nine. He was later ordained an apostle and served valiantly in the
First Presidency and in the Quorum of the Twelve as a great and inspired

man and a prophet in Israel as prophesied by one of the Lord's very best servants, who predicted he would "sit among the highest councils in the church."

A close friend when she was about fourteen lost her mother, which was a heavy blow, and she continued to hurt and anguish about it. Her suffering resulted in anger and rebellion followed by repentance and change. A year later still sorrowing and in great need, she sought a patriarchal blessing. However, when the patriarch checked the tape recorder immediately after the blessing, he discovered that the blessing was not there. She felt devastated by this. It was like God had no blessing for her. Her blessing was a blank. God had taken it away. She sobbed and was heartbroken. The venerable old patriarch, with inspired wisdom, comforted her with the fact that he must have failed to tell her something in the blessing. He told her he would bless her again and instructed her to listen carefully and pick out what was different, what was added so she could discover what he had missed that was so important that a second blessing had to occur. He repeated the blessing almost word for word, but added a most significant sentence, which brought great joy, understanding and comfort to her. He said, "The passing of your mother was to prepare the way for a greater blessing for your father and she is now ready and anxiously awaiting for this important work to be accomplished." This special sentence eased the pain. A beautiful, heavenly feeling enveloped her. It was a direct revelation from God who loved her dearly. It healed her wounded heart and brought the understanding she needed to move ahead with her life. You see, her father was not a member of the Church. Her mom was. Her mom's death would ultimately result in her dad's conversion at some future time. The ground was being prepared for him. Finally things made sense and she could see the big picture and knew it was true. She felt a sweet, peaceful feeling that surpassed all understanding. The much needed relief had come, thanks to divine intervention, through a local man who was also a prophet and patriarch of God.

It is a wonderful, happy privileged to have such great local and general prophets and seers among us—the patriarchs of the Lord to bless us by the spirit of prophecy! This beautiful ancient privilege was restored to encourage us to fulfill the full measure of our creation. They also confer on us the involvement of heaven to a greater degree than we would otherwise enjoy by virtue of the sealing power—the glory of the Holy Priesthood. And patriarchal blessings bear testimony that God lives and fulfills His Word to His faithful and loving children. But they are not to be trifled with. The Lord says, "And all they who receive the oracles of God [which are special revelations which could include patriarchal blessings], let them beware how they hold them lest they are esteemed as a light thing, and are brought under condemnation thereby, and stumble and fall when the storms descend, and the winds blow, and the rains descend, and beat upon their house." (D&C 90:5) Being the Word of God or "scripture," we must take them seriously. Paraphrasing from President Thomas S. Monson, these blessings are to be read, they are to be loved and they are to be followed. (*Conference Report,* October 1986, pp.82-83) The quality and enjoyment of our lives are in the balance.

Vaughn J. Featherstone of the Seventy tell of one extremely successful businessman who was told in his patriarchal blessing he would become a general authority of the Church. However, when he was called to be a mission president by the First Presidency, he delayed so long in accepting the call that someone else was called in his place. His being so slow to answer resulted in a loss of a great privilege, for when names were being considered for general authorities and his name was suggested, he was rejected or passed over. Other men who were more valiant and willing to serve the Lord were given the appointments. In other words, there are consequences and some opportunities can be lost. (*Do-It-Yourself Destiny*, pp.168-169)

Harold B. Lee explained that "even though they [a man] might have been among the noble and great, from among whom the Father declared that he would make his chosen leaders, they may fail of that calling here in mortality." (*Ensign*, January 1974, p.5) The great ones of the pre-existence are not necessarily the great ones on earth. "Hence many are called, but few are chosen." (D&C 121:40) "Because their hearts are set so much upon the things of this world. . . ." (D&C 121:35) However, in the word of Thomas S. Monson, "what may not come to fulfillment in this life may occur in the next." He explained, ". . . for just as life is eternal, so is a patriarchal blessing." (*Conference Report,* October 1986, pp.82-83) It is possible that this man could become one of the one hundred forty-four thousand High Priests spoken of by John, the Revelator, who will, undoubtedly be general authorities. (D&C 77:11) In any case we must trust in our Heavenly Father and repent sincerely, heart and soul, and hope for the best.

In the words of J. Reuben Clark we need to remember that ". . .God has placed in every man's heart a divine spark, which never wholly goes out; it may grow dim, it may become hidden, almost smothered by the ashes of transgression; but the spark still lives and glows and can be fanned into flame by faith, if the heart is touched" and deeply moved. (*Conference Report,* October 1969, p.11) "Those of you," said Robert L. Simpson, "who sit reluctantly in the wings, find your patriarchal blessing, dust it off, and read it again; contemplate deeply the Lord's personal message given to you alone by these wonderful men who are attending this conference, the patriarchs of the Lord. There is yet time. It's never too late to pick up the pieces." (Ibid.) For the greater part of these blessings are eternal and can yet be fulfilled if we repent and obey God, who loves us with a love that is greater and more wonderful than we could ever comprehend in this life. Or, as Brigham Young said, the most loathsome soul that ever lived is "worth worlds," worth more than all the treasures of all the earth, more than all the wealth and riches of all the continents and oceans, than all the heights and depths of this beautiful globe and more, so great is the love of God for each individual man or woman. (*Journal of Discourses* 9:124) Patriarchal blessings are a manifestation of divine love to cheer and encourage us on to the stars of immortality and eternal life.

CHAPTER SIX

THE IMMENSE POWER OF NATURAL PATRIARCHS AND CHURCH LEADERS TO BLESS AND INSPIRE

It is obvious that "all the blessings and all the promises that the Lord has in store for us are not embodied in one written blessing. . . ." (Hyrum G. Smith, *Conference Report,* April 1921, p.185) Therefore, Eldred G. Smith explained that just because you have a patriarchal blessing "that does not mean that you can only have one blessing. If you have a father who holds the Priesthood, he may give you as many additional blessings as you wish. Now these are blessings which are given by a natural Patriarch. If you do not have a father who holds the Priesthood, your bishop is the father of the ward and the home teacher is his official representative, so you could call on your home teacher, you could call on your bishop, you could call on your stake president, or anyone under their direction or anyone who holds the Priesthood, to give you additional blessings as you need them. These may be recorded in your own family record. . . ," if permitted. (*Speeches of the Year,* November 8, 1966, p.5)

Thank God that additional blessings may be sought for that the gift of the prophets may flow into our lives more frequently and the love of God may be more manifestly enjoyed. I have witnessed the power of God many times.in my life This has strengthened my testimony immensely. My own natural father, a spiritually gifted high priest of the Lord—although few knew this about him, had such a gift of the Spirit that he would say exactly what was needed in blessings given to me. Things which only God could know, even things I had asked the Lord secretly in prayer. He would tell me the answer of heaven and predict the future accordingly. This he did with eloquence despite a speech problem that would miraculously vanish while speaking for the Lord. A. Theodore Tuttle once said, ". . . As the Patriarch of his home, a father is also a revelator to his family . . . and . . . in this sense stands in line to receive the revelations from the Lord for the good and bless-ing of that family (see *Doctrines of Salvation* 3:172)." (*Duties and Blessings of the Priesthood, Part B*, p.16) My dad was a good example of this. He was both worthy, gifted and inspired. I honor the memory of his nobility.

But though the mighty priesthood of God and faith like the ancients, "the father may claim the powers of heaven to guide his thoughts and ratify his words." (Victor L. Brown, Jr., *Encyclopedia of Mormonism* 2:504) In addi-tion a former statement of the First Presidency reads "that any father who felt inspired to pronounce the lineage [from one of the tribes of Israel which is to be an heir to exalted and glorious promises] in connection with a father's blessing he was giving to his children should not be prevented from doing so." (*1980 Devotional Speeches of the Year*, p.55) Joseph Fielding Smith said essentially the same thing and this is important. He said, "A father blessing his own child could, if he received the inspiration to do so, declare the lineage of the child," for it confers enormously wonderful things upon us. (*Doctrines of Salvation* 3:172) John Taylor declared that "every father [who holds the higher priesthood] . . . is a patriarch to his own family, which blessings will be just as legal as those conferred by any patriarch to the Church, in fact it is his right. . ." and privilege and duty. (*Gospel Kingdom*, p.146) Bruce R. McConkie explained this same glorious truth that "every person married in the temple for time and all eternity has sealed upon him, conditioned upon his faithfulness, all of the blessings of the ancient patriarchs," which is a prophetic calling to manifest inspired leadership.in the family like the ancient prophets. (*The Millennial Messiah*, p.264)

The father of the home, if he holds and honors the higher priesthood, has the highest blessing and presiding right in his home. This includes the right of prophecy and revelation to foretell and predict the future by the power and gift of the Holy Ghost. Hence, "both ordained patriarchs and priesthood-bearing fathers have the power, through spiritual inspiration, to give a priest-hood blessing that will look down the corridor of time and expand the vision, strengthen the faith, and clarify the life mission of the one receiving the blessing." (Ariel S. Ballif, *Encyclopedia of Mormonism* 3:1065)

Ezra Taft Benson, respecting this holy order, counseled a young man accordingly:

> A young man came to my office a short time ago for a blessing. He had problems . . . he was confused; he was concerned and worried. And so we talked for a few minutes and I said to him, "Have you ever asked your father for a blessing?" "Oh," he said, "I don't know that Dad would do a thing like that. He is not very active." I said, "But he's your father." "Yes." "Does he hold the priesthood?" "Yes, he is an inactive elder." I said, "Do

you love him?" And he said, "Yes, I love him. He is a good man, he's good to his family, good to his children. . . ." I said, "All right, would you be willing to go home and watch for an opportunity, and ask your father if he will give you a blessing? And if it doesn't work out, you come back, and I will be glad to help you."

So he left, and in about three days he came back. "Brother Benson, this has been the sweetest thing that's happened in our home," he said, "Mother and the children sat there, my younger brothers and sisters, with my mother wiping the tears from her eyes. She expressed her gratitude later. Father gave me a lovely blessing." He added, "I could tell it came from his heart." (*Duties and Blessings of the Priesthood, Part A,* p.108)

Joseph F. Smith declared, "This patriarchal order has its divine spirit and purpose, and those who disregard it under one pretext or another are out of harmony with the spirit of God's laws as they are ordained for recognition in the home." He continued, "It is not merely a question of who is perhaps the best qualified. Neither is it wholly a question of who is living the most worthy life. It is a question largely of law and order. . . ." (*Gospel Doctrine,* pp.286-287)

God expects us to respect this order as well. And when we do, greater blessings flow than would otherwise be enjoyed. A faithful, honored father in Israel can be magnified by God with beautiful, impressive miracles and many wonderful and endearing blessings never to be forgotten, and they are given in part because we honor this order. The following is an example of such a father and the results of their loyalty to him:

In March 1961 a terrible storm swept through the Tongan Islands in the South Pacific. Buildings were blown over. Large trees were uprooted. Houses were torn apart and thrown through the air. Many people were injured. Others were killed.

In one village, a Latter-day Saint family huddled together in their small home, fearing for their lives. In describing this experience, the father of the family said that he could feel their home shaking, as if it were ready to fall. He knew that if his family stayed in the house they would die, and if he went outside for help he would die. As he struggled with the decision of what to do, he felt prompted to use his priesthood to protect his family.

Climbing upon a chair, he placed his hand on the part of the roof he thought would go off first. Then he said, "By the power of the priesthood which I hold, and in the name of Jesus Christ, I command you to stand solidly and completely throughout this storm." After he said these words, the house quit shaking, the roof quit rattling.

After the storm, his home was the only one that remained standing. (*Duties and Blessings of the Priesthood, Part B,* p.285)

On special occasions, Melchizedek Priesthood holders "may, on their own initiative, or when called upon, give special blessings" of great encouragement to others as inspired and beautiful as any ever given by any prophet of God. (Ibid., p.46, italics added) Joseph Fielding Smith explained, "A prophet is one who has the inspiration of the Holy Ghost, and every man . . . who has the guidance of the Holy Ghost, and magnifies his priesthood, is a prophet." (J. M. Heslop and Dell R. Van Orden, *Joseph Fielding Smith: A Prophet Among the People*, p.24) Bruce R. McConkie said, "A quorum president should be a prophet to his quorum, a bishop to his ward, a stake president to his stake." (*Mormon Doctrine*, p.606) But each father should be a prophet to his own family. In the words of Spencer W. Kimball: ". . . if you just made the advance [offered to bless your son or daughter], there would be some glorious moments for you." (*Teachings of Spencer W. Kimball*, p.507) Because in the words of Howard W. Hunter, "The Lord never calls a man to any office in His Church but what he will by revelation help that man to magnify his calling. . . ," especially in administering spiritual things. That is, if we seek it diligently, we will have the help of heaven to be better than we are.

"It is your privilege," declared Orson Pratt, "to prophesy to the great and to the low, to the king on his throne, to the great men in high places, to the inhabitants of the earth, and to foretell that which shall befall their cities, villages, nations, countries, and kingdoms—to foretell all these things, not by your wisdom, nor by the spirit of false prophecy, but by the power of that Spirit which rested on Enoch in ancient days." (*Journal of Discourses* 7:312) Enoch shook the earth so powerful were his words and the nations feared and trembled before him. We can likewise work miracles and prophesy in the midst of our families.

For example, Rasmus Julius Smith, a natural patriarch, was impressed to say to one of his granddaughters, Nelda, "Someone in our family will work with the prophets." He continued, "Now, I do not know who it will be, whether it will come through the priesthood line or whether it will come through one of the girls. This promise could be fulfilled through you, or perhaps through your new little cousin Donna." (Lucile C. Tate, *Boyd K. Packer*, p.80) Donna Smith later married Boyd K. Packer who became an apostle of the Lord Jesus Christ and continues to "work with the prophets" as a prophet himself in fulfillment of this faithful grandfather's words.

Joseph Smith explained and declared, "Now if any man has the testimony of Jesus [and we all should], has he not the spirit of prophecy? [These gifts are practically one and the same]. And if he has the spirit of prophecy, I ask, is he not a prophet? [Yes, obviously]. And if a prophet, he can [and should] receive revelation!" (Andrew F. Ehat and Lyndon W. Cook, *The Words of Joseph Smith*, p.230) Unfortunately, "we have many members of this Church who have never [even] received a manifestation of the Holy Ghost," said Joseph Fielding Smith. (*Speeches of the Year*, October 25, 1961, p.4) "And let me tell you," declared John W. Taylor, an early apostle of Christ in this dispensation, "whenever the absence of these gifts and blessings and the administration of holy angels occurs among this people this is not the people of God." (*Conference Report*, April 1900, p.25) Why? Because as Moroni, a great Native American prophet, bore solemn testimony:

> . . .if the day cometh that the power and gifts of God shall be done away among you, it shall be because of unbelief.
>
> And wo be unto the children of men if this be the case; for there shall be none that doeth good among you, no not one. For if there be one among you that doeth good, he shall work by the power and gifts of God.
>
> And wo unto them who shall do these things away and die, for they die in their sins, and they cannot be saved in the kingdom of God; and I speak it according to the words of Christ; and I lie not. (Moroni 10:24-26)

We must be spiritually minded, because "this people can no more live spiritually without these gifts and blessings and inspirations from our Father than you can live [physically] a month without eating [food]. You will die a spiritual death, and there will be nothing left of you in the kingdom of God but a dead form. As the Prophet has said, the letter killeth, but the spirit giveth light [that is, life—the greatest kind of life there is]." (*Conference Report*, April 1900, pp.26-27)

Then Elder Taylor continued and said, "I tell you that among the Latter-day Saints there is a famine for the spiritual gifts of God. That is my testimony unto you. These gifts and blessings are enjoyed among this people, but we do not enjoy them to that fullness that we will when we come up to the standard of keeping the commandments that" we could. (Ibid., p.27) In a similar vein, L. Aldin Porter, in a recent General Conference, discussed a conversation he had with the late Elder LeGrand Richards of the Council of the Twelve. Elder Richards said, "'We have too many in the Church who deny the spirit of prophecy and of revelation.' That was it—he said no more." Elder Porter then stated: "Ours is a day of dwindling faith and increased skepticism about sacred things. . . . The most important knowledge to be gained in this life is that which comes by revelation through the Holy

Spirit. . . . We must never lose this precious gift. We must pay whatever price of faith and obedience is required to retain this great blessing." (*Ensign*, November 1996, pp.10-11)

The spiritual gifts are "not merely to establish the truth of Christianity," declared Orson Pratt, "but as Paul says, 'For the perfecting of the Saints, for the work of the ministry, for the edifying of the body of Christ: till we all come in the unity of the faith, and of the knowledge of the Son of God, unto a perfect man, unto the measure of the stature of the fullness of Christ: that we henceforth be no more children tossed to and fro . . . ,'" but become solid and strong in the Lord. (Ephesians 4:12-14) Elder Pratt continued, "To do away from the Church, apostles, prophets, and other gifts, is to do away the great plan which heaven had devised for the perfection and final salvation of the righteous." (*Orson Pratt's Works*, p.97)

In other words, salvation, revelation and spiritual life are connected. The Lord declared, "If thou shalt ask, thou shalt receive revelation upon revelation . . . that which bringest joy, that which bringeth life eternal." (D&C 42:61) Joy and revelation are companions to the valiant ones in Christ—those who love God and seek the riches and warm privileges of His Spirit. Salvation and exaltation are in the balance.

Elder Bruce R. McConkie wrote, "If spiritual gifts are interwoven with and form part of the very gospel of salvation itself, can we enjoy the fulness of that gospel without possessing the gifts that are part of it? If gifts and miracles shall—inevitably, always, and everlastingly—follow those who believe, how can we be true believers without them? And if we are to seek the gospel, if we are to hunger and thirst after righteousness, if our whole souls must cry out for the goodness of God and his everlasting association, how can we exempt ourselves from seeking the gifts of the Spirit that come from and prepare us for his presence?" (*A New Witness for the Articles of Faith*, p.369)

The scriptures make it clear that being valiant in the testimony of Christ determines whether we go to the highest glory and receive a crown of eternal lives or not. (D&C 76:79) Spencer W. Kimball explains this "means that many of us who have received baptism by proper authority, many who received ordinances, even temple blessings, will not reach the celestial kingdom of glory unless we live the commandments and are valiant." (*Conference Report*, April 1951, pp.104-105) But "what is being valiant? . . . There are many people," continued Elder Kimball, "in this Church today who think they live, but they are dead to the spiritual things. And I believe even many who are making pretenses of being active are also spiritually dead. Their service is much of the letter and less of the spirit." (Ibid.)

Orson Pratt said, ". . . Here is the great center place of gathering, and here should center all the powers of the everlasting Priesthood. Here, in our midst, should be poured out the blessings of that Priesthood to their fullest extent. Here the servants of God should be clothed upon from on high with the glory of God, and be able to foretell all things. . . ." (*Journal of Discourses* 7:312-313) He continued, ". . . why not, ye Elders of Israel—ye servants of the Most High God, rise up in the power of the Priesthood and magnify your callings throughout the settlements? . . . Why give way to darkness. . . . Why suffer a cloud of darkness to hover over your minds, even a cloud of thick darkness that is almost impenetrable? Why suffer your faith to die away, that you cannot prevail with the heavens and obtain the blessings of the Priesthood revealed in the last days? Awake, awake, O ye Elders of Israel, and be clothed with the spirit and power of your callings. . . . It weighs me down by day, and often times I lay awake at nights contemplating the greatness of our privileges and the backwardness of the Saints of God to claim them." (Ibid.) May we cultivate more love for God and thus draw down the blessing of God upon ourselves and His other children.

Unfortunately, many Saints do not live on the high and remarkable level they should, but many, many do. Heber J. Grant said:

> I rejoice in the Gospel, I rejoice in the rich outpourings of the Holy Spirit that have been given in the instructions imparted during this conference. I rejoice with Brother Kimball, that every Latter-day Saint, every humble son and daughter of God that has embraced the Gospel and become a member of the Church of Jesus Christ of Latter-day Saints has received the witness of the Holy Spirit, that the gift of tongues, the gift of prophecy, of healing, and other gifts and blessings, are found in the Church, and are not confined to men that hold responsible positions in the Church. I have listened to some of the most spirited, and able, and some of the finest sermons of my life from men who held no official position. (*Conference Report,* April 1901, p.64)

He then related an experience about how a man who was a home missionary, whose use of the English language was very poor, even an irritation to him, inspired him. He said:

> By my heart was touched, and tears welled up in my eyes because of the rich outpourings of the Holy Spirit upon that man, and there was an impression made upon my heart of the divinity of this work and the fact that Joseph Smith is a Prophet of God that to this day I have not forgotten. It is not position, it is not education that gives the Spirit of God; but it is

keeping the commandments of Almighty God and being lowly in heart and desiring to fulfill the commandments of God in our daily walk and conversation. (Ibid.)

Elder Grant then explained the key to the great enjoyment of the Spirit:

> I bear witness to you here today that no man has ever fallen in this Church, and no man ever will fall in this Church, who is honest in his heart, honest in the payment of his tithes and offerings, who obeys the Word of Wisdom, who attends to his quorum meetings; no man will fall who is doing his duty in this Church. But Satan has power over those who become selfish and sordid and set their hearts upon the things of this earth and fail to render thanks in all things unto God. (Ibid.)

Obviously Church position is not the determining factor. One does not have to be a patriarch or apostle to function as a prophet in giving blessings, and the gifts of God are prevalent locally in the Church. But some who have rarely or never experienced them assume that their own lack of experience applies to everyone. But it doesn't, thank God! Heber J. Grant, speaking of the gift of healing alone, said "it would make a book much larger than the New Testament" to record all the great blessings of Almighty God wrought through the mighty priesthood we bear. He continued, "More miracles have been performed in the Church of Jesus Christ of Latter-day Saints than we have any account of in the days of the Savior and His Apostles" including raising the dead and other marvels of great beauty. (*Conference Report,* October 1910, p.110) Spencer W. Kimball wrote that "if all the spectacular manifestations and visions and pertinent dreams and healings and other miracles were written in books, it would take a great library to hold them." (*Faith Precedes the Miracle*, p.36) Beautiful things are always happening, but many of the Saints know nothing of it on a personal basis.

"Another of the gifts that we believe in," said Robert E. Wells, "is the gift of prophecy. We do not believe that the spirit of prophecy is limited to those who preside. . . ." But we "believe that each of us may from time to time enjoy the spirit of prophecy." (*We Are Christians Because. . . .*, p.60) The Prophet Joseph Smith explained that "every man who possesses that spirit is a prophet." (*History of the Church* 5:408) Brigham Young testified, "My knowledge is, if you follow the teachings of Jesus Christ and his Apostles . . . every person will become a prophet. . . ." (*Journal of Discourses* 1:243) "Revelations, visions, angelic visitations, the rending of the heavens, and appearances among men of the Lord himself—all these things are for all the faithful," declared Bruce R. McConkie. He continued, "They are not . . . a matter of lineage or rank or position or place of precedence." (*The Promised Messiah*, p.575)

As discussed in chapter three, the High Priests are the highest and the greatest of the priests of Melchizedek in the Church. (D&C 107:63-64 and Hyrum M. Smith, *Doctrine and Covenants Commentary*, pp.697, 710) Elders, including the Seventies who are Elders, are the lesser priests of Melchizedek, but the title "elder" literally means "superior in rank, office, or validity" and "one having authority." (*Webster's Ninth New Collegiate Dictionary*, p.460) Elders, therefore, can and should function as prophets in Israel for they hold a superior office and are to administer in the great spiritual things of the last days. In fact, Joseph Smith explained that "if a priest [of the Aaronic order] understands his duty, his calling, and ministry, and preaches by the Holy Ghost, his enjoyment is as great as if he were one of the [first] presidency . . . ." (*History of the Church* 2:478) Thus even a priest of the lesser priesthood can enjoy the beauty and glory associated with a prophetic mantle or status.

Hyrum M. Smith, a past member of the Quorum of the Twelve, taught in general conference that "all men who hold the holy Priesthood are authorities in the Church, and through the Deacon the Lord may speak unto the people, and give His word of praise or reproof, or bestow upon them His blessing. The Priest and the Teacher likewise. The Bishop, the High Priest, the Seventy, the President of a Stake—all of these servants of the Lord are authorities of the Church, and when you have them in your midst you may hear the word of the Lord preached, you may hear and see and feel the inspiration of the Lord." (*Conference Report*, October 1905, p.22)

Wilford Woodruff declared:

> There is one principle connected with the Priesthood that I want all Israel to understand, and that is this: it makes no difference what portion of the Priesthood a man holds, if he holds any at all, he has rights. Whether he be a Deacon or whether he be an Apostle, the Priesthood held by him has rights, on earth and in the heavens. . . . When a man holding any portion of that Priesthood goes before God, the heavens are bound to hear him, if he magnifies his Priesthood. . . ." (*Collected Discourses* 4:8-9)

I have known many local prophets and special witnesses of Christ. One young deacon bore as powerful a testimony of the Book of Mormon as I have ever heard in my life and I can still remember it and the beautiful feeling of absolute truth as he spoke as one having divine authority. One of my bishops ended a blessing with a beautiful promise that a special feeling of gratitude and beautiful, heavenly music would envelope me that very night and testify to the truth of his words or the great and eternal promise of God I had just received in a power blessing. It happened; I enjoyed a sweet and wonderful melody from heaven as prophesied and felt to thank God over and over again for the privilege. I had a stake president prophesy to me that I'd be married when I reached the third position on the High Council. I was then number fourteen as an alternate high councilor. After a few years, and one week after I reached the third position, I was married exactly as promised by this beautiful man. Just a few weeks before this, I had a bishop, another great high priest, prophesy that I would meet the lovely girl I would marry and marry her all within days and weeks but not months and years from that very time. I met her out of the clear blue ten days after the blessing and married her a total of six weeks after that blessing in fulfillment of the word of the Lord. By the way, I thought my bishop was quite presumptuous to tell me I'd be married in a matter of weeks and not months when I didn't even know the person I would marry and had been trying for three years to find the girl of my dreams. But the Lord had spoken it, and I trusted it would come to pass and it did miraculously, which has been one of the greatest things that ever happened to me.in my life I still glory in this thing.

A local patriarch told me in my patriarchal blessing that I'd be a "Priest of the Most High God" or a high priest after the order of Melchizedek and the Son of God, before I married the gal the Lord would provide for me, what I would do for a living, the kind and quality of life I would enjoy, spiritual gifts, such as visions, I would experience, and have experienced, all with amazing accuracy. This all fills me with wonder and awe when I contemplate it.

At an earlier time in my life, a different bishop prophesied what the next Ward I entered would call me to do. My dad, a dear old high priest, who has since passed away, prophesied that I'd do remarkable things among the Native Americans I worked for professionally. Shortly after this they made me the director of their social services and mental health program. In this position, in the year and a half I acted as director, I brought in about five hundred thousand dollars worth of grants and had a 90% success rate in grant writing outcomes. I was twice requested by the Tribe to represent them in Washington as I wrote their statement of needs for the U. S. House of Representatives and the United State Senate. I set up several new programs and started the construction on another. I also gave the only relationship building or enrichment workshops in which the people would actually come back week after week to attend. This had not been done before. Truly I did some remarkable things among them, far beyond my own expectations, amply fulfilling the High Priesthood blessing pronounced upon me. I don't know but what this was one of the greatest works I have ever done worldly speaking.

An very inspired stake president long ago prophesied that my parents would join the Church and I'd have the grand privilege of being sealed to them for time and all eternity, which happened in a beautiful, miraculous way. And I was privileged to baptize and confirm my parents as members of the Church and was sealed to them. A gifted high councilor once prophesied great spiritual blessings I have realized and am still realizing and enjoying. A remarkable bishop was so powerful that occasionally people would enjoy visions under his hands. I did as well. I thank God for these special blessings which have brought me great comfort and dramatically changed the quality and enjoyment of my life. They are happy memories and I hope they will continue. We are so fortunate in this day of inspired men and women.

Local prophets really are very plentiful and a great and beautiful blessing to the people of the earth who have eyes to see it. In fact, "every person who receives revelation," declared Bruce R. McConkie, "has . . . the spirit of prophecy and is a prophet. . . . and "can, as occasion requires and when guided by the Spirit, 'prophesy of all things.'" (*The Promised Messiah*, p.24) This includes all the brethren who hold the priesthood. John L. Ward, while serving as a bishop, tells of setting apart a nonmember and telling her in the name of the Lord "that she would join the Church soon because of the actions of the youth." (*Is There a Patriarch in the House?*, p.51) After a few months as a second counselor in the Young Women's organization and at a final meeting on a trip to Salt Lake City with their youth, as they were kneeling down to pray, this sister said, "'Bishop, excuse me, before we pray I'd like to say something.' She paused, wiped her eyes, and spoke haltingly with emotion. 'This week has been memorable. I've seen your temple, met your apostles, but the reason I know your Church is true is because of the actions and testimonies of the youth kneeling here. I want to be baptized!'" (Ibid.) The spirit and gift of the prophets is alive and well if we seek for it. We have the right, we are entitled to this, we are privileged in the Church to enjoy the gift of revelation and should enjoy it often.

Recently I met with my son-in-law as inspired by the Lord, because the Lord revealed to me that he had the wonderful gift of the prophets and it could be enlarged and enjoyed to a greater degree or level. We had as it were a school of the prophets together and received revelation, even a vision together, on what the Lord's message was to be for his sweet wife, my daughter, who had asked for a blessing. Later, when we were ready, I blessed him and he blessed her. It was a sweet and elevating experience in which every person there wept for the good feeling and wonderful promises expressed. Then Susan, my wife, gave a beautiful, inspired prayer and the Spirit reconfirmed upon me everything which we had done that day and left us with such a beautiful feeling of confidence and an inner sense of peace. Later, I transcribed the words of the blessings from the tape recorder and wept again for joy. Then I typed them and the spirit again rested upon me and I wept again. I have a strong testimony of the Lord and His overwhelming love for His children. Oh, what a glorious privilege it is to be commissioned of Jesus Christ and feel His glorious and endearing spirit!

However, sadly, as Joseph Fielding Smith said, "That great gift comes to us only through humility and faith and obedience. Therefore, a great many members of the Church do not have that guidance. . . ." and do not seek after it and therefore actually miss out on some beautiful, uplifting and glorious experiences that powerfully bear witness that Jesus is the Christ and that He lives and loves us. (*Speeches of the Year*, October 25, 1961, p.4)

These gifts do not always tell us what we want to hear, but they are always true and ultimately fortify us that God lives and loves us and His will was done and all is well after all. Joseph Smith uttered the following prophecy while blessing or setting apart a missionary, Elder Andrew Lamoreaux in 1839:

> [He] laid his hands on Elder Lamoreaux and blessed him, and prophesied upon his head, that he would go on a mission to France, learn another tongue and do much good, but that he would not live to return to his family, as he would fall by the way as a martyr. The Prophet wept, as he blessed him and told him these things, adding that it was pressed upon him and he could not refrain from giving utterance to it. Elder Lamoreaux talked with his family about it when he left them in 1852, and endeavored to persuade them that this was not the time and the mission upon which he should fall, but to believe that he would at this time be permitted to return again. When the "Luminary" brought the tidings of his death, they exclaimed, "Surely, Brother Joseph was a Prophet, for all his words have come to pass. (Duane S. Crowther, *Gifts of the Spirit*, p.221)

Heber C. Kimball, an apostle of Christ felt prompted to prophesy to Parley P. Pratt, another apostle of the living God, in 1836 that his barren, sickly wife would be healed and have a son, that he (Parley) would go to

Canada, Toronto in particular, and find a people ready for the Gospel and they shall receive it and be filled with joy. As a result of this mission, the gospel would spread to the British Isles. And Parley would be given riches to relieve all his debts and have some besides. All of this was fulfilled. And the far-reaching consequences of this prophecy and mission were amazing. Parley did go to Canada and found a people ready for the Gospel who embraced it with joy and remained true to it. Parley was also instrumental in converting John Taylor, a future President of the Church; and some of these people interested people in Great Britain. The remarkable contributions of this one mission can hardly be measured. It resulted in Heber C. Kimball's call to go to England, which mission saved the Church from ruin at a very precarious time. Parley's sickly, wife gave birth to a healthy boy they named Parley, Junior. And Elder Pratt was no longer in debt, but had money to spare.(*Faith of Our Pioneer Fathers*, pp.125-126 and *Autobiography of Parley P. Pratt*, pp.141-142, 165-166, 180-182) The gift of prophecy is enjoyed in the Church today just as it was in the days of Christ and the ancient apostles.

George Teasdale, an earlier apostle of the Lord Jesus Christ, testified, "I know that the Church of Christ is a church of revelation, and that the spirit of prophecy is in the Church. Brethren are set apart to go upon missions and prophecies are made concerning them and their missions, and when they return they invariably tell us that every word predicted was literally fulfilled. Who inspired those blessings? Our Father in heaven, by the power of His Spirit, for He is doing His own work. Man is a manifest failure without the Spirit of God." (*Conference Report*, October 1900, p.38)

Fenton L. Williams, Sr. was a member of an out-going stake presidency. He was invited by the visiting general authority and apostle, Elder Harold B. Lee to stand with him while he blessed and set apart new stake officers. Brother Williams knew each man very very well. However, Elder Lee's contact with them amounted to little more than a handshake. Brother Williams wrote:

> I found myself thinking, "He surely has read these men correctly—almost seems to know them."
>
> As the blessings continued, I began listening intently to every word, tears welling in my eyes, as I began to realize that the pronouncements had not been by chance but by prophetic inspiration.
>
> Here was a new bishop's counselor who would need to "always be on guard" to "honor his priesthood and calling." How well I knew it. Then followed one who had been having a tithing and coffee problem. His blessing

contained specific warnings against those weaknesses. Next was a plodder type, level-headed, honest, and dependable, but not given much to reading. His blessing was a challenge to devote himself to scripture study, the one thing most needed by this fine man.

By this time, my tears flowed freely and I personally did some intense soul-searching about my worthiness to participate in that humbling hour. My hands tingled where they touched his on the heads of my brethren.

The blessings continued. A returned missionary, whose business often interfered with proper Sabbath observance, was told, "The Lord will bless and prosper you if you put his work first." Then followed a college professor who as a bit given to lightmindedness—an occasional vulgar story. "Your potentialities for good are limitless if you keep your thoughts and actions spotlessly clean."

I bear witness that not in one instance did that servant of the Lord fail to strike home. Several of the men who received blessings that day have since borne witness, in my hearing, of the prophetic utterances of our inspired visitor. They were from God. (*Ensign*, February 1974, pp.27-28)

In a remarkable, special blessing, a Brother Terry of Hinckley, Utah was told by a spiritually gifted High Priest some very powerful specific things before he departed for action in World War II:

"As long as you keep those covenants sacred [of the temple], you'll enjoy the same protection and blessing. You will see your companions shot down by your side, but you shall not be injured. Your life will be preserved so that you might perform a great missionary work there. And," I said, "should the only water available to you become contaminated and pronounced by medical science as unfit to drink, if you will not partake of the things that are forbidden of the Lord, he will make the water sweeter to your taste than any water you ever drank and you shall be able to drink of it and it shall not injure you. Those about you will not understand the ways of the Lord and will marvel when they see you drink of that water and live. Remember, however, this blessing will come to you only by observing the Word of Wisdom and not partaking of those things the Lord has declared as not good for man."

It was a highly unusual blessing, but one that gave that young man peace and confidence that he would return unharmed to his loves ones. He then left to join his comrades in battle, knowing the Lord would be his protector.

When he returned from the war, he came and bore his testimony to me. "Twice our division went into action," he said. "The first time, there were five of our group who came back, myself and four others. The next time, three of us returned; the rest were slain."

"One time," he continued, "our water supply became contaminated and our medical men told us not to drink, for it would mean certain death. My buddies, of course, decided not to drink the polluted water, knowing that if they were to enjoy the momentary pleasure of quenching their thirst, they would not live long enough to enjoy the many pleasures that awaited those who would return home from the battlefields. But I trusted in the Lord and the blessing you gave me, which I knew was given through the spirit of revelation. I drank the water and have never tasted better water in my life—it was deliciously sweet and , more importantly, quenched my burning thirst. My companions were completely dismayed and distressed by my actions and feared that they would certainly witness my agonizing death within a very short time. Contrary to the statement of the medical authorities and to the wonderment of those about me, my health was not injured in any way and I was permitted to continue the work that I was asked to do in the service of my country and fellowmen."

"This experience caused many of them to want to know more about the gospel of Jesus Christ and they began investigating the Church. I don't know how many of them finally accepted the gospel, as I soon finished my tour of duty and was sent home, but I do know that many of them were studying the scriptures and reading the literature I had given them that explained the Church of Jesus Christ and its principles."

This young man is now performing a great work in the Church and Kingdom of God and still has a testimony of how his life was preserved by keeping the commandments. He has also been impressed that the Lord preserved his life in such a miraculous and startling manner so that those who saw him drink the contaminated water without ill effects would become interested in the gospel of Jesus Christ and be brought to an understanding of these eternal principles.

This experience has greatly strengthened my testimony that the Lord does honor those who observe the Word of Wisdom and keep his commandments. ("Faith-Promoting Experiences of Patriarch Charles R. Woodbury," in possession of Jennie Lee, pp.9-10—edited with her approval as quoted in *Stories of Insight and Inspiration* by Margie Calhoun, pp.315-317, used by permission)

The following story again illustrates how revelation can comfort and reveal truth and that the priesthood can be immeasurably reassuring in times of great need. Rhonda had a child taken from her through an open window in a car while she was temporarily visiting an elementary school. The community rallied to help, but they were devastated. The story continued:

By the time Rhonda and Mark arrived home that first night, it was very late. The bishop and some members had fed and cared for their other children and put them to bed. They were finally by themselves. They had been thinking about a priesthood blessing all day because in the past these blessings had always given them new information. Mark was nervous about giving Rhonda a blessing, because he was so sad. He didn't know if his emotional state would interfere with his ability to feel and respond to the Spirit.

They knelt down together and prayed that Mark would know the words to say and that the Spirit of the Lord would guide him. As Mark began to give Rhonda the blessing, he recognized the Spirit of the Lord and was prompted to bless Rhonda that she was not to feel guilty for it. Mark could almost feel guilt and anguish going into the soul of the kidnapper for what he had done.

Mark promised Rhonda that she would be sustained, and both Rhonda and Mark received a firm confirmation that Sarah would be okay. They received the knowledge that Sarah had many more important things to do in this life and that there was no power that would be able to harm her. The Spirit told them that angels were attending and supporting her. When the blessing was finished, they just sat and cried. They knew she would be protected from the elements and would not suffer for food and water. They knew Sarah would come back to them and grow up in their home. They hugged each other and cried for a long time because they knew their daughter would be okay.

When they awoke up the next morning, they had the feeling that they would get Sarah back on Friday, which was three days away. On Friday morning they looked at each other and said, "Well, today is the day. The trial is about over." Sarah was found about nine-thirty that morning. Hunters found her wandering in a desert wash about ten miles outside of town. She had a few scratches and bruises but that was the extent of her physical injuries.

Rhonda and Mark first saw Sarah again in the emergency room, where she shared with them what had happened to her. Sarah said that she had been dropped off in the desert and had felt really scared. Then she saw a little girl that looked like her younger sister playing in the desert. This girl was building a great big pile of rocks, and when the rocks would fall down, she would laugh and laugh. Whenever Sarah felt really scared again, she said, this girl would come back and play with the rocks until she was not afraid anymore. As Mark and Rhonda heard this, they knew that angels really had assisted their daughter.

Sarah said that no one told her but that she just knew what to do for the days and nights that she was alone. She stayed near some trees for two of the days and nights. When it rained Thursday night, she got under the trees and did not get wet. Mark and Rhonda had been home praying that if she was out in the elements she would somehow find shelter and stay dry. They had told the Lord that if he could part the Red Sea, he could part a few raindrops.

On Friday morning Sarah knew she was to leave the trees and begin to walk. She said she knew where to walk because there was a pathway to guide her. This pathway led her out of the desert and to the hunters who found her. All of the promises the Lord had made in the priesthood blessing had come to pass. (Alan K. Burgess and Max H. Molgard, *Stories That Teach Gospel Principles,* copyright Bookcraft, Inc., 1989, pp.37-39, used by permission. Further reproduction of this material without the written consent of the publisher is prohibited.)

There is great power in the priesthood that can bring great comfort, consolation and change lives. Joseph Smith said, ". . . Search the revelations of God; study the prophecies, and rejoice that God grants unto the world seers and prophets." (*Teachings of the Prophet Joseph Smith*, p.12) And I would add, local ones who touch our lives so deeply and profoundly and who are near at hand. Dallin H. Oaks gave some examples of such in a General Conference address. Note how God's greatest blessings can go unnoticed especially by outsiders, who would never know that a miracle had happened. He said:

About a hundred years ago, Sarah Young Vance qualified as a midwife. Before she began serving the women of Arizona, a priesthood leader blessed her that she would "always do only what was right and what was best for the welfare of her patients." Over a period of forty-five years Sarah delivered approximately fifteen hundred babies without the loss of a single mother or child. "Whatever I came up against a difficult problem," she recalled, "something always seemed to inspire me and somehow I would know what was the right thing to do" (L. J. Arrington and S.A. Madsen, *Sunbonnet Sisters: True Stories of Mormon Women and Frontier Life,* Salt Lake City: Bookcraft, 1984, p.105).

In 1864, Joseph A. Young was called on a special mission to transact Church business in the East. His father, President Brigham Young, blessed him to go and return in safety. As he was returning, he was involved in a severe train wreck. "The whole train was smashed," he reported, "including the car I was in to within one seat of where I sat, [but] I escaped without a scratch" (*Letters of Brigham Young to His Sons,* ed. Dean C. Jessee, Salt Lake City: Deseret Book Co., 1974, p.4). (*Ensign,* May 1987, p.38)

Priesthood blessings can be very powerful, and far reaching, and extend special divine providence throughout ones whole life time. Dallin H. Oaks said, "Let us remind you that you have been set apart [or blessed] by a power so great that you can't even comprehend it." (Ibid.) This is the same authority which Jesus used to heal the sick and afflicted and which created all life and organized the awesome universe itself. When divine reservoirs of heavenly power are tapped, lives are changed forever. Another example of those quiet workings happened to a man in his forties in Vancouver, Washington:

> He was coming back into full activity in the Church but was hampered by his lifetime habituated to coffee. After confessing his weakness to his bishop and asking for help, the bishop gave him a blessing to overcome the temptation. The following day at work he walked into the employee lounge and was greeted by the smell of coffee. But instead of the usual urge to drink some, he was overcome with nausea. Never again did he have the desire to drink coffee. That was nearly thirty years ago. He has been faithful ever since, enjoying the blessings of the priesthood and the ordinances of the temple with his family. . . . Such blessings are possible because those pronouncing the blessing have the power to speak for God. (*Ensign*, February 1993, p.19)

Powerful and beautiful priesthood blessings, after the order of the Son of God, are sometimes pronounced upon groups of people, or on places and even nations are dedicated and prophetically blessed. Vaughn J. Featherstone, while President of the Utah South Area, pronounced the following inspired blessing on the people over whom he presided at the time. He said:

> God bless the Utah South Area. The Lord has planted and is planting giants in the land. Apostles and prophets are being born in your homes. Some of your youth will walk in the Highest places in this kingdom. Your sons who are on missions will return and fill the most sacred callings. You do not know who your children are.
>
> As we faithfully commit and follow through with a great missionary thrust, God will bless us. Our children will see visions, our leaders will dream sacred dreams. Angelic and unseen beings will watch over and protect you and your children. Employers hearts will be softened, bounteous blessings will flow. Satanic influences will be thwarted. Our people will walk in holiness protected and blessed as the "children of light." Homes will be protected from evil and destroying powers will pass us by. You will come to the shade of trees to cooling fountains, to the Haven of Rest. Peace, love, and hope will be yours.
>
> This Utah South Area will be the fountain head of blessings that flow to every people on this earth. Let us fulfill our divine destiny to prepare for these promises. ("Extra"—a Utah Salt Lake City South Mission monthly notice for February 27, 1987)

James E. Faust declared that "such individual [including general] blessings are part of the continuous revelations that we claim as members of The Church of Jesus Christ of Latter-day Saints." (*Ensign*, November 1995, p.62) For "those called to preside over quorums, wards, stakes, or other organizations in the church," according to Bruce R. McConkie, "should be prophets to those over whom they preside." (*A New Witness for the Articles of Faith*, p.349) In fact, "Joseph Smith has said in substance, a man is a prophet if he has the testimony of Jesus, and, therefore, every man should be a prophet who is keeping the commandments of the Lord." (Joseph Fielding Smith, *The Restoration of All Things*, p.67)

However, the only way this magnificent gift can be fully realized and personally enjoyed is for our faith and devotion to increase enough to enable the Lord to show greater manifestations of His endearing love like He did for the Nephites of old to whom He said, "So great faith have I never seen among all the Jews; wherefore I could not show unto them so great miracles, because of their unbelief." (3 Nephi 19:35-36) We need to grow in faith that God may show great miracles among us as he did for the ancients.

John H. Groberg of the First Quorum of the Seventy, as a young Elder in the South Pacific, enjoyed a most glorious experience and feeling of love and awe and reverence beyond mortal description and was informed by the sweet, endearing gift of the Spirit that his father was just made a patriarch that very day. Three weeks later this was confirmed by the receipt of a letter that his father was indeed made a patriarch that very day in one of the Idaho Stakes. He wrote of some other impressions he had on that special day as well, ". . .I felt a deep reverence for the calling of a patriarch and sensed there is a stronger link between patriarchs and heaven than we now understand. I had the feeling that we will have a much deeper appreciation for our patriarchal blessings at a later time as we see things more clearly. I also felt we should try to follow our blessings better and be more appreciative of them," for they are greater and more important than we realize. (*In the Eye of the Storm*, p.121)

It is important to realize in the words of Joseph F. Smith that "no endowment or blessing in the house of the Lord, no patriarchal blessing, no ordination to the Priesthood can be taken away, once given," because they are eternal and endless as God himself. (*Gospel Doctrine*, p.166) Wilford Woodruff testified on this by saying:

If I have a blessing given to me by the holy Priesthood, or if I receive a blessing from a Patriarch, those gifts and blessings will reach into the other world; and if I am true to my covenants through this life, I can claim every blessing that has been conferred upon me, because that authority by which they were conferred is ordained of God; and it is that by which the sons of the Most High administer unto the children of men the ordinances of life and salvation; and those official acts will have their effect upon those persons beyond the grave as well as in this life. These are the true riches; they are riches that will last to all eternity, and we have power through these blessings, conferred by the Gospel, to receive our bodies again, and to preserve our identity in eternity. (*Journal of Discourses* 9:163)

God bless us to ask for more inspired Priesthood blessings and live worthy of them. And may God bless us to develop and cultivate the spirit and gift of the prophets and thus manifest this great gift among the people. Wilford Woodruff explained, "I think sometimes that we do not fully comprehend the power that we have with God in knowing how to approach him acceptably. All that these men holding the priesthood, and all that our sisters need do, is to live near to God, and call upon him, pouring out their soul's desires in behalf of Israel, and their power will be felt, and their confidence in God will be strengthened," or in other words, our faith will grow mighty and strong. (*Discourses of Wilford Woodruff*, p.222) It takes effort and determination to really do our part. The requirement of heaven is that we love the riches and honors of eternity and seek the gifts and blessings of the Spirit with zeal and devotion. Otherwise, a lame effort equals a half baked product, and instead of enjoying the magnificence which is our right, we experience very little of the glory and beauty of God's love and personal involvement with us.

As George Q. Cannon explained:

The natural man is at enmity with Christ and with God; and unless he seeks to conquer his nature by bringing it into subjection to the mind of God, he is not a son, or she is not a daughter of God. This is the labor that devolves upon us. This is why we meet together at conference; it is to impress upon the people the character and magnitude of this work that rests upon each individual man and woman. As I have said once before in this Tabernacle, we may be heralded through the earth as famous; but unless we conquer ourselves it is in vain that our names are known and that our deeds resound through the earth. I care not how famous a man in this Church may be—he may be an apostle, he may be a high priest, a bishop, or hold any other important office or position; but unless that man conquers himself and carries on the work within himself of self-improvement, and brings himself and all there is within him in subjection to the mind and will of

God, I tell you his fame is as empty as the sound of a trumpet when it passes away. We hear it; it strikes the ear, but it presently dies away, and that is the end of it. So it is with fame of this character. Therefore, I say to you that that which is applicable to the individual is applicable to us as a people. Our fame my go forth for great works and mighty things that we have done; but unless we ourselves bring forth fruits of righteousness in our lives; unless we conquer our evil passions, our evil habits, our evil inclinations, our evil desires, and bring them under complete subjection to the Spirit of God our labor is comparatively profitless, for that is the object of preaching the Gospel to us. (*Journal of Discourses* 21:79)

The Lord has told us that "many will say to me in that day [in the day of judgement]: Lord, Lord, have we not prophesied in thy name, and in thy name have cast out devils, and in thy name done many wonderful works? And then I will profess unto them: I never knew you; depart from me, ye that work iniquity." (3 Nephi 14:22-23 and Matthew 7:22-23) Commenting on this scripture John Taylor said, "You say that means outsiders? No, it does not. . . . Sometimes they will do things in the name of God; but it simply an act of blasphemy. This means you, Latter-day Saints, who heal the sick, cast out devils and do many wonderful things in the name of Jesus. And yet how many we see among this people of this class, that become careless, and treat lightly the ordinances of God's house and the Priesthood of the Son of God [in other words, they have become lukewarm or lost the divine spark. They are no longer aglow with an adoring, loving spirit for the things of God]; yet they think they are going by and by to slide into the kingdom of God; but I tell you unless they are righteous and keep their covenants they will never go there." (*Doctrine and Covenants Commentary*, pp.462-463)

President Taylor explained that "while many men are diligent and their whole hearts are engaged in the work of God, there are a great many astride the fence. . . ." (Ibid., p.462) So even though they may have worked beautiful miracles before the Lord in the past, or given wonderful blessings and prophesied beautifully before God as Church leaders, they will meet with disaster in eternity, unless they repent and set their whole hearts and souls on loving and obeying God.

May we great things happen inside our own selves in the silent chambers of the heart where the greatest battles of life are fought out. We must put Christ supreme and triumphant above everything or anything else in our lives and in the affections and feelings of our hearts. This is cleansing the inner vessel. Then we will be beautifully magnified of heaven and give mighty blessings of great joy, consolation and encouragement more frequently as local and general prophets in Israel, for we have limitless possibilities and unlimited potential. And in the words of President Brigham Young, if we obey and love God and magnify the Priesthood, "everything the most fruitful mind can imagine shall be yours, sooner or later," even "all that my Father hath. . . ." (*Journal of Discourses* 2:125 and D&C 84:38)

CHAPTER SEVEN

CULTIVATING THE SPIRIT AND GIFT OF THE PROPHETS

Bruce R. McConkie explained that "nothing more than the testimony of Jesus is needed to make a person a prophet. . . ." (*Mormon Doctrine,* p.605) And after he has received this testimony, "he is then in a position to press forward in righteousness and gain other revelations including those which foretell future events. On this basis, should the necessity arise [such as the request to give a blessing be received], those who are prophets are in a position where they 'could prophesy of all things.' (Mosiah 5:3.)," for to prophesy is to bring great comfort and encouragement to all who struggle and want the Lord's blessings. (Ibid.)

John A. Widtsoe explained that "since patriarchs [and other prophets of the Higher Priesthood] are but men, they are subject to human frailties. Their manner of speech and thinking is reflected in their blessings. Different men express the same idea in different words. The Lord does not dictate blessings to them word for word." (*Evidences and Reconciliations*, p.324) Hence, the great need to develop and cultivate the spirit of the prophecy to ensure that we perform accurately this and other special callings to give inspired priesthood blessings after the Holy Order of the Son of God. But "patriarchs who are ordained have sealed upon their heads the right of revelation and prophecy," declared Joseph Fielding Smith. ("Address of President Joseph Fielding Smith, June 15, 1956, p.3) This is to help them measure up to their exalted calling. Nevertheless, every man ordained to the priesthood of the living God is a prophet, for "no man is a minister of Jesus Christ without being a prophet," declared Joseph Smith, the head of this, the greatest of all dispensations. (*Teachings of the Prophet Joseph Smith*, p.160)

It was never intended that the generally accepted prophets (members of the First Presidency and the Quorum of the Twelve) should give all the blessings, cast out all the devils, work all the miracles, heal all the sick and comfort all those who are in real need. Yet these great blessings require great inspiration and power which is exactly what God has given all those ordained after the order of Melchizedek, which is to be ordained after the likeness or to be similar to the ancient prophets. That is, we have the ordained right to be prophets in Israel and manifest great power among the people. And this is of far-reaching importance. We need to live up to this privilege, for the general authorities will not run every ward and stake or every primary, young womens or relief society. They will not and should not be required to write all the inspired poetry, plays, music or books. Revelation and inspiration given to every member should cause beautiful outpourings of love for every courageous endeavor. The general membership of the Church should paint the greatest paintings, build the most beautiful of buildings, deliver the greater sermons and lessons, sculpt, sing and glorify the great God of heaven in beautiful power. As Moses declared, "Would God that all the Lord's people were prophets, and that the Lord would put his spirit upon them." (Numbers 11:29)

So, asked Bruce R. McConkie, "Who may prophesy? Who can receive revelation? To whom are visions and heavenly manifestations vouchsafed? Not to members of the Council of the Twelve only, not to bishops and stake presidents alone, not just to the leaders of the Church. . . . Prophecy is for all: men, women, and children, every member of the true Church; and those who have the testimony of Jesus have the spirit of prophecy. . . ." (*Doctrinal New Testament Commentary* 2:387) John Taylor said that "any man that has the testimony of Jesus has the spirit of prophecy; for 'the testimony of Jesus is the spirit of prophecy' so says the old Bible: and consequently, such a man is a prophet." (*Journal of Discourses* 5:147) Joseph Fielding Smith explained that "every man who can say knowingly that Jesus Christ is the Son of God, and the Savior of men, is a prophet," for "a prophet is one who has the inspiration of the Holy Spirit . . ." and therefore can do many wonderful things for humankind. (*The Way to Perfection*, pp.158-159)

"Wherefore, brethren, covet to prophesy . . . ," for "he that prophesieth edifieth the church," declared the Apostle Paul. "For ye may all prophesy one by one, that all may learn, and all may be comforted." (1 Corinthians 14:39,4,31) Commenting on these scriptures, Elder McConkie wrote, "What better desire can members of the Church have than this? In effect it means, Seek the Spirit, and the companionship of the Spirit is the greatest gift men can receive in this life." (*Doctrinal New Testament Commentary* 2:388)

To prophesy is "to act as a prophet" and speak inspired words according to the dictionary. (*New Webster's Dictionary and Thesaurus of the English Language,* p.801) The word prophet is from the Greek *pro* and *phanai* and the Hebrew word *nabi.* Both mean one who speaks for God as well as one who foretells. (Gerald N. Lund, *The Coming of the Lord*, p.6) Hence, a prophet is "A person who, by divine inspiration, declares to the world the divine will. . . ." (*New Webster's Dictionary and Thesaurus of the English Language,* p.801) "The mission of prophets is not alone to foretell the future," declared Bruce R. McConkie, but "even more important is the witness they bear to living persons of the divinity of Christ, the teachings they give of the plan of salvation, and the ordinances which they perform for their fellow men." (*Mormon Doctrine,* p.606) This definition is more in line with the Greek term for prophet which literally means "inspired spokesman" or one who proclaims the divine message of God speaking forth the mind of the Lord on the matter. (Joseph Fielding McConkie, *Prophets and Prophecy,* pp.7-8)

The Lord told Moses: "I have made thee a god to Pharaoh: and Aaron thy brother shall be thy prophet. Thou shalt speak all that I command thee: and Aaron thy brother shall speak unto Pharaoh. . . ." (Exodus 7:1-2) That is, to be a prophet is to be again an "inspired spokesman" who proclaims divine truth whether that truth is about current events, the future or historical verities. To do so one must enjoy the mighty gifts and powers of the Holy Ghost which was conferred upon us when we were confirmed members of the Church.

But "the genius of the kingdom," declared George Q. Cannon is ". . . to make every man a Prophet. . . ." (*Journal of Discourses* 12:46) "Are you entitled to it?," asked President Cannon, "Yes, every one of you—the same spirit of revelation that Moses had, the same spirit that all the prophets and apostles had, it is your privilege, it is the privilege of every man and woman who possesses the Gospel . . . and the more we seek after it and cherish it the more we will have." (*Journal of Discourses* 21:272) This is the great gift every priesthood holder should cherish and cultivate.

Many of the great gifts of God are interrelated and build one upon another to higher more advanced expressions of the Holy Ghost. To have the spirit of the prophets or gift of prophecy, for example, one must have faith, hope and charity as well as having personal revelation and a testimony. Hence, Bruce R. McConkie could and did say, "Prophecy stands supreme, the greatest of all the gifts of the Spirit," because to enjoy this gift means we must have and enjoy many of the other gifts as a foundation. (*Doctrinal New Testament Commentary* 2:386)

So important are these gifts that Bruce R. McConkie made the statement that "visions and revelation are always found in the true church. They always abound among the saints of God, and without them there would be no divine kingdom on earth. Without them there is no true religion, no salvation, no hope of eternal glory, no way in which man can be as his Maker. They are as much a part of true religion as sunshine and rain are part of mortal existence." (*A New Witness for the Articles of Faith*, p.375)

Brigham Young said, "Every man and woman may be a revelator, and have the testimony of Jesus, which is the spirit of prophecy [which again constitutes a prophet], and foresee the mind and will of God concerning them, eschew evil, and choose that which is good." (*Journal of Discourses* 2:189) But, in the words of Lorenzo Snow, "The gifts of the Gospel must be cultivated by diligence and perseverance. The ancient Prophets when desiring some peculiar blessing, or important knowledge, revelation or vision, would sometimes fast and pray for days and even weeks for that purpose." (Ibid., 23:195) Certainly there is a price to pay, but it is worth it.

Brigham Young said:

Thrust a man into prison and bind him with chains, and then let him be filled with the comfort and with the glory of eternity, and that prison is a palace to him. Again, let a man be seated upon a throne with power and dominion in this world, ruling his millions and millions and without that peace which flows from the Lord of Hosts—without that contentment and joy that come from heaven, his palace is a prison; his life is a burden to him; he lives in fear, in dread, and in sorrow. But when a person is filled with the [sweet] peace and [endearing] power of God, all is right with him." (*Discourses of Brigham Young*, p.33) After giving a blessing recently to a pregnant woman giving birth and feeling the divine presence so overwhelmingly and beautifully strong and, under the glory of that influence, I could honestly say I'd rather have that feeling and experience of joy and glory than a million dollars. It was so beautiful. I know there are great things to come for those that love the Lord, because I have tasted it on numerous occasions.

Anthon H. Lund, another earlier apostle, in general conference told the following story to illustrate the beautiful reality of spiritual gifts in the kingdom of God:

When President Peterson of the Sanpete Stake was a young man he attended a meeting in Illinois. There were many present, and the spirit of the Lord was poured out upon the Saints in a great measure. He felt urged by the spirit to talk in tongues, and when he sat down a young girl arose and interpreted it. She was but seventeen years of age, perhaps younger, and she interpreted what Brother Peterson had spoken. Some of the brethren there, then in good standing but who afterwards left the Church, were told that if they did not take heed they would apostatize, and that the balance of the branch should emigrate to the West and travel in wagons like houses, across large plains. This was the interpretation of the tongue. They did not then know that there would come a time when they should travel in covered wagons and go to the west. But a remarkable thing happened at that meeting. Two young girls that had been stolen while children, by the Indians, and been brought back by the government, were present. They heard Brother Peterson speak in tongues, and they declared that he spoke in an Indian tongue, which they had heard before, and they understood most of it, though they said he spoke it better than they ever heard the chiefs speak it, and the young girl, they said, had translated what they understood correctly. This is a great testimony of the truth of that gift, and many other instances could be mentioned, showing that this gift is in the Church. The gift of prophecy we know is in the Church. (*Conference Report,* April 1900, pp.33-34)

Orson Pratt was told in a revelation to lift up his "voice" and "prophesy." (D&C 34:10) This was very hard for him. He feared being wrong. He soberly declared, "I would rather have had my head severed from my body than to have been guilty of so great a crime [as to prophesy falsely]. . . . Such a man in ancient days was to be cut off from the midst of Israel," that is, he was executed or stoned. (*Journal of Discourses* 7:311) To prophesy presumptuously is an evil that amounts to taking the name of God in vain having no authority or permission to speak for Him. It is to impersonate a prophet of God.

Hence, "If a patriarch is to be a prophet, he must have inspiration from the Lord and he must live so he can receive it," declared Joseph Fielding Smith. (Meeting of Patriarchs, October 11, 1958, p.3) That is a mighty challenge, but nothing is impossible for God because he sustains and magnifies His servants who diligently seek Him. Nevertheless, it still requires the exercise of faith to be brave enough to say what God wants said and to accurately discern His messages to an individual or nation.

Heber C. Kimball declared, "I say that every man and woman who will live their religion, be humble, and be dictated by the Holy Ghost, the spirit of prophecy will be upon them." (*Journal of Discourses* 5:176) The spirit of prophecy, according to Orson Pratt, "makes a Prophet of him who has it." (Ibid., 16:139) This spirit is the testimony of Christ that He lives and is the Son of God and our Redeemer. Of course, as Bruce R. McConkie explained, "Most of the great prophets are possessors of the Melchizedek Priesthood," that is, the greatest prophets are priests of the Higher Priesthood order, because there are "ranks and grades of prophets in responsibility and authority." (*Mormon Doctrine,* p.606) That is, there are grades in the priesthood one above another till one obtains that "which is the greatest of all," which is the office of High Priest. (D&C 107:64) Joseph Smith declared that the High Priests should "be better qualified . . . than the Elders. . . ," because it is the highest and most advanced office in the Church. (*Teachings of the Prophet Joseph Smith*, p.21) Joseph F. Smith declared that no one should excel them, that is, they are expected to excel in everything that really matters. (*Conference Report*, April 1908, pp.5-6) The most important type of prophet a "priest of the Most High" can become is a member of the First Presidency which is over all the members of the Church in all the world. This is the highest position a man can hold on earth. (D&C 107:22 and 76:57)

The Lord declared that the School of the Prophets, as restored in modern times, was originally for "all the officers of the church, or in other words, those who are called to the ministry in the church, beginning at the high priests, even down to the deacons." (D&C 88:127) In other words, all priesthood holders are to be prophets and inspired men according to their divinely appointed responsibilities. Therefore, Bruce R. McConkie could declare that every "elders quorum should be a school of the prophets. . . ," because we should live up to our exalted callings. ("Only An Elder," a talk given on October 3, 1974 and printed as a pamphlet by the Church, p.9) He likewise understood that from "the high priests, even down to the deacons," from the greatest to the least, we should all be special and outstanding for God, because "he that is ordained of God and sent forth, the same is appointed to be the greatest, notwithstanding he is the least and the servant of all." (D&C 50:26)

Hence, from the least Deacon's quorum to the quorum of the great and eternal office of the High Priests, these priesthood quorums, according to Bruce R. McConkie, are an important "Church agency that administers salvation to its members and their families . . . [and each] is a local school of the prophets," if we are true to our individual and collective ordinations before the Lord. (*The LDS Speaker's Source Book*, p.350) For, as already quoted, "no man is a minister of Jesus Christ without being a prophet," declared Joseph Smith. (*History of the Church* 3:389) Therefore, we must be prophets or great men inside in the inner man to be true servants of the living God. And this means we must be inspired and develop the wonderful gift of revelation in our lives.

The connection between priesthood and revelation is so vital and so essential that James E. Talmage wrote, ". . .it is evident that in the absence of direct revelation the Church would be left without authorized officers, and in consequence would become extinct. The prophets and patriarchs of old, the judges, the priests, and every authorized servant from Adam to Malachi, were called by direct revelation manifested through the special word of prophecy. This was true also of John the Baptist, of the apostles, and of lesser officers of the Church, as long as an organization recognized of God remained on the earth. Without the gift of continual revelation there can be no authorized ministry on the earth; and without officers duly commissioned there can be no Church of Christ." (*Articles of Faith*, p.304) Therefore, according to J. Golden Kimball, "under the influence of the Holy Ghost men are entitled to inspiration, to revelation, to dreams and visions, for their own salvation" and to bless, heal and console others as well as perpetuate the priesthood. But any man who is so inspired, he continued, "who thinks he is living so close to God that he can direct this Church, unless he repents he will apostatize, as surely as God lives. God never gave us inspiration and revelation to [replace or to] take the place of the Prophet of the living God," that is, the Lord's special anointed servant who presides over all Israel in our day and generation. (Arnold Dee White, *J. Golden Kimball's Golden Moments*, p.34)

Wilford Woodruff explained, "He [Brigham Young] is a prophet, I am a prophet, you are, and anybody is a prophet who has the testimony of Jesus Christ, for that is the spirit of prophecy. The elders of Israel are prophets." But "a prophet [deacon, teacher, priest, elder, seventy or high priest] is not so great as an apostle. Christ had set in his Church, first, apostles; they hold the keys of the kingdom of God." (*Discourses of Wilford Woodruff*, p.90) "It is not the business," said Joseph F. Smith, "of any individual to rise up as a revelator, as a prophet, as a seer, as an inspired man, to give revelation for the guidance of the Church, or to assume to dictate to the presiding authorities of the Church. . . ." Nevertheless, "it is the right of individuals to be inspired and to receive manifestations of the Holy Spirit for their personal guidance," etc. (*Gospel Doctrine*, p.41)

An example of this, from the Old Testament, is how Aaron and his sister Miriam in ancient Israel complained against Moses their brother. They thought why should he be the highest of all the prophets? They said, "hath the Lord indeed spoken only by Moses? hath he not spoken also by us?" In other words, we receive revelation and enjoy spiritual gifts as well. The Lord gave them an important answer. He said of his special appointed leader, "Hear now my words: If there be a prophet among you, I the Lord will make myself known unto him in a vision, and will speak unto him in a dream. My servant Moses is not so, who is faithful in all mine house. With him will I speak mouth to mouth, even apparently, and not in dark speeches; and the similitude of the Lord shall he behold: wherefore then were ye not afraid to speak against my servant Moses? And the anger of the Lord was kindled against them; and he departed," but not without some serious temporary consequences for Aaron and Miriam. (Numbers 12:6-9) It all boils down to the fact that "the Lord's house 'is a house of order.' It is not governed by individual gifts or manifestations, but by the order and power of the Holy Priesthood as sustained by the voice and vote of the Church in its appointed conferences," as President Joseph F. Smith explained. (*Messages of the First Presidency*, p.286)

This, however, is rarely the problem. More likely it is that some members "have never received that gift [inspiration and revelation from the Holy Ghost], that is, the manifestations [or the enjoyment] of it. Why? Because they have never put themselves in order to receive these manifestations. They have never humbled themselves." Sadly, "they have never taken the steps that would prepare them for the companionship of the Holy Ghost." (Joseph F. Smith, *Conference Report,* October 1958, p.21) Thus they miss out on all the greater rewards and enjoyments of God's great love.

George Q. Cannon said that after baptism "when the Holy Spirit is sealed upon a person's head, they have received that which comprehends within itself every other blessing which is in the power of the Priesthood at that time to bestow." (*Gospel Truth*, p.140) And there is essentially no limit to the greatness and glory and intensity of blessings that can be bestowed including all the beautiful gifts and blessings promised by the Savior to all believers which includes the spirit of prophecy. In fact, B.H. Roberts declared that "the Holy Ghost is the spirit of prophecy. . . ," which is the testimony of Jesus Christ.

Hence, Wilford Woodruff could testify "that there is no greater gift, there is no greater blessing, there is no greater testimony given to man on earth. . . . I claim that the gift of the Holy Ghost is the greatest gift that can be bestowed upon man." (*Collected Discourses* 1:224) Bruce R. McConkie stated that "his companionship is the greatest gift that mortal man can enjoy," and "those who enjoy the companionship of the Holy Ghost have the spirit of revelation." (*Mormon Doctrine*, pp.359,651)

"And the more His promptings we receive," said Ezra Taft Benson, "and follow, the greater will be our joy." (*The Teachings of Ezra Taft Benson*, p.343) Joseph F. Smith said, "The feeling that came upon me was that of pure peace, of love and of light." (*Gospel Doctrine*, p.96) John Taylor said that "receiving that heavenly treasure is one of the greatest manifestations of the faithfulness of God, in sanctifying the acts of his elders that it is possible for us to conceive of." (*Journal of Discourses* 21:346) It is beautiful beyond description, for the Spirit brings such wonderful feelings with it—grand feelings of sweetness, peace and joy. It was meant to be a daily or at least weekly renewal, if not a constant experience, of inner wonder, love, glory and awe. It is to be baptized with fire and the Holy Ghost re-establishing feelings of hope and our faith in God and in the future. It is so important that President Ezra Taft Benson said, "The most important thing in our lives is the Spirit. I have always felt that. We must remain open and sensitive to the promptings of the Holy Ghost in all aspects of our lives." (*Ensign*, April 1988, p.2)

Orson F. Whitney proclaimed that we should seek and enjoy this gift always and perpetually. He said:

> I heard a veteran Elder once say to a youthful convert, who was brimming over with zeal and enthusiasm in the good work: "Oh, you'll get over that. We all feel that way in the first place." I have often pondered upon those words, and when I have heard aged men, who for 30, 40, or 50 years have been engaged in preaching the Gospel, bearing testimony to its truth in burning words, I have come to the conclusion that that man was mistaken, and that there is no reason why our testimony of the truth should grow dim, or our zeal abate, if we live and labor as we should. As long as a man will live for the testimony of the Spirit, he will have it. . . . Latter-day Saints who will lead chaste and pure, temperate, faithful lives, will never have occasion to say that the fruits of the Gospel are less sweet to them than formerly. But if we practice fraud and trickery, if we worship Mammon, if we are jealous of, and conspire against each other, if we lust after forbidden things, we are very liable to say, "I once felt full of enthusiasm and zeal, but I've gotten over it now." There is always a good reason why a tree fails to blossom and bear fruit. The testimony of the Gospel in the bosom of a man who lives as he should live, will grow brighter and brighter unto the perfect day. (*Collected Discourses* 2:63)

But "the Lord will not force himself upon people," declared Spencer W. Kimball, "and if they do not believe, they will receive no visitation. If they are content to depend upon their own limited calculations and interpretations, then, of course, the Lord will leave them to their chosen fate. . . ." (*Teachings of Spencer W. Kimball*, p.454) They miss out on all the glory and beauty that flows out of the heavens. May we truly "receive the Holy Ghost" as we should and enjoy all it's special, unique blessings, which only members of the Church can do to the fullest extent.

Before he was a general authority, Paul H. Dunn interviewed President

David O. McKay for his Institute class and asked him what was the biggest problem facing the Church. His answer was "spiritual illiteracy." That is, we stumble and make mistakes and fail to obtain the greater gifts and blessings, because of a lack of love and desire for the things of God enough to educate ourselves or do something about it. And this is serious, because all is not well in Zion! (2 Nephi 28:24-25) Yet many, many things are right, but we miss out on the greater and more beautiful blessings, because the Lord "doth grant unto the children of men, [only] according to the heed and diligence which they give unto him." (Alma 12:9) Alma explained that if we harden our hearts, "the same receiveth the lesser portion of the word; and he that will not harden his heart, to him is given the greater portion of the word, until it is given unto him to know the mysteries of God [in other words, be a prophet and enjoy the great glory and beauty of the Spirit to a marvelous degree] until he know them in full." (Alma 12:10) To do this, we need to want the right things so much that we seek after them, even hunger and thirst for them, that the Holy Ghost may sweetly fill us to overflowing and richly comfort our souls and we actually grow "brighter and brighter [or more beautiful and glorious within] until the perfect day." (D&C 50:24)

George Q. Cannon said, "There is nothing like communion with the Holy Spirit, there is no blessing to equal it. I have proved it abundantly. . . and I rejoice that I can bear this testimony to you to-day." (*Journal of Discourses* 17:130) He continued that there is "nothing of greater importance than teaching men and women how to live so as to be always in the enjoyment of light and wisdom and the peaceful Spirit of God. . . ." (Ibid.)

Bruce R. McConkie concluded with the following statement. He said, ". . .All saints, all true believers, all who have faith in the Lord Jesus Christ, all who love and serve him with all their hearts, receive revelations and spiritual gifts, enjoy signs, and work miracles. Suffice it to say that true greatness, from an eternal standpoint, is measured not in worldly station nor in ecclesiastical office, but in possession of the gifts of the Spirit and in the enjoyment of the things of God." (*The Promised Messiah*, pp.574-575) This enjoyment represents greatness within, that is, in the heart, to be so honored and trusted of heaven to enjoy its rich treasures. But, in the words of Elder McConkie again, "Men must seek the[se] honors—revelations, visions, companionship of the Holy Spirit, and the like—which it is the Father's good pleasure to confer; otherwise such are not obtained. As long as men's hearts are centered on the things of the world and the honors of men, they never seek the blessings of eternity with that fervor and devotion which leads to the receipt of spiritual gifts. What greater honor can a man receive than that which comes from God?" (*The Mortal Messiah* 2:79)

John A. Widtsoe said, "Revelation [that is, the Spirit of the Lord] is inseparably connected with the Priesthood, as an unchanging principle from all eternity to all eternity." (*Priesthood and Church Government*, p.36) But the essence, or the bottom line, of this gift is the ability to discern what is being communicated to us. This takes practice and training. Boyd K. Packer described how his son got some radio equipment and he would listen with him as he talked to people from around the world. "I could hear static and interference and catch a word or two, or sometimes several voices at once. Yet he could understand, for he had trained himself to tune out the interference." (*Ensign*, November 1979, p.19) Then he concluded, "It is difficult to separate from the confusion of life that quiet voice of inspiration. Unless you attune yourself, you will miss it. . . . You can learn to respond to that voice," which "is the key, the foundation stone of all revelation." (Ibid., pp.19-20 and *Discourses of Wilford Woodruff*, p.46)

It is true that the influence of the endearing Spirit of God is sweet and enjoyable. It warms the heart and carries with it the desire to love God, love life, love people and dearly love righteousness. But we can also learn to be good listeners and discern what the Spirit of the Lord is communicating to us. Joseph F. Smith said, "After you get the Spirit of inspiration [just discussed] . . . , you are then entitled to the title prophet, because you are a prophet; you possess the spirit of prophecy . . . ," which is the gift and privilege of being a prophet. (*Millennial Star* 68:723) This is the gift that makes a man a true servant of God, overflowing with the gift of the Holy Ghost, guidance and revelation. It brings joy, sweetness, the love of heaven and divine assistance. It empowers us to be effective as true followers of the Lord and bless the people like the ancient prophets did.

But we need to be careful to discern God's will and carefully follow it. "Better far to do this," said Abraham H. Cannon, an earlier apostle:

> than by faith . . . rescue the sick from death, and yet see these same children who have been saved by our faith suffer something that is worse than death; for some children who have apparently been snatched from the grave by the faith exercised by the servants of God and their parents, have in time lost the faith, and have brought sorrow and affliction to the family to which they belong. There are things in this life far worse than death. There are sins which burden our hearts with grief far worse than to follow to their last resting place the bodies of our loved ones. It is better by far that we take to the tomb our loved ones and bury them in their purity and holiness than that by our faith and our constant wrestling with God we save them from temporal death and consign them to an eternal punishment. (*Collected Discourses* 4:29)

We must have the gift of revelation to prevent us from doing what is wrong or foolish with the great power that God has given us. With this authority sometimes people have suffered terribly because through the exercise of our faith, we have kept people alive when they should have died. We must say and do like our Lord who said, "For I came down from heaven, not to do mine own will, but the will of him that sent me." (John 6:38) There is great safety in this, and to do it, we must be in tune with the fountain of all truth. That is, we must receive revelation and follow it.

Bruce R. McConkie explained, "Some are sustained as prophets, seers and revelators to the Church. . . . But all of us are entitled to the spirit of prophecy and of revelation in our lives, both for our personal affairs and in our ministry." (Mark L. McConkie, *Doctrines of the Restoration,* pp.244) The scriptures are so important in helping us achieve this that Elder McConkie commenting on the Doctrine and Covenants said that all the beautiful things in it "makes this book of great value to the human family and of more worth than the riches of the whole earth." ("Explanatory Introduction" to the Doctrine and Covenants) He declared, "The prayerful study and pondering of the holy scriptures will do as much, or more than any other single thing, to bring that spirit, the spirit of prophecy and the spirit of revelation, into our lives." (*Doctrines of the Restoration*, pp.244) We need to be diligent in feasting on the word of the Lord and become intimately acquainted with the voice of the true Shepherd.

"I want to say, however," said John W. Taylor, "that while these gifts and blessings are the right and privilege of the Latter-day Saints, we should not depend upon them for our salvation in the kingdom of God. The gift of prophecy will not save a man. It is not a saving principle; it is a gift. It is to comfort our hearts. It is to give us the testimony of the mind and will of God concerning things which are to come. As Elder Grant has said, I may prophesy from now till the coming of the Son of Man, and if I fail to keep the commandments, I will not be saved in the kingdom of God." (*Conference Report,* April 1900, p.26) That is, it is more important to obey than manifest great gifts. Abraham H. Cannon said:

> . . .it is not the outward appearances; it is not the healing of the sick, nor the hearing of tongues, that gives a man or woman the greatest strength in the work of God. . . . Better by far for us to possess is the still small voice of the Spirit—the inward feeling which is experienced in every fibre of our [being or] organization, which tingles in our veins, which reaches the extremities of our bodies, and tells our whole being [indelibly] that this is the work of God. This testimony is possible for each to obtain and to retain

by a constant observance of the requirements of the Gospel of the Son of God. (*Collected Discourses* 4:27)

However, revelation and spiritual gifts are necessary to give us life and vitality, to comfort and encourage us to carry on and endure to the end. Orson Pratt declared that "without these gifts . . . , we could not enter into the fullness of His glory," because we "would be altogether unprepared for the reception of still greater powers and glories of the eternal world." (*Orson Pratt's Works*, p.97) Therefore, Bruce R. McConkie said, "We should be very careful not to lightly esteem the gifts of God [for they are incredibly important], for by them we live, and without them we can never be saved in his kingdom." (*Millennial Star* 51:18)

These gifts are essential and we should greatly desire them and cultivate them; and when we do, revelation and love sweetly flows out of the heavens and endears us to every good and beautiful thing, and we learn to love God all the more from the deepest part of our inner selves. To have these gifts is to be rich in the inner man or to have great wealth within. It is to taste of the tree of life, the fountain of living water or the love of God. The fruit of which filleth "with exceeding great joy," is "most sweet, above all," "most desirable," most "white," most "pure," "most joyous," and most perfect and beautiful. (1 Nephi 8:10-12; 11:21-23)

Orson Pratt declared, "The Prophets, Patriarchs and Saints in olden times received great and glorious blessings, and why should we not be blessed, the same as they were blessed? . . . it is our privilege to live for them and enjoy them in their fullness according to our faith." (*Journal of Discourses* 25:144-145) However, "we [often] do not receive them in their fullness, because we do not seek for them as diligently and faithfully as we should." (Ibid. 25:145) "And so it is with the promises made to you in your confirmations and endowments, and by the patriarchs, in your patriarchal blessings; we do not live up to our privileges as saints of God and elders of Israel. . . ." (Ibid. 25:145-146) ". . .We have received oftentimes the gift of prophecy and revelation, and have received many great and glorious gifts. But have we received the fullness of the blessings to which we are entitled? No, we have not. Who, among the Apostles have become seers, and enjoy all the gifts and powers pertaining to that calling? Still it is our privilege to become prophets, seers and revelators, for these blessings were promised us. . . ." (Ibid. 25:145) "These and other blessings are given to us on condition that we are diligent and faithful. If we fail to receive them, the failure is not on the part of the Lord, nor in His servants who preside over us, but the fault lies in ourselves alone." (Ibid.) "And I have thought the reason why we have not enjoyed these gifts more fully is, because we have not sought for them as diligently as we ought." (Ibid.)

Shortly after Lorenzo Snow was ordained an apostle of the Lord Jesus Christ in 1849, he was called to go to Italy by Brigham Young in 1850 and open up the gospel. The promise of the Lord was that "whosoever ye [the Lord's servants] shall send in my name, by the voice of your brethren, the Twelve, duly recommended and authorized by you, shall have power to open the door to my kingdom unto any nation withersoever ye shall send them." (D&C 112:21) However, Elder Snow was not getting anywhere. The people wouldn't listen. They were closed and unyielding. He prayed with all his heart for an opportunity to awaken the people to the Restoration of the Gospel. He had God's promise for success, but it doesn't always come easy, "for after much tribulation come the blessings. . . ," sometimes. (D&C 58:4) That is, miracles when they are needed.

Elder Snow noted that the Grey family in Piedmont, Italy, where he was working, had a little boy who was very sick and probably dying. He felt deeply if he could get permission or the assurance from the Lord to heal him, the door would open and the gospel could prosper and flourish. He felt to save this child would ultimately bring salvation to a nation. It was that important. He prayed late into the evening and fasted. The spirit of prayer filled his being and he poured out his soul. He continued the next day struggling for six, long hours petitioning and pleading for the privilege of exercising this great blessing miracle. He wanted it so much he offered anything, even his life (the supreme sacrifice) if only God would open up the door of salvation. And he meant every word of it. His whole life proved that he meant it. In the words of Max B. Skousen from whom this story was obtained:

> At last, at the end of six hours, the answer came! The reply was "Yes."
> He would be granted the privilege. Oh, the joy that must have surged through his being when he knew that God had heard and answered his prayer. The "powers of the world to come" had been poured out upon him through this direct response to his earnest petition. As an agent of the Almighty God, filled with a consuming joy, he walked down from the mountain side in perfect faith to save a dying child.
>
> I might add that the effect of this incident was marvelous. For the first time people gladly opened their doors and listened to his message. Within a few short months, a large branch was organized for scores of newly baptized converts. Lorenzo Snow rejoiced in thanksgiving for this blessing. It

was over a year later, however, when he returned home, then he heard the other side of the story. It should be a lesson for us all, for the path of the righteous has never been easy. Those whom the Lord desires to make the greatest, He seems to test the hardest. Evidently the Lord had taken Lorenzo Snow at this word, for when he returned, he found that his wife, his childhood sweetheart, had died. She had passed away suddenly on the very day he had healed the dying child in Italy. (*How to Pray and Stay Awake*, pp.1-5)

Jedediah M. Grant, a member of the First Presidency long ago, said:

[If I discovered] the best [water situation] that could be found, I should have no occasion for going to another and more distant place to procure water. And if I should find ice there, should I say it was too much trouble to break it? No, but I should labor to break that ice; and the thicker the ice, the more persevering I should labor, until I got some of the water of the crystal fountain.

While paying attention to the prayers of some persons in their family devotions, I sometimes notice that they often stop praying without breaking through the darkness and obtaining the Holy Spirit. If I found that it was necessary to pray three hours I would keep praying for that length of time, or until I got the Spirit . . . I would keep praying until I broke the ice and obtained the Holy Ghost. (*Journal of Discourses* 4:150-151)

Prayer is critically important. The Living Water that springeth up unto eternal life is the gift of the Holy Ghost and is the binding tie between us and the Godhead. We need to do whatever is necessary to enjoy this great gift of gifts. (See Appendix A and B) Prayer is obviously extremely necessary for the enjoyment of the greater gifts and powers of God.

The Lord declared, "Pray always, and I will pour out my Spirit upon you, and great shall be your blessing—yea, even more than if you should obtain treasures of earth and corruptibleness to the extent thereof." (D&C 19:38) That is, a fullness of earthly treasures could not equal the rich, sweet warmth and delight that the Spirit imparts to the heart of a worthy and adoring son or daughter of Almighty God. If we could really comprehend this glorious promise, that is truly ours to enjoy, we would rejoice and be filled with gladness. And we would "pray always" and "always remember him" as requested. (Ibid. and Moroni 4:3)

The following was originally given as a challenge about forgiveness by Spencer W. Kimball, but it can equally apply to the great spiritual gifts we need to cultivate. He wrote, ". . . One good brother asked me, 'Yes, that is what ought to be done, but how do you do it? Doesn't that take a superman?' 'Yes,' I said, 'but we are commanded to be supermen. Said the Lord, 'Be ye therefore perfect, even as your Father which is in heaven is perfect.' (Matt. 5:48) We are gods in embryo, and the Lord demands perfection of us.' 'Yes, . . .Christ [could]. . . , but he was more than human,' he rejoined. And my answer was: 'But there are many humans who have found it possible to do this divine thing.' Apparently there are many who like this good brother, hold the comfortable theory that . . . [this] is more or less the monopoly of scriptural or fictional characters and can hardly be expected of practical people in today's world. This is not the case. . . . [It] can be developed today. . . . Hard to do? Of course. The Lord never promised an easy road, nor a simple gospel, nor low standards, nor a low norm. The price is high, but the goods attained are worth all they cost." (*The Miracle of Forgiveness*, pp.286-87,299)

Joseph Smith explained that "the nearer a man approaches perfection, the clearer are his views, and the greater his enjoyments, till he . . . like the ancients, arrives at that point of faith where he is wrapped in the power and glory of his Maker. . . ." (*History of the Church* 2:8) We must also be diligent and determined, then marvelous things will happen in our own lives, for "how long can rolling waters remain impure? What power can stay the heavens? As well might man stretch forth his puny arm to stop the Missouri river in its decreed course, or to turn it up stream, as to hinder the Almighty from pouring down knowledge from heaven upon the heads of" those who love God and obey Him with all their hearts. (D&C 121:33) In other words, they will enjoy the spirit, glory and richness of the holy prophets and thus be prophets and inspired men themselves.

To do this work and develop within is a great work, so great and important that Brigham Young asked, ". . .Who in the eyes of the Almighty ought to . . . be countenanced, adored, loved, and reverenced in his capacity, and be justified therein by the heavenly hosts? It is that [local] man who is sanctified before God, and who loves the Lord Jesus with all his heart, or in other words, who is endowed with wisdom from on high, and has revelations, visions, and dreams, giving him understanding . . . [making him a local prophet and inspired man] for the good and benefit of all. In the eyes of eternal justice, only such a man has a right to [any high and elevated] office." (*Journal of Discourses* 2:188-189) This is because he has such a good heart for God and people and has so much to contribute, to offer and to share. May we do our part and enjoy the greater blessings reserved for the faithful, diligent and determined.

CHAPTER EIGHT

RECOGNIZING REVELATION AND BLESSING THE PEOPLE

One of the most important abilities required of a patriarch or priesthood holder who wants to be inspired and effective is the ability to recognize revelation when it comes. Too often when faith promoting experiences are told, the trial and inner strivings that created the intervention of God are left out. Therefore, the work required to obtain revelation is rarely told. As a result, the rank and file membership of the Church think all one need do is pray and then expect a wonderful outpouring of beautiful blessings all without much effort. Or, knowing that they have the right to inspiration, they pray and then believe that the first thought they experience must be right, or the word of the Lord. Neither of these ideas is accurate and both have negative consequences. Only the truth can make us free to be true servants of the Lord. (John 8:32)

Glenn L. Pace of the First Quorum of the Seventy wrote "that inspiration would come only after intense, agonizing study, research, and meditation. In other words, I learned that revelation is 95 percent hard work." Elder Pace declared, "Every time I hear it [the statement 'I feel really good about it'], I see a red flag go up." He explained that this "is a perfectly good way of expressing a feeling of the Spirit, but too often the literal translation is, 'I haven't done my homework.' Some bad decisions have been made by people who 'feel really good' about something they have failed to . . ." pay the price for. (*Spiritual Plateaus*, pp.20, 19) Oliver Cowdery was rebuked for taking "no thought save it was to ask me," that is, he didn't really work at it. He was counseled to "study it out," then "ask" and either "your bosom shall burn within you" and "you shall feel it is right" or "you shall have a stupor of thought" and "forget the thing which is wrong." (D&C 9:7-9)

Revelation takes energy and determination as well as fasting and prayer [which is] . . . rejoicing and prayer" according to the Lord. (D&C 59:14) But "To get this revelation," declared Brigham Young, "it is necessary that the people live so that their spirits are as pure and clean as a piece of blank paper that lies on the desk before the inditer [composer], ready to receive any mark the writer may make upon it. When you see Latter-day Saints greedy, and covetous of the things of this world, do you think their minds are in a fit condition to be written upon by the pen of revelation? When people will live so that the Spirit of revelation will be with them day by day, they are then in the path of their duty, if they do not live according to this rule, they live beneath their duty and privileges." (*Journal of Discourses* 11:240-241) In the words of Heber C. Kimball, "There is no person . . . who can increase in the knowledge of God, in the spirit of revelation, in the gift of prophecy, in visions or in dreams, unless they cleave unto God with full purpose of heart, but by being faithful these gifts will be multiplied unto the Saints." (*Journal of Discourses* 10:245)

Therefore, Bruce R. McConkie could write that "all faithful brethren should be prophets in their own right" to bless those who are worthy of divine counsel with the gift of prophecy and revelation. (*A New Witness for the Articles of Faith*, p.349) One lady, Charlene Hansen, was told by her physician to terminate her pregnancy which put her in a moral dilemma. The strong medication used for some physical disorders were sure to cause extreme birth defects and deformities or create a severely handicapped child. Three "second opinions" confirmed the same; but in a blessing from their Bishop, an inspired high priest of the Most High God, the Lord told them "that all the problems concerning this pregnancy would be forgotten in the birth of a perfect child" and she would enjoy "a normal delivery." Not only this, but she was told she'd have the joyous experience of personal revelation to see the lovely little girl before she was born. As told by her husband, "One night, during her eighth month of pregnancy, Charlene saw in a dream the daughter that was to be sent to our home. She had rosy cheeks, blue eyes, and long, dark hair, and she was surrounded by a bright light. Immediately, my wife awoke and excitedly recounted every detail to me. Our dark-haired little girl was born healthy, normal, and right on schedule—just as we had been promised. Today Amy is a testimony to the truthfulness of the gospel of Jesus Christ and the importance of obeying the Spirit." (*Ensign*, February 1988, pp.56-57)

Men who are able to do this, who have developed within themselves these beautiful gifts, declared Bruce R. McConkie, "are always sought for to serve as patriarchs and in other positions of church responsibility and leadership." (*Mormon Doctrine*, p.760) Wilford Woodruff declared that "the spirit of revelation belongs to the priesthood." (*Discourses of Wilford Woodruff*, p.57) And Joseph Smith declared that "every man who possesses that spirit is a prophet." (*History of the Church* 5:408) This is our full duty and responsibility to develop this precious spirit within us as a gift to be of greater benefit to our fellowman and more effective servants of the Lord. For "no man, in this or any other generation," declared Wilford Woodruff, can ". . .edify the inhabitants of the earth without the inspiration of the Spirit of God." (*Journal of Discourses* 15:275)

But this is easier said than done. Boyd K. Packer explained that "the spirit does not get our attention by shouting or shaking us with a heavy hand. Rather it whispers. It caresses so gently that if we are preoccupied we may not feel it at all." (*Ensign*, January 1983, p.53) Spencer W. Kimball said, "Sometimes we don't recognize them when they come." (*Teachings of Spencer W. Kimball*, p.454) And this is a big part of the problem. For "expecting the spectacular, one may not be fully alerted to the constant flow of revealed communication." (Ibid., p.457)

Revelation is rarely spectacular. Boyd K. Packer, as an apostle of the Lord Jesus Christ, explained, "I have learned that strong, impressive spiritual experiences do not come to us very frequently." (*That All May Be Edified*, pp.337-338) That is, most revelation is in common dress, even a "still small voice." (1 Kings 19:11-13) H. Burke Peterson declared that, "Answers from the Lord come quietly—ever so quietly. In fact, few hear his answers audibly with their ears. We must be listening so carefully or we will never recognize them. Most answers from the Lord are felt in our heart as a warm comfortable expression, or they may come as thoughts to our mind. They come to those who are prepared and who are patient." He explained that we must "have a sincere heartfelt conversation with him. Confide in him, ask him for forgiveness, plead with him, enjoy him, thank him, express our love to him and then listen for his answers." (*Ensign*, January 1974, p.18-19) All of this because as taught by Joseph Smith, "The things of God are of deep import; and time, and experience, and careful and ponderous and solemn thoughts can only find them out." (*History of the Church* 3:295) It isn't easy. Much is expected of us. But we can train ourselves to tune into the great spirit of the Lord.

Lynn Packham wrote how the Lord's refusal to give him a great spiritual manifestation in the temple ultimately strengthened him and his ability to discern the promptings of the Spirit. He wrote:

> No manifestation occurred. Nothing. . . . Afterward, in response to the questions in my prayers, I realized why the Lord kept the veil drawn that day for me. I've had to learn, and I'm still learning, how the Lord's communication differs from my own subjective mental and emotional states. Had any manifestation been given that day in the temple, I probably would have ended up questioning it, because I had been expecting it so much.

By saying "no" to my sign-seeking, and later by manifesting his power through priesthood authority on many other occasions when it was necessary for purposes other than my own desires, and by sending the Holy Spirit's prompting, often unsolicited and unexpected, the Lord has proven to me that he is an entity outside my mind; that this is his work and he directs it as he wishes. . . . (*Ensign*, August 1974, pp.65-66)

We don't direct the Spirit, the Spirit and the Godhead direct us if we are receptive, loyal and true.

The only thing that is constant is God's love and comfort. Whether we can feel this warmth and enjoyment or not depends on getting ourselves mentally, emotionally and physically in tune with Him. Bruce R. McConkie explained what can realistically be expected in the enjoyment of this gift. He said, "Even a righteous person is often left to himself so that he does not at all times enjoy the promptings of revelation and light from the Holy Ghost." (*Mormon Doctrine*, p.313) But this is actually a great blessing in a number of ways. Orson Pratt said:

Supposing a person were thus guided all the time, from waking in the morning until they retired to rest at night; and then when asleep if his dreams were given by the same spirit, and this should be the uninterrupted condition of an individual, I ask, where would be his trials? This would lead us to ask, is it not absolutely necessary that God should in some measure, withhold even from those who walk before him in purity and integrity, a portion of his Spirit, that they may prove themselves, their families and neighbors, and to the heavens whether they are full of integrity even in times when they have not so much of the Spirit to guide and influence them? I think that this is really necessary. . . . (*Journal of Discourses* 15:233)

There appears to be three basic reasons why it is important that we do not always have the constant companionship of the Spirit, and they are all guiding principles and vital to our lives. They are:

(1) We won't be commanded in all things or be compelled to do what's right, when we don't want it or have no heart for it, which would result in slothfulness, rejection and condemnation. (D&C 58:27-28) God loves us too much for this to occur.

(2) Being left to ourselves, we can be tested and prove ourselves that we are full of integrity and truly love what is right. That is, we can choose to do good of our own free will and choice and thus be accountable for it and be rewarded and abundantly blessed for our righteous decisions and choices. (D&C 58:27-28)

(3) And we can experience the darkness and learn by contrast how beautiful and glorious the light really is. That is, we can taste the sour or bitter of life so we can appreciate the sweetness, beauty and glory of heaven.

By being devoid of the Spirit at times, we can learn to really miss it and instead of taking it for granted, we love it and hunger for it all the more. We can also learn to appreciate, adore and thrive on the wonderful gift of the Holy Ghost as an unfailing source of happiness, joy and peace.

Bruce R. McConkie in an address to students at Brigham Young University, said:

> All the revelations of eternity are here, but you and I who have assembled in the devotional are probably not receiving them. This field house is full of the visions of eternity, and yet we are not viewing visions at this moment, but we could . . . , if at any time we manage to tune our souls to the eternal wave band upon which the Holy Ghost is broadcasting, since he is a Revelator, we could receive the revelations of the Spirit. If we could attune our souls to the band on which he is sending forth the visions of eternity, we could see what the Prophet saw in Section 76, or anything else that it was expedient for us to see. . . . Now I am not able to explain how this takes place." But I "can state, as one having authority, that these things do take place in the spiritual realm, and that it is possible to receive revelation and direction and guidance in our personal affairs. (*Speeches of the Year*, September 29, 1964, pp.4-5) (Joseph Fielding McConkie, *The Spirit of Revelation*, pp.17-18)

But just like trying to describe salt to a person who has never tasted it, or color to a blind man, Bruce R. McConkie said, "I cannot use any language that describes to you what a revelation is. Somebody said, 'How can I tell if I have had a revelation? I have had a feeling that such and such is true. How can I be sure?' Nobody can tell you how to be sure. Revelation is not something that you describe. Revelation is something that you experience." ("Personal Revelation," address delivered to the Salt Lake Institute of Religion, January 22, 1971, p.7) Hence, we need to seek to love and obey all His counsels, and learn the sweet and glorious art of communing with God. And by doing this we "may grow into the principle of revelation." (*Teachings of the Prophet Joseph Smith*, p.151)

But spiritual growth and enjoyment takes time. You can't just reach into your pocket and give another years of rich, spiritual experiences in striving to follow Christ. Nor can we really share the glory and beauty of the love we've developed for the Lord. We simply cannot pull rabbits out of a hat. It takes time; and being in a hurry, or being impatient and not waiting for an answer may be one of the major reasons why we don't receive more answers. We need to stay on our knees, exercise our faith, practice, get experience, wait, listen, feel, and adore our Heavenly Father deeply in our hearts. It takes time and experience.

Neal A. Maxwell wrote that this is a "special territory one enters for which detailed maps are not available. The guides who know the country well speak of such things only in hushed tones, if at all. Suffice it to say that if we truly hunger and thirst after such things, we will be led to living water!" (*Wherefore, Ye Must Press Forward*, p.122) President Boyd K. Packer gave a good analogy of how we can train ourselves to listen. He told about the naturalist John Burroughs who was walking through a park in a noisy city one summer and heard a bird sing. "He stopped and listened! Those with him had not heard it. He looked around. No one else had noticed it. It bothered him that everyone should miss something so beautiful. He took a coin from his pocket and flipped it into the air. It struck the pavement with a ring, no louder than the song of the bird. Everyone turned; they could hear that!," but not something so positive and beautiful as the song of a bird. (*Conference Report,* October 1979, p.27) We don't ordinarily develop an ear for things we habitually ignore or consider of little value.

President Packer gave another example of developing the ability to hear. He described how he and his wife divided two small children into "his" and "hers" for night tending. Elder Packer would get up for the one who was cutting teeth, and sister Packer would get up for the new baby. Eventually, he said, "we came to realize that each would hear only the one to which we were assigned, and would sleep very soundly through the cries of the others." (Ibid., p.28) Again we can learn to hear the still small voice of revelation. And, "when we learn to distinguish between the inspiration that comes from the Spirit of the Lord and that which comes from our own uninspired hopes and desires, we need make no mistakes. To this I testify," declared Marion G. Romney as one of the great past councilors in the First Presidency. (*The New Era*, October 1975, pp.34-35)

Revelation is a gift that must be cultivated with energy and diligence. And this is not given as advice or as a suggestion to us. It is the high command of the living God. The Lord said, "But ye are commanded in all things to ask of God . . . considering the end of your salvation . . . and that which the Spirit testifies unto you even so I would that ye should do. . . ." (D&C 46:7 order changed) Wilford Woodruff added, "When a man becomes acquainted with the whisperings of the Holy Ghost, which is revelation, he should be very careful to obey it, for his life may depend upon it." (Duane Crowther, *Gifts of the Spirit*, p.8) In fact, his eternal life does depend on it. It is so important that Bruce R. McConkie, in all soberness, could write that we must "get personal revelation to be saved" and ". . . without it, no one can be saved in the kingdom of heaven." (*A New Witness for the Articles of Faith*, p.487) And Joseph Smith said, "Salvation cannot come without revelation; it is in vain for anyone to minister [or give a blessing] without it. . . ." (*History of the Church* 3:389-390) It is just that important.

But "all inspiration does not come from God. (See D&C 46:7.)," declared Boyd K. Packer. He wrote, "The evil one has the power to tap into those channels of revelation and send conflicting signals which can mislead and confuse us. There are promptings from evil sources which are so carefully counterfeited as to deceive even the very elect. (See Matthew 24:24.) Nevertheless, we can learn to discern these spirits. Even with every member having the right to revelation, the church can be maintained as a house of order" and safety. (*Ensign*, November 1989, p.14) But "nothing," said Joseph Smith, "is a greater injury to the children of men than to be under the influence of a false spirit when they think they have the Spirit of God." (*Teachings of the Prophet Joseph Smith*, p.205)

Joseph F. Merrill, an apostle of Christ, said:

> Satan tempts us where we are most vulnerable. He misleads a few into believing that the promptings that come from him are divine revelations. These false prophets in turn are seemingly so devout, so humble, so earnest and sincere that they, with Satan's help, are able to deceive and mislead many others—only those, however, who profess a belief in modern revelation. . . .
>
> The foolish who have been blinded have been led to believe that they are serving the cause of the Master when the fact is they are dupes of the devil. . . .
>
> When in doubt go on your knees in humility with an open mind and a pure heart with a real desire to do the Lord's will, and pray earnestly and sincerely for divine guidance. Persist in praying in this way until you get an answer that fills your bosom with joy and satisfaction. It will be God's answer. If obedient to this answer you will always act as the President indicates. You will then be safe. (quoted in *Church News*, February 20, 1993, p.14)

"Thus there is no possibility of a person's ever being deceived," declared Orson Pratt, "who follows the teachings and revelations of the Holy Ghost," which is revelation. (*Orson Pratt's Works*, p.70) This is protective, provided of course we really love everything pertaining to God and His Kingdom upon the earth. Heber C. Kimball said, "When a man revolts against the work of God and against the counsels of his servants, and will not be subject to the Holy Ghost, which dwells in him, he commits treason against God, and against his authority on the earth, and neither the Father, nor the Son, nor the Holy Ghost will take up their abode with such a man, and he may bid farewell to the guidance of good angels." (*Journal of Discourses* 11:145)

As explained, revelation and spiritual promptings were never meant to be constant. It was never meant that we should receive revelation on every little thing, or as a result there would be no free agency—one of the greatest principles of life. Nor would we experience or learn much during our mortal probation—the school of mortality would be thwarted. Hence, "those who pray that the Spirit might give them immediate guidance in every little thing throw themselves open to false spirits that seem ever ready to answer our pleas and confuse us. . . . The people," continued William E. Berrett, "I have found most confused in this Church are those who seek personal revelation on everything. They want the personal assurance from the Spirit from daylight to dark on everything they do. I say they are the most confused people I know because it appears sometimes that the answer comes from the wrong source." ("Teaching by the Spirit," pp.102-103) (quoted in *The Holy Ghost* by Joseph Fielding McConkie and Robert L. Millet, pp.29-30) George A. Smith explained that when we are "guided by the Spirit of God, it leaves the mind happy and comfortable, and the understanding clear." (*Journal of Discourses* 8:255) It is not confusing.

To help us, the Lord set up a safety net in his Church to protect us from the danger of being led astray. He said, "And unto the bishop of the church, and unto such as God shall appoint and ordain to watch over the church and to be elders [leaders or presiding officers] unto the church, are to have it given unto them to discern all those gifts lest there be any among you professing and yet not be of God." (D&C 46:27) In other words, "the gift of discerning [distinguishing between] spirits will be given to the Presiding Elder" or officer of the Church, because "no man nor sect of men without the regular constituted authorities, the Priesthood and discerning of spirits, can tell true from false spirits." (*Teachings of the Prophet Joseph Smith*, pp.162, 213) Therefore, "The gifts," declared Orson Pratt of having priesthood offices, presiding officers or brethren who are prophets of the living God locally in our midst, "were given to prevent the people from being carried about by every wind of doctrine. Take away these gifts—the gift of revelation, prophecy and miracles, which were enjoyed by the Saints in ancient days, and the people are liable to be tossed to and fro by every wind of doctrine that may be sounded in their ears." (*Journal of Discourses* 16:138)

There are, in addition, a number of other ways to judge and discern true revelation besides those mentioned above. One is that it edifies us and we feel to rejoice over it. To edify according to the dictionary means to uplift, enlighten and inform. Some synonyms for the word edify are beneficial, helpful and useful, and the Lord reminds us that if we love the truth, it will cause us to rejoice and feel happy inside and lifted up. (*Merriam Webster's Collegiate Dictionary*, p.367; *Roget's International Thesaurus*, 672, 21 and D&C 50:22) Joseph Fielding Smith said: "There is no saying of greater truth than 'that which doth not edify is not of God.' And that which is not of God is darkness, it matters not wether it comes in the guise of religion, ethics, philosophy or revelation. No revelation from God will fail to edify and it is a wonderful promise. . . ," because we can distinguish the good from the evil. (*Church History and Modern Revelation* 1:184 and D&C 50:13-24))

Joseph Smith wrote, "They can all tell the Spirit of the Lord from all other spirits; it will whisper peace and joy to their souls; it will take malice, hatred, strife and all evil from their hearts; and their whole desire will be to do good, bring forth righteousness and build up the kingdom of God." (Journal History, February 23, 1847) Hyrum Smith was told to "put your trust in that Spirit which leadeth to do good—yea, to do justly, to walk humbly, to judge righteously; and this is my Spirit. Verily, verily, I say unto you, I will impart unto you of my Spirit, which shall enlighten your mind, which shall fill your soul with joy; And then shall ye know, all things whatsoever you desire of me, which are pertaining unto things of righteousness, in faith believing in me that you shall receive." (D&C 11:14) George Q. Cannon taught, "I want to give you a rule by which you may know that the spirit which you have is the right spirit. The Spirit of God produces cheerfulness, joy, light and good feelings." (*Gospel Truth*, p.144) Obviously, the Lord's spirit is very positive and reassuring and leadeth to do good.

Sometimes we can experience a glorious taste of heaven in prayer. Parley P. Pratt wrote that "on a sudden the Spirit of God came upon me, and filled my heart with joy and gladness indescribable; and while the spirit of revelation glowed in my bosom with as visible a warmth and gladness as if it were fire," he then received a beautiful message. (*Autobiography of Parley P. Pratt*, p.294) Prayer can be a beautiful, rewarding experience. Spencer W. Kimball wrote, "Learning the language of prayer is a joyous, lifetime experience." (*Ensign*, October 1981, p.5) It takes time. It is not an overnight venture, but if we make the effort, God will answer us in various ways.

President Kimball continued, "Sometimes ideas flood our mind as we listen after our prayers. Sometimes feelings press upon us. A spirit of calmness assures us that all will be well. But always, if we have been honest and earnest, we will experience a good feeling—a feeling of warmth for our Father in Heaven and a sense of his love for us." (Ibid.)

Joseph Smith taught, "You say honey is sweet, and so do I. I can also taste the spirit of eternal life. I know it is good. . . ," because "it tastes good." (*Teachings of the Prophet Joseph Smith*, p.355) "The kingdom of God," wrote Paul to the Romans, "is not meat and drink; but righteousness, and peace, and joy in the Holy Ghost." (Romans 14:17) For the fruit of the tree of Life, which is "the love of God," is most sweet, wonderful and delicious. (1 Nephi 8 and 11) Hyrum G. Smith, one of the Patriarchs of the Church, declared, ". . .as a rule, I have discovered that the adversary's agencies, in their promptings, are usually of an urging, crowding, hurrying nature, while the Spirit of the Lord and his agencies are always of a quiet, sweet, peaceful and convincing character. . . . The spirit of conviction, of peace and of charity, which is the love of the Lord and his work, is not in a hurry, but has time to decide, time to weigh, time to consider; does not act in haste, but in calm deliberation." (*Conference Report,* October 1931, p.27) And this is the endearing spirit we need to cultivate.

George Q. Cannon said, "You should never leave your bed chamber until you get that calm, serene and happy influence that flows from the presence of the Spirit of God and that is the fruit of the Spirit. So, during the day you are apt to get disturbed, angry and irritated about something. You should stop and not allow that influence to prevail or have place in your heart." (*Gospel Truth*, p.504) That is, in our hearts we need to treasure and hold on to a grateful, happy, endearing spirit that is in harmony with the Spirit of God, which bring joy and gladness, and be prayerful and upright in all that we do.

Joseph Fielding Smith declared that "a great many members of the Church do not have that guidance [of the Holy Ghost] . . . . and without that guidance which is promised to us through our faithfulness, people are unable to discern and are led astray. It depends on our faithfulness and our obedience to the commandments of the Lord if we [are to] have the teachings, the enlightening instruction, that comes from the Holy Ghost." (*Speeches of the Year*, October 25, 1961, p.4) And this is of enormous importance.

Harold B. Lee concluded, "We [will] get our answer from the source of the power we list to obey. If we're keeping the commandments of the Devil, we'll get answers from the Devil. If we're keeping the commandments of God, we'll get the commandments [the inspiration and revelation we desire] from our Heavenly Father for our direction and for our guidance." (*Speeches of the Year*, October 5, 1952, p.181) Or in the words of Wilford Woodruff, "if a man had the spirit of God [which means he dearly loves and obeys the Lord] he can tell the difference between what is from the Lord and what is not." (*Journal of Discourses* 22:333)

In Joseph Smith's translation of Matthew chapter twenty-four, one verse representing the word of God reads, "And whoso treasureth up my word, shall not be deceived. . . ." (Joseph Smith-Matthew 1:37) That is, if we treasure, love, value, cherish, adore and thrill in God and His words, we will know them and that knowledge will protect us from a deviant path that leads to nowhere. Also a letter from the First Presidency, when Joseph F. Smith was president, makes a very clear statement of how to judge good and evil in regard to spiritual things. We read, "When visions, dreams, tongues, prophecy, impressions or any extraordinary gift or inspiration conveys something out of harmony with the accepted revelations of the Church or contrary to the decisions of its constituted authorities, Latter-day Saints may know that it is not of God, no matter how plausible it may appear." (As quoted by Harold B. Lee in *The Improvement Era*, June 1970, p.64)

Of course, to be protected, one must know what is and is not in harmony with the standard works of the Church and the presiding prophets and apostles of the living God. This takes a love for and an enjoyment of the things of God, and a strong desire to be right with God—so much so, that we love the truth, search it out, live it and thrive on it. In other words, when one is full of a rich, abundant spiritual life, the love of God, purity and correct knowledge, one is on a good foundation for accurately interpreting revelation when it comes. And it will bring him or her much comfort and the sweet assurances of God's love.

Orson Pratt said, ". . .The time will come when this people will become more fully revelators, and prophets, and seers themselves . . . as the waters cover the great deep." (*Journal of Discourses* 19:219) But to do so, we must advance to higher levels of spirituality and a greater closeness to the great God of heaven. Unfortunately though, because revelation is easily misunderstood and we are spiritually underdeveloped problems continue.

George Q. Cannon, a great prophet and general authority who lived in the eighteen hundreds, soberly warned that "every Elder who lays his hands upon a child to bless it should be careful that he is not led by fancy or by a desire to say some wonderful things instead of being prompted by the Spirit of the Lord. For when the Spirit of the Lord does not dictate, however many blessings an Elder may promise and fine things he may say, disappointment is sure to follow. The parents of the child have their expectations raised only to be dashed again to the earth. It is too often the case that in blessing children the Elder entertains the idea that they ought to pronounce upon its head every good thing they can think of. . . ." (*Gospel Truth*, p.193)

This is totally out of order and almost criminal. We have no right to promote fantasy or make believe! That is, no desire to heal or promise great things can justify false prophecy. Much grief and sorrow can be avoided through careful, sincere preparation. Otherwise we can do irreparable damage or sow confusion and disillusionment among the people. In fact, this is so serious that the Lord warned us that, "Whosoever shall offend one of these little ones which believe in me [like being a false prophet among the people], it were better for him that a millstone were hanged about his neck, and that he were drowned in the depths of the sea." (Matthew 18:6)

Therefore, if we do not have the inspiration to know what to say, we should either give the person a generic blessing, which would be true for anyone, or pray so sincerely for the individual that he or she is truly blessed of heaven for "the effectual fervent prayer of a righteous man availeth much." (James 5:16)

Tragically, however, if we do not pay the price of revelation, we hurt people and sin a very heavy sin before the great God of heaven. Bruce R. McConkie explained that "since a true prophet is a minister or religious teacher who receives revelation from God, it follows that a false prophet is a person who pretends . . . who does not in fact receive revelation." (*Doctrinal New Testament Commentary* 2:121-122) A complaint from the past is very applicable today. In 1880 Emily Dow Partridge Young said, ". . . we suffer with disease year after year and children die. . . ." And she continued:

> Who is responsible for this state of things. Is it not those who are entrusted with the priesthood; holding the power and authority to rebuke the Destroyer? Are they not responsible in a great measure for the lack of faith among the people. Mothers having sick children send for the Elders according to the revelation; they come from their work feeling in a very great hurry. They cannot take time to bow down before the Lord and dedicate themselves, then administer and act concerned to His Glory, but go through the ceremony in a hurried manner, their minds filled with the cares of business. They think not of the result of their administration; but leave the patient or friends to exercise faith if they can under the circumstances. Who can wonder that distrust creeps into the minds of the people . . . rather than trust in an Elder when sickness is raging. . . .

We lose confidence in the Priesthood. J.S. and his brethren obtained blessings through much prayer. If there were two or three together, they would pray in turns and if they did not prevail at first, they would pray again and again until the Lord would grant them their desires. I have known Elders to lay on hands with no effect at first; but after the second or third time, the patient was healed." (*Diary of Emily Dow Partridge Young,* pp.55-56)

"Present levels of performance," President Spencer W. Kimball declared, "are not acceptable either to ourselves or to the Lord." (*Church News,* March 22, 1975, p.5) We have a great responsibility to be diligent, to wrestle and plead and work at these things for the faith to thrive in Israel. George Q. Cannon lamented and pleaded with the Saints about this. His exact words are worth thinking about. We must capture the high vision of it all. He said:

> We do not look upward as we should do. We do not plead with the heavens for the bestowal of greater gifts, greater powers, greater qualifications, as we should. We should plead with our Father to give us more of the Holy Ghost, more of the gifts thereof, more revelation, more of the gift of prophecy, and more of all those gifts that He has promised unto His Church. We should not be content to remain on the level we have reached, and think, "Oh, that is the height we ought to go, and there is no need for us to seek to climb any higher." This is wrong. It is my duty as a servant of God, to qualify myself by faith for the office that God has given me. It is the duty of the First Presidency to do this, that we shall not be stagnant, and that the Church will not stand still; but that we shall be alive, and filled with the spirit, power and gifts of our office and calling; that the revelations of Jesus will be given to us, and the Twelve Apostles also, until angels will minister to us, the heavens be opened to us, the revelations of God be multiplied upon us, until everything necessary for the guidance of this people to redemption will be revealed to us. This is our duty. It is also the duty of every officer in the Church in his place and station—every President of a Stake, every High Councilor, every Bishop, and every Teacher and Deacon in the Church of Christ—to live in such a way that there will be constant communication between the heavens and each soul. (*Collected Discourses* 5:327)

It seems that the parable of the talents that Christ taught is more than applicable here. (Matthew 25:14-30) Joseph Fielding Smith commented on this and said:

> Each man holding the Priesthood should learn his duty from this parable, for when the Lord shall come, like rewards shall be given us. Many

who have promised to magnify their Priesthood, and who have failed to do so, shall be cast out. Their Priesthood shall be taken from them. . . . Theirs shall be a condition of weeping and gnashing of teeth. Now what is meant by the saying: "For unto every one that hath shall be given . . . but from him that hath not shall be taken away even that which he hath?" Simply this: We are under obligation as men holding the Priesthood to put to service the authority which we have received. If we do this then we shall have other responsibilities and glory added, and we shall receive an abundance, that is, the fulness of the Father's kingdom; but if we bury our Priesthood, then we are not entitled to receive any reward, we cannot be exalted. (*The Way to Perfection*, pp.220-221)

"Now, I think that above all else in the world," President Joseph Fielding Smith declared, "I, and you, and all members of the Church should seek to be guided by the Spirit of the Lord. To the extent that we gain the guidance of that Spirit we will be prophets to ourselves and in our own affairs, and we will also find ourselves in harmony with those prophets whom the Lord has placed in the First Presidency and in the Council of the Twelve." (*Joseph Fielding Smith—A Prophet Among the People*, pp.24-25) That is, we will be spiritually gifted and enjoy the rich inner comfort and treasures that flow out of the Spirit enjoyed by all the prophets, whether elders, seventies or high priests, who minister in the sacred name of the Lord.

For "when the Lord's servants perform ordinances, they act in the place and stead of Christ. . . . Their commission and charge is to do what the Lord wants done, a goal which can be gained only if the plan and purpose of the Lord is manifest by revelation. . . . Thus the secret of giving an approved and proper blessing is to act under the direction of the Spirit." (*On Earth and In Heaven*, pp.129, 143) "And the Spirit," the Lord declared to us, "shall be given unto you by the prayer of faith; and if ye receive not the Spirit ye shall not teach [or give a blessing]. (D&C 42:15) But if we do have "the Comforter [the Holy Ghost], ye shall speak and prophesy as seemeth me good; For, behold the Comforter knoweth all things, and beareth record of the Father and the Son." (D&C 42:17) That is, the spirit strengthens us and any blessing from God should fortify our testimonies and encourage our faith.

Faith in God is deeply rooted in prophecy. Faith is, in fact, a belief or near certainty that something will happen, such as, good will triumph over evil eventually, Christ will redeem us and deliver us, the resurrection will bring to us perfection and beauty and rest, or the Lord will intervene is some important area of our lives. Is it any wonder, then, that God's servants must be prophets and speak about future events to build and fortify our faith? Great rewards are at stake. Will the man live or die? Will the infant grow up and become a productive adult? Will I be able to succeed in this important calling? Can I do it? It is not only appropriate, but we are often expected to prophesy. People need and want the Lord's comfort and encouragement, the consolation of heaven, the oil of gladness, good tidings of truth, the balm that heals, lifts and thrills. We need the help of God in our lives.

In this regard, I know one great high priest, who has the wonderful gift to lay hands upon people and bless them beautifully according to the will and word of the Lord. He is always prepared. And I know there are others, but I think for most of us, myself included, and a patriarch I knew, we need to inquire of the Lord first and get His personal message for the individual requesting the blessing. We need to bless, in effect, "having first obtained [our] . . . errand from the Lord." (Jacob 1:17) That is, we first obtain revelation. To do this, "Ye shall call on the Father in my name, in mighty prayer; and after ye have done this ye shall have power that to him upon whom ye shall lay your hands, ye shall give the Holy Ghost [that is, give a great blessing]; and in my name shall ye give it. . . ." (Moroni 2:2) When the Spirit is present in rich abundance everyone is happy and thrilled and full of love and rejoices. "Mighty prayer" must become a wonderful habit and a prelude to greater things so we can function beyond our natural ability. Preparation in this way also fills us with divine confidence, which is critical, because fear is the opposite of faith and is the enemy to enjoying the full rights and privileges of the Priesthood.

George Q. Cannon said, "The feeling of fear when it rests upon a man, drives away the Spirit of God. The two spirits cannot exist in the same bosom. One must have the mastery. If the Spirit of God has the mastery, it drives away all fear, and enables a man to speak under its influence with power. If the spirit of fear has the mastery, the Spirit of God is checked, and the man is not able to tell the people the will and counsel of the Lord." (*Gems For The Young Folks*, pp.42-43) The Lord has told us, ". . . if ye are prepared ye shall not fear." (D&C 38:30) Two well known sayings come to mind. One is, "Preparation precedes power" and the other, "If you fail to prepare, you are prepared to fail." If one knows ahead of time the special divine messages for an individual, one can stand with the utmost assurance, stand with great faith that God is with it and, therefore, speak with great power and authority.

But, we need to keep in mind that "puny preparation precedes puny revelations" and blessings. (Joseph Fielding McConkie, *Prophets and Prophecy*, p.134) Only to those who truly "hunger and thirst after righteousness" is the promise given that they shall be "filled with the Holy Ghost." (3 Nephi 12:6) No such great blessings are "given to those satisfied to nibble at the gospel or who fill themselves with spiritual junk food." (*Prophets and Prophecy*, p.134) Members of the Church miss out on wonderful, soul-stirring experiences when leaders are not skilled in matters of the Spirit or are spiritually immature and undeveloped.

The Prophet Joseph Smith in translating the Bible changed Paul's definition of faith to read. "Now faith is the assurance of things hoped for, the evidence of things not seen." (Hebrews 11:1) It used to read "substance" instead of "assurance." Therefore, true faith involves revelation or divine assurances. Again, faith is a gift of divine assurance or a confirming revelation. Such assurances make for great and beautiful blessings from on high. Heber C. Kimball explained: "When the Holy Ghost dwells in us [for the Holy Ghost is filled with revelation], it will . . . show us all things to come, and bring things to our remembrance, and will make every one of this people prophets. . . ." (*Journal of Discourses* 4:119) And Bruce R. McConkie wrote that "the greater the faith [an accumulation of divine assurances] the more wondrous are the forthcoming revelations," or prophetic words of immense power. He continued that "all saints, all true believers, all who have faith in the Lord Jesus Christ, all who love and serve him . . . receive revelation and spiritual gifts, enjoy [the great] signs [of the last days], and work miracles." (*The Promised Messiah*, pp.573-574)

Ian Llewwllyn wrote:

> Ever since my baptism thirteen years ago, I had been confused about priesthood blessings. The sheer responsibility involved frightened me. How could the priesthood holder be sure, when he gave a blessing, that he spoke the words of the Lord and not his own well-meaning phrases? Naturally he wants the sufferer to be made well, but what if the Lord has other plans? How would the person receiving the blessing feel if, instead of becoming better as the blessing indicated, his or her condition worsened? How would the family feel if the sufferer died? I never wanted to be in a position where I said something that the Lord didn't want me to say. But an experience I had one spring enlightened my understanding of priesthood blessings and, more important, removed my fear. (*Ensign*, September 1990, p.54)

And that was that he received revelation before he blessed the person. He wrote that "suddenly the strangest thing happened," that is, it was unexpected. He continued, "Quite unmistakably, I received a clear message:

Beverly was going to get better. This was not wishful thinking on my part—the message came directly from the Spirit." (Ibid.) Therefore he blessed her to get well and she did. Hence, he acted as a prophet and told her the truth. (Ibid.)

George A. Smith declared that "to be a Prophet is to have the Spirit of Prophesy," which is revelation. (*Journal of Discourses* 10:67) This inspiration is absolutely necessary to give inspired blessings like the great prophets of ancients times did with wonderful skill. To do otherwise, is to take the Lord's name in vain and be a false prophet, which is a very serious offense. Also, "there are instances when individuals should work out their problems without a priesthood blessing. No clearly defined rule can be made to designate what to do in every instance except to seek inspiration from the Lord." (*Duties and Blessings of the Priesthood, Part B,* p.46) But we need to be right. We need inspiration from heaven. And in the words of B. H. Roberts, "if an Elder's heart is filled with blessing [that is, he feels a beautiful, heavenly feeling to exercise his great authority] . . . and the Spirit prompts him to pronounce blessings upon them for their encouragement, . . . or if he is prompted to tell them what particular gift of the Holy Ghost will develop within them, or to admonish them against evil, all well and good; [and] with one of old we say, 'Quench not the Spirit, neither despise prophecy,'. . . ," for it is sometimes great and wonderful. (Ben E. Rich, *Scrapbook of Mormon Literature*, 2:112)

One of the great secrets of giving beautiful and inspired blessings was given to me by an old patriarch. He told me to prayerfully practice saying blessings and giving possible promises quietly, or in my mind, for the individual in question and what the Spirit bears witness to or I feel a sense of confidence in, I should remember, and whatever falls flat or I get a sense of confusion or an uncomfortable feeling about it, forget. That is, inquire about what the unique needs are for this individual—what counsels would be most helpful and appropriate—what great things are in his or her future—what would encourage and have special meaning for this precious and dear person—what is the Lord's special and unique message for him or her? In other words, I was not to suppose that He would give it to me when I took no thought save it was to ask Him. I was to study it out in my mind, and if it was right, I would feel it is right and if it was wrong, I would have a stupor of thought. (D&C 9:7-9) This beautiful old man told me that I must do my homework, I must know things about the individual, when possible, to guide me in my search for the words, phrases, warnings and promises that God will bear witness to and sustain. In other words, he counseled me to ask for and receive specific revelations in order to get the unique blessing of heaven for the precious soul requesting the word of the Lord. Harold B. Lee said, ". . . When these whisperings come it is a gift and our privilege to have them. They come when we are relaxed and not under pressure of appointments. (I want you to mark that.)" (*Teachings of Harold B. Lee*, pp.414-415) We need to take time for spiritual success.

Occasionally, the old patriarch told me, he would at times, and he said I would as well, see a quick vision, sometimes looking through a glass darkly, that is, sometimes dim, but nevertheless, a vision, which would have to be translated into words for the individual receiving the blessing. I have experienced this as he promised I would, and I was also promised this in my patriarchal blessing. But whether I was so fortunate or not, after discovering the basic message of the Lord to that individual and a few specific promises and perhaps what predicates each unique blessing, I needed to be full of fillers. That is, since you can't get water out of an empty well, one needs to have his heart full of possible promises that could be given, by inspiration, to anyone to fill in the empty spaces and create an uplifting and edifying blessing. Then, armed with this beautiful truth and glory within, we say the very things that are needed and administer in a way that is truly beautiful and fortifying.

However, when inquiring or preparing oneself to bless another and we feel prompted to promise something unusually grand or alternatively if we personally receive an extraordinary promise from another priesthood holder, we should pray for a confirmation, because if we are truly faithful, we have a right to two or three witnesses or promptings. For "in the mouth of two or three witnesses ever word may be established," saith the Lord. (Matthew 18:16 and Deuteronomy 19:15) This is a law of heaven. Hence, one patriarch, while blessing the son of a friend, hesitated for several minutes until he could reconfirm a remarkable prompting, which was in fact a vision, as described above, because it could fall flat or be unfulfilled and therefore hurt the individual, if it were false. If no reassurance comes, after sincere inquiry, the idea may be regarded as unreliable or unworthy of mentioning.

Helaman, a Nephite prophet wrote that "we did pour out our souls in prayer to God, that he would strengthen us and deliver us" and later "the Lord our God did visit us with assurances. . ." or a confirmation of the original promise to spare their lives and give them success, "insomuch that he did speak peace to our souls. . . ." (Alma 58:10-11) This is the glorious right and privilege of the Saints who deeply desire to love and obey God in their hearts, for the gifts of the Spirit "are given for the benefit of those who love me and keep all my commandments, and him that seeketh so to do. . . ." (D&C 46:9)

If one has difficulty receiving revelatory answers to prayer, or feels a need for help, one could request the help of a bishop or any other faithful priesthood holder to confirm or disconfirm any special promise important to ones own life or someone else's life to which one has personal stewardship responsibility. For, in the words of Bruce R. McConkie, even a "teacher is expected to be a prophet and to know for himself of the truth and divinity of the work . . ." or the truth of the prophetic words he is declaring. (*The Holy Ghost*, p.113)

In some cases, a higher order of revelation is required. That is, not just a strong, sweet impression or conviction, but the hearing of the still small voice or seeing a vision or even enjoying the presence of an angel in extremely rare cases. Also one must be especially careful if personal feelings are involved. Boyd K. Packer said, "The spiritual part of us and the emotional part of us are so closely linked that it is possible to mistake an emotional impulse for something spiritual." (*That All May Be Edified*, p.342) For example, our own hearts can leap within us for joy over an idea or possibility and this can deceive us into thinking that the feeling was a revelation from God. Hence, greater care, such as the confirmation of a third party and a higher, more sure word of revelation needs to be sought after when personal feelings are involved. This is because they can so easily distort good reception and result in false conclusions or ideas.

Also, my experience has been that I need time between giving blessings. I am so full of the images, privileges and future of the one I just finished to give an appropriate blessing to the second person immediately after the first. I might give some of the first persons blessing to the second individual, which could so easily happen and result in an uninspired or partially inspired blessing without full authority or validity. That is, and I shutter to think of it, it could make me a false prophet to that individual. Personally, I need time to let go of the beauty and glory of the first blessing so as to discover the unique, personal counsels of the living God for the second. This takes some time and prayer. I realize there are individuals who do not have the same problem as I do—again, my friend and former bishop. But I cannot do this very easily and need special preparation. Others may feel the same need. But as a result of my experience, I can really relate to the idea that lousy preparation precedes a lousy, half-baked blessing or an uninspired blessing.

We need to "remember that that which cometh from above is sacred, and must be spoken with care, and by constraint of the Spirit; and in this there is no condemnation, and ye receive the Spirit through prayer; wherefore, without this there remaineth condemnation." (D&C 63:64) However, "our

Heavenly Father," declared George Q. Cannon, "will not hold him a trans-
gressor for a slip of the tongue or a verbal inaccuracy caused by nervousness
or misapprehension." (*Gospel Truth*, p.193) But, "every officer should do his
very best when ministering in the things of God. . . ." Continuing Elder
Cannon explained that "carelessness or slovenliness in the handling of holy
things or the performance of sacred rites is very displeasing to Him in whose
name we are officiating." (Ibid.)

The Lord told Hyrum Smith not to declare His Word until he first
obtained it. That is, we need to know the Lord's specific counsels, promises
and blessings for the individual first by revelation, "then shall your tongue
be loosed; then, if you desire, you shall have my Spirit and my word, yea,
the power of God unto the convincing of men." (D&C 11:21) To have this
great privilege the Lord tells us to "treasure up in your minds continually the
words of life, and it shall be given you in the very hour that portion that shall
be meted unto every man." (D&C 84:85) Notice that this great promise is
predicated on the idea that we "treasure up . . . continually the words of life,"
including the beautiful truth revealed about the particular individual we are
to bless.

Neal A. Maxwell of the Council of the Twelve explained one critically
important way we could treasure up the things of God and therefore be full
of the glory and beauty of the Spirit within ourselves that can flow out and
enrich others lives. He wrote:

> We need to feast upon the words of Christ in the scriptures and as
> these words come to us from living prophets. Just nibbling occasionally
> will not do. (See 2 Nephi 31:20 and 32:3.) Feasting means partaking with
> relish and delight and savoring—not gorging episodically in heedless
> hunger, but partaking gratefully, dining with delight, at a sumptuous spread
> carefully and lovingly prepared by prophet-chefs over the centuries. These
> words plus the gift of the Holy Ghost will tell us all things we should do.
> (*Wherefore, Ye Must Press Forward*, p.28)

Hence, we must do more than read about the spiritual feast of others. We
too must approach the table and feed our own souls. But "when we are dis-
obedient," said Joseph Fielding Smith, "when our minds are set upon the
things of this world rather than on the things of the kingdom of God, we cannot have the manifestation of the Holy Ghost." (*Speeches of the Year*,
October 25, 1961, p.5) Therefore, we need to invest in spiritually feeding
ourselves for friendship with the Spirit needs feeding or it will starve
because of our inattention. But if we fill up our hearts, adore and treasure

beautiful things, we sanctify ourselves with true delight and love for God, and we glory in Him. We then overflow with inner good.

Heber C. Kimball said, "If your heart is right you cannot speak without speaking what is right." (*Journal of Discourses* 3:111) That is, treasuring, cherishing, loving, valuing, adoring and thrilling in the things of God goes a long way toward creating the right internal atmosphere for the Lord to write upon our hearts His message for each unique individual. Of course, this takes time and energy, but it is worth it for this is what we were ordained for—to be like Christ and be revelators and prophets of God to the people. Being ordained after His order and likeness, we, of all people, should strive with all our hearts to live up to being great and inspired men after the order of Melchizedek and the Son of God.

Unfortunately, as Bruce R. McConkie noted:

> . . .it is an almost universal practice among most Church leaders—to get so involved with the operation of the institutional Church that we never gain faith like the ancients, simply because we do not involve ourselves in the basic gospel matters that were the center of their lives.
>
> We are so wound up in programs and statistics and trends, in properties, lands, and mammon, and in achieving goals that will highlight the excellence of our work, that we 'have omitted the weightier matters of the law.'
>
> However talented men may be in administrative matters; however eloquent they may be in expressing their views; however learned they may be in worldly matters—they will be denied the sweet whisperings of the Spirit that might have been theirs unless they pay the price. . . .
>
> May I suggest, based on personal experience, that faith comes and revelations are received as a direct result of scripture study. . . . Those who study, ponder, and pray about the scriptures, seeking to understand their deep and hidden meanings, receive from time to time great outpourings of light and knowledge from the Holy Spirit. (*Doctrines of the Restoration*, pp.321-240)

The Apostle quoted above goes on to say that we should believe the scriptures, center our lives around them, quote them, ponder and pray about them, mark them, live them and testify of their truth; and, he promised, if we do, our lives would be sweetened with loftier, happier views, greater enjoyments, heavenly, spiritual treasures and abundant power to overcome the world and all our inner enemies. (Ibid.)

Joe J. Christensen of the Seventy testified that "impressive personal revelations and increased spirituality are directly associated with reading and pondering over the scriptures." (*To Grow in Spirit*, p.10) What this means in practical everyday life is that we should spend at least twenty to thirty minutes twice a day savoring and treasuring the things of God through sincere, fervent prayer, pondering and feasting on spiritual food and cultivating a thankful, appreciative heart for every beautiful and glorious thing created by the hand of God, but most importantly for His Son, the Great Redeemer, and His atonement, the center of all things, which is the gospel of joy and endless opportunities—things beyond words to express. For nothing can hold a candle to the gospel of Jesus Christ! It has a beautiful, happy effect on those that love Him deeply for they develop attributes similar to the greatest men and women who ever lived.

But, "We need to remember that "it is by magnifying one's calling in the higher priesthood that men obtain exaltation in the eternal worlds." (Bruce R. McConkie, *Doctrinal New Testament Commentary* 3:320) These are the individuals who obtain the sweet and uplifting whisperings of the Spirit in their lives. To be mediocre or without real enthusiasm for the Lord and His kingdom is to lose out on the richest rewards and most beautiful blessings and enjoyments possible on earth. For of the valiant and brave for God and man, it is written: "Great shall be their reward and eternal shall be their glory." (D&C 76:6)

But also happy shall be their hearts or inward parts. Brigham Young explained, "If you find it out that you are a Saint, then all is right with you; your heart is comforted, it is lighted up, and you feel happy, and will meet with your Brethren with a joyful countenance. . . . How does the spirit of the Lord make you feel? Does it make you feel cheerful or sad, gloomy, cast down and melancholy? . . . There is not a man or woman on this Earth, whose peace is made with God, . . . but their countenances are lit up with a lamp of divine cheerfulness." (Fred C. Collier, *Teachings of President Brigham Young*, pp.337-338)

Heber C. Kimball said to those who had long faces in his day, "You think our Father and our God is not a lively, sociable, and cheerful man. He is one of the most lively men that ever lived; and when we have that sociability and cheerfulness, it is the Spirit of the Lord. God delights in a glad heart and a cheerful countenance." (*Journal of Discourses* 5:180) At a later time, he continued on this subject and said, "I feel very cheerful and happy today. . . . I find that the more that I have of the Spirit of God, the more cheerful I am; and it is so with all men of God. I know that those Prophets who have lived in my day loved to tell stories and be cheerful: they delighted in a glad heart and a cheerful countenance." (Ibid. 8:351) And describing what a true prophet of God is like, Elder Kimball said, "Father Smith [the Presiding Patriarch] was one of the most cheerful men I ever saw, and he was harmless as a child." (Ibid.)

A beautiful example I'm grateful for, of an exceptional local leader ,who developed and nurtured the gift of revelation, is from Chauncey C. Riddle. He paid the price and grew step by step into a whole new and wonderful world of joy and inner peace. He concluded that random revelation was just not enough. He decided:

> To be a rock, a bastion of surety, revelation must be something on which one can count and receive in every occasion of real need. I began to seek for it actively. I prayed, I fasted, I lived the gospel as best I knew. I was faithful in my church duties. I tried to live up to every scruple which my conscience enjoined upon me. And dependable revelation did come. Intermittently, haltingly at first, then steadily, over some years it finally came to be a mighty stream of experience. I came to know that at any time of day or night, in any circumstance, for any real need, I could get help. That help came in the form of feelings of encouragement when things seemed hopeless. It came in ideas to unravel puzzles that blocked my accomplishment. It came in priesthood blessings which were fully realized. It came in whisperings of prophecy which were fulfilled. It came in support and even anticipation of what the General Authorities of the Church would say and do in general conference. It came in gifts of the Spirit, as the wonders of eternity were opened to the eyes of my understanding. That stream of spiritual experience is today for me a river of living water that nourishes my soul in every situation. It is the most important factor of my life. If it were taken away, all that I have and am would be dust and ashes. It is the basis of my love, life, understanding, hope, and progress. My only regret is that though this river is so wonderful, I have not been able to take full advantage of it as yet. ("What a Privilege to Believe!," *Sunstone*, May 1988, p.10)" (as quoted in *Spiritual Survival in the Last Days* by Blaine and Brenton Yorgason, pp.199-200)

George A. Smith, an early apostle of Christ, declared that as a man "improves upon his gift [the great gift of the Holy Ghost which is to receive revelation] he becomes a Prophet." (*Journal of Discourses* 10:67) B. H. Roberts said: "And where the Elder has learned his duty [to follow the Spirit] . . . a beautiful and powerful administration is usually the result." (*Scrapbook of Mormon Literature* 2:489) And according to Joseph Fielding Smith, "if he is so inspired [of the Holy Ghost], he is a prophet" of the living God. (*Doctrines of Salvation* 1:186)

Connie LaVall Foy was being set apart for a calling at a Brigham Young University Ward. The counselor in the Bishopric, a presiding high priest of the Lord, who was mouth, hardly knew her or anything about her family, but pausing in the blessing, she could feel the sweet and endearing influence of the Spirit intensify around her. And "he told me that great and important things were happening in my home. He said the blessings of heaven were being poured out upon my family. He told me to humble myself before the Lord and put my life in order so that I might be worthy to receive the great blessing that would soon come to me. I didn't have any idea what Brother Beal was talking about, but I was so touched that I cried. As I turned to shake his hand after the blessing, I found that he, too, had tears streaming down his cheeks." (*Ensign*, October 1991, p.27) Within a year her father had quit smoking, they became active in their Ward, he was ordained an elder in the Melchizedek Priesthood, and the family was sealed for time and all eternity in a temple of the Most High God. (Ibid.) What a beautiful and unforgettable experience for all involved. When we feel inspired to say such things, Joseph Smith asked, "Is he [the priesthood holder] not taking upon himself or assuming the character of a Prophet? . . ." (*The Words of Joseph Smith*, p.230) Yes, and what a beautiful testimony of His servants who speak for him showing that God lives and loves us.

David A. Smith, a past counselor in the Presiding Bishopric, told in general conference in 1927 how:

> Day after day it was my pleasure to be with my father [Joseph F. Smith] as he gave blessings to those boys—your boys—going out to serve their country in a righteous cause [World War I]. And in every case, as I recall, the blessings pronounced upon their head, gave them the promise that if they would keep themselves clean, obey the laws of the land, remember their God, they would go and return uninjured. As I heard father pronounce those words time and again on those boys, and as I saw them leave, not knowing what minute they would be on their way, yet with joy in their souls because of the comforting promise, I paused to wonder! One day in the lull, I turned to father and asked, "What is there that impresses you to make this promise? When we read of the great slaughter and destruction on the other side, it seems to me the only possible thing that can cause your promise to come true will be the termination of the war before the boys get there." He answered: "I do not know whether they shall be called to go to battle or not, but this I do know, for the Lord has given me to understand and know; that promise is made to these young men through their faithfulness, and if they abide the commandments of God, they shall return." Well, the rest of the story you know. They served and met every requirement and returned home again to engage in their pursuits of life uninjured. (*Conference Report,* October 1927, p.118)

These blessings were powerful.They stand as an evidence of not only the power of the prophetic spirit, but God's loving intervention in the lives of each young man who remained faithful and true to the Lord through the whole ordeal.

Norman Vincent Peale, a prominent Protestant religious leader some years ago visited Spencer W. Kimball, while he was President of the Church, and sensing his deep spiritual nature asked him to pray for him. He described how President Kimball laid his hands on his head and in a quiet, sincere and loving manner prayed and blessed him beautifully. Then all of a sudden he felt a "wondrous feeling of the [divine] Presence." (*Ensign*, February 1977, p.84) He knew God was near. To this uncommonly thrilling experience, Reverend Peale bore fervent testimony to all the world, who heard him, in a radio broadcast that he felt God ever so wonderfully close to him while the Mormon prophet prayed for him and blessed him. (Ibid.) I have also enjoyed this wonderful and enjoyable experience in giving blessings. I have seen others do it as well on local and personal levels. God is indeed with His priesthood when they seek Him in faith so fervently that they are rewarded with special outpourings of His rich, sweet spirit.

I testify that by following the principles outlined in this book, I and others have worked wonderful miracles in the name of the Lord, trembled under the endearing power of God, felt heaven surround us and basked in the arms of His love, enjoyed the beauty and encouragement and upliftment of heaven, prophesied great things and small, and seen their fulfillment, healed the sick and the lame, seen engaging visions, cast out devils and many other impressive things. Yet despite such experiences I feel my weakness and know I have no power in and of myself. But I know it is a sweet and glorious ministry, beyond words to express, when we are able to tap into divine sources of heavenly power and glory and enjoyment.

In conclusion, we live in a precious time of local and general prophets, whether as elders, seventies or high priests, and enjoy blessings that the world at large will never know. We are in the words of Wilford Woodruff involved in "as great and as mighty a work as ever was committed to any man on the earth, and that too in the midst of the last dispensation and fulness of time." He also declared soberly that "we cannot [or must not] sleep any longer with the Priesthood of Almighty God resting upon us, and the work that is required at our hands. . . ." (*Journal of Discourses* 4:148,147) That is, we should not be sleeping giants, but be head and shoulders above mediocrity. We should be great. We have enormous power to do good. May we wake up and manifest the endearing glory and love of our great

Redeemer, the Great Jehovah of eternity, in administering powerful blessings to the people that are memorable and so beautiful that they will never be forgotten.

CHAPTER NINE

GREAT FAITH AND INSPIRATION

George Q. Cannon taught that "the people should be taught that great and mighty works can be accomplished by the exercise of faith." (*Gospel Truth*, p.427) But not without effort. For example, Ezra Booth joined the Church in 1831 after seeing Joseph, the Prophet perform a miracle. He was advanced to be a High Priest of the Lord, but did not remain faithful and true. Joseph Smith said, "When he actually learned that faith, humility, patience, and tribulation go before [a great] blessing, and that God brings low before He exalts. . . , he was disappointed. . ." and fell away. (*History of the Church* 1:216) Great effort often precedes great miracles.

A friend, who was having trouble with his eyes, asked me to give him a priesthood blessing, so I inquired of the Lord and received the answer to use the best language I could in the blessing to convince him to exercise his faith and that he would be permanently, totally and absolutely healed, but not without a personal effort. He reported feeling a soothing feeling come over his eyes and all the pain he'd been experiencing was removed—a feeling to rejoice also rested upon him, but he went right back to work and forgot about everything but the tasks and business of his job. Then the pain returned and he wondered what he should do. Should he go to the emergency room? Then he remembered the words of the blessing and the miracle of peace and relief it brought, so he prayed and exercised his faith and the soothing feeling returned and he felt happy once more.

But he soon forgot God and became preoccupied with work, and the pain returned. Facing the dilemma again, he decided he would once more attempt to retrieve the gift of God he had received through the priesthood blessing, but this time with this one difference, he would stay with God in his thoughts and desires all the rest of the day even though he had to complete important tasks for his employer. Then came again the enjoyment and wonderful relief he had previously felt which stayed with him all day as he continued to abide and enjoy communion with the Lord. He learned that the Lord really does mean business when he asks us to "pray always" and "when you do not cry unto the Lord, let your hearts be full, drawn out in prayer unto him continually for your welfare, and also for the welfare of those who are around you." (Alma 34:27)

It is so easy to be distracted by the things of the world and be deceived into thinking that God does not require us to pray without ceasing. In Appendix A and B are a list of some of the scriptures throughout the Standard Works that require us to pray "always" and "continually," which raises the question: Why would the Lord say this over and over—again and again and again unless it was one of the most important things we could ever do—so important that it should be repeated and repeated again? The greater glory, power and potential of the priesthood depends on this kind of inward obedience. That is, He cannot abide with us fully and completely unless we abide in Him. We must sanctify ourselves and welcome Him into our innermost feelings often. In other words, we must "always remember him . . . that [we] may always have his Spirit to be with us." (Moroni 4:37)

Great blessings are at stake for "all victory and glory is brought to pass unto you through your diligence, faithfulness, and prayers of faith," saith the Lord. (D&C 103:36) Prayer is so important that Boyd K. Packer wrote that "no message in the scriptures is repeated more often than the invitation, even the command, to pray—to ask. Prayer is so essential a part of revelation that without it the veil may remain closed. . . ." Prayer is your personal key to heaven. (*Ensign*, November 1994, p.59) In fact, "we can gauge the faithfulness and spirituality of men," wrote Spencer W. Kimball, "by the degree and intensity of the communication between them and God." (*Faith Precedes the Miracle*, p.22)

A different friend years earlier worked at a hospital in Salt Lake as a pharmacist in training. He was asked to administer to a man who looked like death warmed over. Most of his family were less active and about fifteen of them were present to witness the blessing. The Lord in an unmistakable way let my friend know that this man would be out of the hospital within three days and would be in good health. However, he feared to say this. He was filled with the vision of how badly this man looked and feared being wrong in front of all these people. He could not muster up the courage to say something so contradictory to what was so eminently obvious—that the man may die and that very quickly or any second. How could he tell this man and his family that he would be out of the hospital in three days and would be fine? He later learned that the man was released within three days and was in good health. He felt bad and regretted not being brave enough to be the prophet of the Lord he was called to be at the time to strengthen the faith of these people whom the Lord dearly loved and wanted to speak to.

Bravery is an act of faith or inspiration. One good brother, Louis Principe, was told by an emergency room physician that his son had a brain tumor the size of a golf ball. His son was having difficulty breathing and was limp. He asked his bishop Jonathan Harmon to bless his son. The Bishop felt prompted to say this was a trial but he told Joey, "You will be well." Later the parents were told an operation was absolutely necessary to save his life, but the tumor was in the motor reflex area and would leave him at least fifty percent paralyzed or handicapped for life. The next day before the operation, Joey lost the use of his right arm and then his right leg. On the day of the operation, the physician said Joey's tumor was pretty bad because it was deeply rooted and they had better prepare for the worst. The Bishop was disconsolate in the face of all this grim news. He momentarily feared he may have given the parents false hope. However, on reflection, knew that he'd been impressed by the Spirit to say, "You will be well."

The operation proceeded. Two hours passed. And the doctor came and said, "I don't know how to tell you this—Joey is in the recovery room moving all of his limbs. It's the most amazing thing I've ever seen. When I went back, the tumor was completely defined and sitting on the top of his brain. It's as if someone put his hand into Joey's brain and lifted the tumor out. Your boy is going to be well." Later he shrugged his shoulders and said, "The tumor just lifted right out. I can't explain what happened, but Joey is looking at a cure." Two weeks later Joey was back in school healthy and well. The surgeon reported, "This brain scan is as perfect as that of any normal child." A miracle was experienced and was documented in their hearts if not in hospital records. The Bishop, a Presiding High Priest in Israel, had been a prophet and had bravely and faithfully delivered the Lord's word of comfort in the midst of contrary news. (Louis Principe, *Ensign*, July 1990, p.61)

Bishop Manual Sanchez in a California town was asked to bless one of the children in his Ward. The six year old boy had been run over by a car. He had extensive brain damage, a cracked skull, damaged ribs and heavy trauma over the rest of his body. He was dying. Yet this faithful, brave and valiant man obeyed the prompting and blessed him in front of the doctors and nurses to live. He said, "You could have heard a pin fall. The doctors, the nurses, everybody. There was complete silence." The little boy Mario Espinoza was transferred by helicopter to the hospital in Van Nuys. The next day he was responding to muscle stimulation. The doctor said that the way he'd been the day before he should have died or become a vegetable. But in a few days, Mario was walking and completely recovered. He amazed the neurologists and surgeons. "He was the miracle of the floor. All the nurses wanted to see him. How could it have happened that Mario, who was in such critical condition could have made such a remarkable recovery." A year of so later, the Bishop commented, "That boy is really special. Ever since the day of the accident, his attitude has changed. He is so heavenly." ("We couldn't bear to lose the little boy," *Church News*, July 21, 1990, p.10) We can work miracles, because God, who we represent, is a God of miracles.

Vaughn J. Featherstone of the First Quorum of the Seventy tells the following story of faith and righteousness:

> Some time ago I had the privilege of being involved with a young man and his father. The youth and a friend had been hiking in the foothills near Cody, Wyoming. The friend jumped across a high-power line that was down, but the young man got tangled in it and was electrocuted. The friend ran all the way back to where the father lived—and it wasn't a short distance—and told the father that his son had been electrocuted and was dead. The father, who was not a young man, ran all the way back up, taking about fifteen minutes. When he got to where the boy was lying across the wires, he managed somehow to remove the youth from the wires with a board or a large stick.
>
> Then he picked his son up in his arms [remember he had been dead over thirty minutes] and held him, saying, "In the name of Jesus Christ and by the power and authority of the Holy Melchizedek Priesthood, I command you to live." The dead boy opened his eyes and talked with his father. (*Charity Never Faileth*, p.102)

Mormon in speaking about one man said he "was a just man who did keep the record—for he truly did many miracles in the name of Jesus; and there was not any man who could do a miracle in the name of Jesus save he were cleansed every whit from his iniquity." (3 Nephi 8:1) Elder Featherstone at another time concluded on this father who raised his son from the dead by saying, "This great brother could not have possibly done that had he been looking at a pornographic piece of material a few nights before or if he had been involved in any other transgression of that kind. The priesthood has to have a pure conduit to operate." (*Ensign*, May 1975, p.66)

The simple truth is, "the powers of heaven cannot be controlled nor handled only upon the principles of righteousness." (D&C 121:36) If we try to "cover our sins, or to gratify our pride, our vain ambitions, or to exercise control or compulsion upon the souls of the children of men, in any degree of unrighteousness, behold; the heavens withdraw themselves. . . ." (D&C 121:37) And we are left powerless, helpless and alone. With God we can do the impossible, without Him "ye can do nothing." (John 15:5) But nothing comes from nothing. We must pay the price. Lorenzo Snow said:

> When our friends are stricken down by sickness and disease, or when our little ones are in the agonies of pain and death, there should be Elders in our midst who have educated themselves so thoroughly in developing the gifts of the Spirit within them, and in whom the Saints have such perfect confidence, that they would always be sought after. . . . There are men among us who possess the gift of healing, and might have great faith; but they do not exercise the gift, they do not live for it, and, therefore, do not have the power to use it so effectively as they might. There are men in this Church who are as good in their hearts and feelings as men ever were, but lack faith and energy, and do not obtain really what is their privilege to receive. If their faith, their energy and determination were equal to their good feelings and desires, their honesty and goodness, they would indeed be mighty men in Israel; and sickness and disease and the power of the evil one would flee before them as chaff before the wind. Yet, we say we are a good people and that we are not only holding our own but making great advances in righteousness before God; and no doubt, we are. But I wish to impress upon you, my brethren and sisters that there are Elders among us endowed with Spiritual gifts that may be brought into exercise through the aid of the Holy Ghost. The gift of the Gospel must be cultivated by diligence and perseverance. The ancient Prophets when desiring some peculiar blessing, or important knowledge, revelation or vision, would sometimes fast and pray for days . . . for that purpose. (*Journal of Discourses* 23:194-195)

To do this, we must learn the laws that predicate these blessings, for knowledge is empowering, while ignorance is self defeating and gets us nowhere. Grant Von Harrison tells of a home teacher who blessed a man to get well only to find out a week later that he was not any better, but in danger of losing his ability to provide for a family of eight in the only way he knew. He "became perplexed in that the blessing was not realized. He turned to his Father in Heaven in secret prayer, desiring to know why this blessing had not been realized. It was revealed to his mind that his mind had become very preoccupied with the other demands in his life—his schooling, job, etc., and that if this blessing was to be realized, it would necessitate his making this request and this desire a matter of focus in his daily prayers as well as during other times during the day." (*Drawing on the Powers of Heaven*, pp.69-70) He then went back to the hospital, shared what he had learned, blessed the man all over again to be completely healed and resolved to remember the Lord and this good brother continually everyday. The next week he returned only to discover that the man no longer had any damage to his heart, but every indication was he would be restored to full health. (Ibid.) We have a responsibility beyond just giving an inspired blessing. We must do more. We must exercise our faith and plead with the Lord and that on a continual basis. (See Appendix A and B)

Bishop Leon W. Gourdin blessed a member of his Ward who was hospitalized for a brain hemorrhage. It was very serious and looked bleak. He wrote:

> I had performed this ordinance many times before, but this time I was compelled by a force within me to continue a silent prayer for her through the night and the next day. Never before had I experienced such a strong feeling. I would pause and find myself praying to the Lord to bless this sister. That afternoon her husband called my wife at home, and in a choked voice he indicated that the X-rays showed no evidence of damage and that his wife was going to be all right. He said the doctor was amazed and couldn't believe or understand what had happened. We all knew what had happened: through the power of the priesthood and the faith of those involved, the Lord had answered our prayers. (*The Improvement Era*, July 1966, p.646)

Lorenzo Snow, after having a vision and promising the Saints of St. George rain, if they paid their tithing, had to continue to pray and wrestle with the Lord to fulfill his inspired words. A trial ensued. It appeared that his words would fall flat and the Saints would not harvest anything that season as promised. He had exercised faith in mighty and sustained prayer for months and never gave up. Then miraculously rain came late in the season, but the plants did unusually well for being starved for water and a better than usual harvest was achieved. The scriptures say "for ye receive no witness until after the trial of your faith," and "after much tribulation come the blessings"—even "glory . . . shall follow after much tribulation." (Ether 12:6 and D&C 58:4,3) That is, the laws of heaven require that we prove ourselves that our faith and desires are genuine even through the furnace of affliction in some cases.

Also, it is not in the mind of God that we should be given power to heal everyone. Suffering often brings a greater blessing than healing. Even the Son of the Eternal God of heaven, the Great Redeemer, Himself, who had all power, did not heal everyone. Being without honor in his home town, "he did not many mighty works there because of their unbelief." (Matthew

13:58) Brigham Young asked, "Do you suppose that Jesus Christ healed every person that was sick or that all the devils were cast out in the country where he sojourned? I do not. . . . Once in a while the people would have faith in his power, and what is called a miracle would be performed, but the sick, the blind, the deaf and dumb, the crazy, and those possessed with different kinds of devils were around him, and only now and then could his faith have power to take effect, on account of the want of faith in the individuals." (*Journal of Discourses* 3:45-46) James E. Talmage explained that "faith is of itself a principle of power; and by its presence or absence, by its fulness or paucity, even the Lord was and is influenced, and in great measure controlled, in the bestowal or withholding of blessings; for He ministers according to law, and not with caprice or uncertainty." (*Jesus the Christ*, p.296)

Even, the original Twelve Apostles of the meridian of times, who are such great men that they will one day sit upon twelve thrones and judge the whole house of Israel, could not cast a devil out of a young man. (Matthew 17:19-21) They were not invincible. They did not have absolute power. It was never in the mind of God to make them or anyone else that way in mortal life. Spencer W. Kimball explained:

> The power of the priesthood is limitless but God has wisely placed upon each of us certain limitations. I may develop priesthood power as I perfect my life, yet I am grateful that even through the priesthood I cannot heal all the sick. I might heal people who should die. I might relieve people of suffering who should suffer. I fear I would frustrate the purposes of God.
>
> Had I limitless power, and yet limited vision and understanding, I might have saved Abinadi from the flames of fire when he was burned at the stake, and in doing so I might have irreparably damaged him. He died a martyr and went to a martyr's reward—exaltation. . . .
>
> With such uncontrolled power, I surely would have felt to protect Christ from the agony in Gethsemane, the insults, the thorny crown, the indignities in the court, the physical injuries. I would have administered to his wounds and healed them, giving him cooling water instead of vinegar. I might have saved him from suffering and death and lost to the world his atoning sacrifice. (*Faith Precedes the Miracle*, pp.99-100)

In other words, we could do enormous harm and ruin everything. Elder Kimball wrote:

> If all the sick for whom we pray were healed, if all the righteous were protected and the wicked destroyed, the whole program of the Father would

be annulled and the basic principle of the gospel, free agency, would be ended. No man would have to live by faith. . . . There would be no test of strength, no development of character, no growth of powers, no free agency, only satanic controls. (Ibid., p.97)

Elder Malcolm S. Jeppsen, a former member of the Seventy and a doctor, said:

I soon learned in my medical practice that the ultimate healing process for an injured or sick body was already provided by our Heavenly Father. I also learned that a patient's attitude has much to do with healing. Those who would rely on Heavenly Father and exercise faith in the power of the priesthood often enjoyed faster recoveries.

I have witnessed miracles! Many times when my medical training suggested a dismal prognosis, I have seen individuals fully recover. I have also witnessed others who relied with faith on the Lord and sought blessings with their prayers, which prayers were not answered in a way the person or loved one desired.

The Lord had given a condition for healing blessings: "He that hath faith in me to be healed, and is not appointed unto death, shall be healed" (D&C 42:48; emphasis added). Even when a person relies in faith on the Lord for blessings, if it is his or her appointed time to die, there will not be restoration of health. Indeed, "death [must come] upon all men, to fulfil the merciful plan of the great Creator" (2 Ne. 9:6) (*Ensign*, May 1994, p.17)

Truly, not all will be healed, but in the words of Spencer W. Kimball, "There are infinitely more healings today than in any age and just as wondrous." He continued, "Today the libraries would bulge their walls if all the miracles of our own time were recorded." (*The New Era*, October 1981, p.48) In a letter by a missionary from Scotland to Orson Pratt in 1849, the difference between the doctors success and the power of the priesthood was quite astonishing. We read:

. . .The differences between the treatment of cholera by the Latter-day Saints and those learned ignoramuses, called doctors, may be easily perceived by the following: 'By a report of the Board of Health, we find that at least two-thirds of those who have been attacked by the cholera have died'. . . Whereas, out of at least one hundred cases that have been administered to by the elders of the Church, in and around Glasgow, only four have died. (Lindsay R. Curtis, *Church News*, March 25, 1967, p.7)

"The accounts of miraculous healings in the Church [today] are numerous," declared James A. Cullimore, a past member of the First Quorum of the Seventy. "They warm one's soul and give great strength of testimony to the divinity of this great work." (*Ensign*, November 1974, p.28) I have also experienced astounding things and so have many of my acquaintances.

Richard G. Scott of the Quorum of the Twelve told how the use of the priesthood opens up channels of special divine help otherwise unavailable, but emphasized that there is no guarantee for the outcome without effort on our part. He told how:

> A relative [once] asked Elder Spencer W. Kimball for a blessing to combat a crippling disease. For some time Elder Kimball prepared himself spiritually; then, fasting, he was prompted to bless her to be healed. Some weeks later she returned, angry and complaining that she was "fed up" with waiting for the Lord to give the promised relief.
>
> He responded: "Now I understand why you have not been blessed. You must be patient, do your part, and express gratitude for the smallest improvement noted."
>
> She repented, followed scrupulously his counsel, and eventually was made well. (*Ensign*, November 1990, p.85)

Obviously, we need to be patient. Blessings take time sometimes years even a lifetime. Abraham yearned for a son for over seventy years, but he continued in the hope he would have an heir even when no hope was possible except by a miracle. This was accounted unto him for righteousness and ultimately caused the fulfillment of his fondest dream. (Romans 4:9-22)

Elder Scott continued, "It is through the combination of our doing what is within our power to accomplish and the power of the Lord that the blessing is realized." (*Ensign*, November 1990, p.85) Therefore, a sobering responsibility rests upon both the priesthood bearer and the person receiving the blessing. The priesthood holder must be inspired to speak for God as a prophet would, by revelation or the prophetic spirit, which is required of all true servants of the Lord God of heaven. The receiver must exercise faith, be patient, express gratitude for all improvements and do all within their power to resolve the problem. Bruce R. McConkie said, ". . .except in special and unusual circumstances. . . , healing miracles are and should be performed as a result of the faith of the one receiving the divine blessing." (*The Mortal Messiah*, 2:287) And Brigham Young said we might as well go to a graveyard and try to raise the dead as to bless a people who will not help themselves. (*Journal of Discourses* 4:24-25) This is true for all priesthood blessings whether for comfort, for health, for a decision, for success in a new venture or whatever. We have a responsibility as great or greater than the one giving the blessing to make it come true. If we do all that we can, all the great and enormous powers of the godhead will converge and focus on it, and the blessings will ultimately come to pass as promised through the Lord's servants. Hence, these blessings can bring a wonderful comfort to our souls and strengthen our faith.

Victor L. Ludlow wrote, "Giving blessings is an exhilarating opportunity for priesthood leaders as they struggle to become in tune with the Spirit and to give counsel that the Lord himself would give if he were speaking." (*Principles and Practices of the Restored Gospel*, p.93) He continued, "These blessings can offer personal, specific direction and revelation to their recipients." (Ibid.) They are "a form of revelation." They "draw upon the powers of revelation," as well as "inspiration and revealed counsel as they perform priesthood ordinances, set members apart to Church callings, anoint the sick, and perform other priesthood blessings." (Ibid., pp.92-93) If done in the right spirit, "those who give and receive blessings at the hands of the priesthood in this spirit are lifted up and sustained, and healed in mind, body, and spirit." (J. Elliot Cameron, *Encyclopedia of Mormonism* 3:1140) That is, "both are edified and rejoice together." (D&C 50:22)

An example of such an uplifting healing was given by Janet Gunderson Parberry who said:

> As my father placed his hands upon my head, his words, ". . .this oil consecrated for use in the households of the faithful. . ." anointed comfort to my soul. And then an unforgettable sensation: it seemed the oil held an unusual warmth, yes, an unusual warmth, and that warmth was flooding through me. Apprehension drained away. My entire being was suffused with the healing power of a loving Father-God and I felt most strongly that burning in the bosom referred to in scripture. Tears welled in still closed eyes. Soothed and healed by God, the symptoms vanished. In November our beautiful baby boy was born. And still this experience testifies to me. God is Love." (*Ensign,* January 1982, p.65)

Spencer W. Kimball told of an experience he had. He said:

> I learned a valuable lesson once long ago from a sweet lady, Sister Lucy Grant Cannon, who became violently ill while visiting her daughter in Arizona. We elders were promptly called, and we administered to her. The next day she was asked if she wished to be administered to again and her

reply was, "No, I have been anointed and administered to. The ordinance had been performed. It is up to me now to claim my blessing through my faith. (*The New Era*, October 1981, p.47)

President Kimball continued that "the need of faith is often underestimated. . . ." (Ibid.) It is one of the critical elements. Faith is a recognized principle of power on earth and in heaven. In fact, Joseph Smith said, it "is the first great governing principle which has power, dominion, and authority over [nothing less than] all things" in the universe. (*Lectures on Faith*, pp.5, 8) However, faith is a mystery or even an elusive quality to most. The question is: what is it and how can this gift of God be exercised or developed? The answer is important, because the full enjoyment of the beautiful healing and comforting power of God depends on it.

First of all, faith is a gift, but it is also very positive attribute of all those who are truly devoted. In fact, a synonym for faith—"optimism," defines it as a cheerful or bright outlook, a pleasant anticipation, a positive reliance on something or a hope that is confident and assured. (*The Synonym Finder*, pp.392, 812) Thus faith is a happy and glad hearted trust or complete acceptance of a truth which cannot be demonstrated or proved; wherein one is convinced so much that one believes and acts on the assumption. In recognition of its positive qualities, and how very positive love and hope are, is it any wonder that the Lord admonishes us 248 times in the Standard Works to have joy and be joyful, 56 times to be happy, 20 times to be cheerful, 49 times to be delighted, 142 times to be glad, 137 times to be thankful and 217 times to rejoice. That's 869 times we've been admonished to be positive. (*A New Concordance of the Holy Bible*, pp.62, 98-99, 182-183, 201, 236-237, 346-347, 426-427 and R. Gary Shapiro, *An Exhaustive Concordance*, pp. 166, 240, 380-381, 424, 491-492, 795-796, 955) Surely the Lord would not ask us over and over again to be filled with such positive feelings unless this was of eternal importance.

In General Conference, Sterling W. Sill said, "One of the greatest handicaps to spiritual growth, or any other kind of growth, is to have a negative mind, and I suppose that one of the functions of a great faith is to lift our thoughts upward, to houseclean our minds, to sweep out our 'temptations down,' and fill our minds with 'temptations up.' (*The Improvement Era*, June 1955, p.440) George Q. Cannon testified that:

> We of all people should be happy and joyful. When the clouds seem the darkest and most threatening, and as though the storm is ready to burst upon us with all its fury [including disease and death], we should be calm,

serene and undisturbed, for if we have the faith we profess to have[,] we know that God is in the storm; in the cloud or in the threatened danger, and that he will not let it come upon us only as far as is necessary for our good and for our salvation, and we should, even then, rejoice before God and praise him. (*Journal of Discourses* 15:376)

Faith is a way of thinking, an attitude toward something, a view, or opinion, a strong belief in something that is true. It is a state of mind that influences everything we do. Joseph Smith said, ". . . It is the foundation of all righteousness." And it "is the moving force of all action." (*Lectures on Faith*, pp.1-2, 6) Hence, it is one of the greatest and most important of all things. And Joseph explained that "when a man works by faith he works by mental exertion instead of by physical force." (Ibid., p.72) Hence, the Lord's admonition to, "Look unto me in every thought; doubt not, fear not." (D&C 6:36) For "thoughts make us what we are." (reference unknown) James Allen said, "Let a man radically alter his thoughts, and he will be astonished at the rapid transformation it will effect in the material conditions of his life. Men imagine that thoughts can be kept secret, but it cannot, it rapidly crystallizes into habits, and habit . . ." determines almost everything we will do for the rest of our lives. (*As A Man Thinketh*, pp.30-31) Therefore, in the words of David O. McKay, "Each of us is the architect of his own fate. . . ." (*The Instructor*, January 1964, p.1)

Brigham Young declared, "The greatest mystery a man ever learned, is to know how to control the human mind, and bring every faculty and power of the same in subjection to Jesus Christ; this is the greatest mystery we have to learn while in these tabernacles of clay." (*Teachings of President Brigham Young*, p.90) Orson Hyde, another of the original apostles chosen in this dispensation, said, "Let the mind be concentrated, and it possesses almighty power. It is the agent of the Almighty clothed with mortal tabernacles, and we must learn to discipline it, and bring it to bear on one point. . . ." (*Journal of Discourses* 7:153) The reason for this is that attention equals power, and it will determine our direction in life. In practical terms, this means one must take control of ones thoughts, for "if ye do not watch yourselves, and your thoughts, . . . ye must perish," so said a great ancient prophet of the Western Hemisphere. (Mosiah 4:30)

The Lord has told us to "let virtue [beauty or heavenly things—the things of God] garnish [decorate, beautify or adorn our] thoughts unceasingly," that is all the time. (D&C 121:45) The promise, if we do this, is that "the doctrine [or laws] of the priesthood [which pertains to love and pure knowledge] shall distil upon thy soul as the dews of heaven" and "the Holy Ghost [that gift of gifts] shall be thy constant companion"—as a comforter and revelator. (D&C 121:45-46) Paul, the great missionary apostle of the New Testament, admonished us in like fashion with the following important counsel. He said, "Finally, brethren, whatsoever things are true, whatsoever things are honest, whatsoever things are just, whatsoever things are pure, whatsoever things are lovely, whatsoever things are of good report; if there be any virtue, and if there by any praise, think on these things." (Philippians 4:8) And if we do, great faith, great miracles and great rewards will follow.

Spencer W. Kimball quoted the following by an unknown author, "The greatest battle of life is fought out within the silent chambers of the soul. A victory on the inside of a mans heart is worth a hundred conquests on the battlefields of life." (*The Miracle of Forgiveness*, p.235) We must pray, look to God and ponder, meditate and read the scriptures and feast on everything right and noble and good. Every man is what he is because of what he thinks in his mind. "Such is the power—and the outcome—of our thoughts," taught Elder Kimball. (Ibid., p.115)

Faith is a positive thought, immersed in truth, that moves one to action. It is the alpha and omega, the beginning and the end, the grand and beautiful key to the treasures of heaven, because of Christ, the Great Redeemer. Faith involves the heart, our deeper being, the moving force of our lives. And we are shaped and fashioned by what we dearly and deeply love inside ourselves. Therefore, "what lies behind us and what lies before us are tiny matters compared to what lies within us," as expressed by Ralph Waldo Emerson. (Reference unknown) In other words, it is an inside job. The real target is the heart. That's where the roots of human happiness are as well as a great abiding faith. Such that, the quality inside our hearts will determine the inner quality and enjoyment of our lives. The point is, if you can change your heart, you can make life so rewarding and enjoyable that you treasure it. But you must make a solid, iron clad, determination or deeply felt commitment for things to change where it really counts, that is, in the deeper part of yourself.

You must powerfully ponder and tightly hold on to everything beautiful, attractive, loveable, precious, and endearing about the God of heaven and the people you should love. You must gladly, beautifully, happily and sincerely relish, treasure, delight in, savor, cherish, value, enjoy, love, favor and adore these things with all your heart and soul for love to prevail above the powerful distractions, sandbars, traps and lifeless decoys that easily beset most people and can turn your attention away from that which will make life sweet and beautiful. You see, we make life largely what we are inside.

The cheerful man makes a cheerful world around him. The grumpy man makes a grumpy world around him, which is but the reflection of his own mood. That is, if I focus on everything exquisitely wonderful, sweet, rich, thrilling, happy, magnificent and beautiful in life, I will become those very things—gorgeously thrilled, rich, loving, tender and wonderfully uplifted inside.

To focus on the good and beautiful is not a denial of reality—the good exists. It is merely a matter of what kinds of thoughts we hold in our minds and hearts. Positive faith is a choice and you can develop the habit of living happily with God. This is not advocating rose colored glasses, but "rosy reality" or "rosy truth." That is, you see everything, the full and the empty, the good and the bad, but you focus on the good and let life nourish, uplift and feed you and thus fill you up so that you overflow with good. You do this through constant prayer, feasting on spiritual food and cultivating a grateful heart. All of this sweetens up life itself. That is, we should develop an ability to enjoy even small insignificant things. Just like learning to play a piano, you won't make beautiful music at first, but if you keep practicing and practicing and practicing, you can become very good at enjoyment or loving life. And it becomes second nature to be that way.

Since enjoyment, delight, gladness and thankfulness are about eighty percent identical in meaning, gratitude becomes at least as great as or equivalent to the others, but may indeed be of greater importance. Cicero said, "The grateful heart is not only the greatest virtue, but the parent of all the others." (reference unknown) It is so important that Joseph Smith "once remarked that if you will thank the Lord with all your heart every night for all the blessings of that day you will eventually find yourself exalted in the kingdom of God." (Truman G. Madsen, *Joseph Smith, the Prophet*, p.104)

James E. Faust, a member of the Twelve at the time, said, "A grateful heart is a beginning of greatness. . . . It is a foundation for the development of such virtues as prayer, faith, courage, contentment, happiness, love, and well-being." (*Ensign*, May 1990, p.86) The Lord has told us that "he who receiveth all things [good and bad] with thankfulness shall be made glorious. . . ," and the Lord promises many other great and beautiful rewards to such an uplifted soul. (D&C 78:19) For we are admonished to "live in thanksgiving daily" or rejoice and have joy in life. (Alma 34:38) "The bright word gratitude is set like some rare jewel in the heart; always its brilliance is both caught and shared. It is a basic part of all great souls. . . ." (Christie Lund Coles, reference unknown) May we be free of the sin of ingratitude and learn the virtues and delight of a grateful heart.

Because repentance is also a positive quality of mind and heart, no wonder the Bible Dictionary in the Standard Works states that "the Greek word of which [repentance] is the translation denotes a change of mind, i.e., a fresh view about God, about oneself, and about the world." (p.760) Repentance is a thankful, loving view, attitude or way of thinking deeply within, which is "a turning of the heart and will to God" in a believing way, a cleansing of the inner vessel, so much so that we change our ways forever, "because of the goodness of God." (Ibid. and Mormon 2:13)

Brigham Young said, "It is the privilege of the Saints to enjoy every good thing. . . ," but you had better "learn to be happy when you have the privilege." (*Discourses of Brigham Young*, pp.237, 235) "Thinking negatively does not require any effort," declared Grant Von Harrison, "maintaining a believing frame of mind, however, requires an exerted effort over a sustaining period." (*Drawing on the Powers of Heaven*, p.36) There is no free lunch. We have to learn how, and to practice it over and over and over until we get it right. It is like the saying, "Live to learn, learn to love, and you'll love to live." (reference unknown) If we learn to be glad, we'll be glad to live. If we learn to enjoy, we'll enjoy living. If we learn to be positive, we'll be positive about life and everything that happens. In other words, if you think cheerful, optimistic thoughts, you'll be a cheerful, optimistic person.

George Albert Smith said, ". . .unless we have the spirit of contentment in our hearts we are miserable." That is, "if we become discontented[,] the Spirit of the Most High leaves. . . ." So "unless we enjoy that spirit which brings happiness, inspires the soul and makes heaven. . . , we shall be constantly uneasy." He continued, ". . .if they [the great men of the priesthood of God] do not get uneasy and unsettled in their minds[,] they have no fear of death, but they rejoice in the enjoyment of the Spirit of the Lord and the spirit of mercy, then the light of revelation, peace, happiness and contentment are and for ever will be their portion. So will it be with all of us." (*Journal of Discourses* 9:349) For, in the words of Spencer W. Kimball, ". . .the man [or woman] who yields to the sweet influence and pleadings of the Spirit and does all in his [or her] power to stay in a repentant [or faithful and loving] attitude is guaranteed protection, power, freedom and joy." (*The Miracle of Forgiveness*, p.176) Or, in the words of Wilford Woodruff, ". . .the nearer we live to God, the closer we obey his laws and keep his commandments, the more power we will have, and the greater will be our desire for building up. . . the kingdom of God. . . ." (*Journal of Discourses* 21:191)

Ezra Taft Benson admonishes us to "be cheerful. . . . Live joyfully. Live happily. Live enthusiastically, know that God does not dwell in gloom and melancholy, but in light and love." (*The New Era*, September 1979, p.42) In order to do this the important question becomes, are you truly awake, alive and aware of all the rich color, beauty and glory that surrounds you? Do you appreciate it? Does it nourish, uplift and feed you? Do you drink it in? "Every normal function of life holds some delight," said Will Durant. (reference unknown) Our job is to enjoy what is. As James M. Banie said, "The secret of happiness is not doing what one likes, but in liking what one has to do." (reference unknown) It is being thankful for everything—seeing the beauty, the glory, the wonder, the greatness of it all and being awed by it all. We must train our eyes to see it, our ears to hear it and our hearts to be dearly lifted, thrilled and delighted by it. In summary, we must live to learn, so that we learn how to really live happily ever after by a habit of happiness, which is a habit of appreciating everything that comes our way, so that all that is makes us feel whole and complete, rich, contented and full.

The prophets were usually very good at this. Joseph Smith said he had a "cheery temperament." (Joseph Smith—History 1:28) He drank in of the good of life. He explained to Jedediah M. Grant something very special about Brigham Young's disposition. He said, "How is it that Brother Brigham is able to comfort and soothe those who are depressed in spirit, and always make those with whom he associates so happy? I will tell you how he makes us feel so happy. He is happy himself, and the man who is happy himself can make others feel so, for the light of God is in him, and others feel the influence and feel happy in his society." (*Journal of Discourses* 3:12)

In the book *Christ's Ideals for Living*, published in 1955 for the Sunday Schools of The Church of Jesus Christ of Latter-day Saints, it says Christ, "the greatest of all" (D&C 19:18), "loved life and wanted men to be happy. He had a cheerful temperament. The Gospel, He said in effect, is like an invitation to a royal banquet. . . . He loved children. . . . He loved nature. . . . He was exuberant and joyful. . . . He said to His disciples: 'Be of good cheer . . .' [and] 'rejoice and be exceedingly glad.' . . .Here was a spirit unmatched in radiance and gladness, victorious over all that men and circumstances could do to Him." (pp.229-230) No man was greater.

Neal A. Maxwell said of Christ, "Though He was called 'man of sorrows,' that description refers to His bearing of our sorrows—not His; it does not describe His day to day bearing! Indeed, given the overarching and resplendent realities, Jesus was able to teach His disciples to have a spirit of rejoicing about life." (*Even As I Am*, p.163 and Isaiah 53:3-4) Alma Sonne said these positive virtues, the Lord exemplified, "are evidences of a great soul" in anybody. (*Speeches of the Year*, October 27, 1964, p.3) And Joseph

Smith said, "Our Savior was 'anointed with the oil of gladness above his fellows.'" (*Teachings of the Prophet Joseph Smith*, p.245) He was happy and cheerful and He asked us, ". . .what manner of men ought ye to be? His answer was, "Verily I say unto you, even as I am." (3 Nephi 27:27)

Being in the mental health field for over fifteen years, I have noted how affirmations (see Appendix C) and the technique of savoring or treasuring for at least ten minutes a day (sometimes called emotional restructuring) have dramatically changed a number of lives, if used consistently over a long period of time. All one need do for this, which is an exercise in learning to enjoy things, is savor each member of ones family, thinking and dwelling on every fond memory, everything you adore, admire and delight in, as well as love, value and favor, combining it with your best feelings for them. This could be done in prayer and God should be included. It is a process of teaching oneself to dearly love and appreciate others, so one becomes integrated with such positive, hopeful qualities as faith and charity for "then," as the scriptures say, "ye will always abound in good works." (Alma 7:24) Upon this basic foundation and principle "hang[s] all the law and the prophets." (Matthew 22:36-40) For love is a river of life, joy and inner glory. It is so rewarding and uplifting that beautiful things always flow from it, which includes a merry, happy heart. And the scriptures declare that "a merry heart doeth good like a medicine . . . ," and "a merry heart hath a continual feast." (Proverbs 17:22 and 15:15) In other words, it makes us healthy and happy within.

Antoine R. Ivins, a former member of the First Council of the Seventy, declared, "This is a time when we need faith, faith of a very definite and positive nature, the faith that will lead us to optimism. I believe that pessimism grows out of a lack of faith, and that if we have the right type of faith, we will be optimistic about the future." (*Conference Report*, October 1950, p.53) President Gordon B. Hinckley said, "We have every reason to be optimistic in this world. . . . You can't, you don't, build out of pessimism or cynicism. You look with optimism, work with faith, and things will happen." (Jack H. Goaslind, *Ensign*, April 1997, p.25) In fact, "'Things will work out,' may well be President Hinckley's most repeated assurances," noted Elder Jeffrey R. Holland of the Quorum of the Twelve Apostles. "'Keep trying,' he will say, 'Be believing. Be happy. Don't get discouraged. Things will work out.'" (*Ensign*, April 1997, p.25) We need to remember that the gospel of Jesus Christ is a wonderful gospel of unusually glad tidings—something of great joy. It is not a gospel of gloom. The Lord says, "Be of good cheer, and do not fear. . . ," because we are expected to trust God and bask in the endearing warmth of His love and delight. (D&C 68:6)

"It seems to me," said Paul H. Dunn, "that dwelling on negative thoughts and approaches is, in fact, working directly opposite of hope, faith, and trust—in the Lord, ourselves, and others—and causes continual feelings of gloom, while the positive lifts and buoys us up, encourages us to forge ahead, and is an attitude that can be developed, a habit that we can cultivate." (*Ensign,* May 1987, p.74)

One of my favorite scriptures, which is full of important insight, is Proverbs 3:5, which says, "Trust in the Lord with all thine heart; and lean not unto thine own understanding." When I get down, it is because I'm dwelling on my own limited understanding of things instead of truly trusting in God who knows all things, and has all power and actually loves me with a greater love than I could ever imagine. When I do trust Him, I am untroubled and free to enjoy whatever is happening.

All of this is consistent with King Benjamin's admonition, ". . . as ye have come to the knowledge of the glory of God, or if ye have tasted of his love, and have received a remission of your sins, which causeth such exceedingly great joy in your souls, even so I would that ye should remember, and always retain in remembrance, the greatness of God . . . and his goodness. . . . And . . . I say unto you that if ye do this ye shall always rejoice, and be filled with the love of God. . . ." (Mosiah 4:11-12) This is because, in the words of George Q. Cannon, "The Spirit of God always produces joy and satisfaction of mind. When you have the Spirit you are happy; when you have another spirit you are not happy. The spirit of doubt is the spirit of the evil one; it produces uneasiness and other feelings that interfere with happiness and peace. . . ." (*Journal of Discourses* 15:375)

Hence, barring biochemical depression, which is a disorder that can often create static or a barrier or get in the way of spiritual progress, to paraphrase President David O. McKay, the man who diligently feeds and nourishes his spiritual nature will find his life wonderfully sweetened and enriched, his discernment sharpened, his feelings tender and compassionate, yet his spirit will be strong and valiant. Spirituality is the highest acquisition of the soul—the divine in man. It is the supreme crowning gift that makes him king of all created things. It energizes all the beautiful concepts and ideals and endearing deeds and makes them real and attractive, such that, we love the truth so much that we live it and thrive on it and grow to our full potential. (*True to the Faith*, pp.244-245) Therefore, President McKay said, "With all my soul, I plead with the members of the Church and people everywhere, to think more about the gospel; more about developing of the spirit within; to devote more time to the real things of life, and less time to those things which will perish." (*Conference Report*, April 1968, p.144)

The more humble part of the people in the days of the prophet Nephi, the son of Helaman, did this very thing. ". . .They did fast and pray oft, and did wax stronger and stronger in their humility, and firmer and firmer in the faith of Christ, unto the filing of their souls with joy and consolation, yea, even to the purifying and the sanctification of their hearts, which sanctification cometh because of their yielding their hearts unto God." (Helaman 3:35) Bruce R. McConkie explained that "faith is a gift of God bestowed as a reward for personal righteousness. It is always given when righteousness is present, and the greater the measure of obedience to God's laws [including the laws that develop positive feelings in our hearts] the greater will be the endowment of faith." (*Mormon Doctrine,* p.264) And the greater our faith, the greater are the miracles and the revelations we enjoy.

Heber C. Kimball said, "I know that every man and woman can be [a prophet and a revelator] if they live for it. To enjoy this blessing they must walk in the channel of the Priesthood, being subject to the order and government of heaven; then they are all [full of glorious] revelation and they cannot predict anything that will not come to pass." (*Journal of Discourses* 3:112)

Dallin H. Oaks, of the Quorum of the Twelve, declared in general conference, "It is a very sacred responsibility for a Melchizedek Priesthood holder to speak for the Lord in giving a priesthood blessing." (*Ensign,* May 1987, p.37) For "not only was Joseph Smith to be a prophet," declared Joseph Fielding Smith, "not only his counselors and the Council of the Twelve were to be prophets, but every person who would be willing to accept the truth, who would humble himself, and come into the Church, might speak in the name of God, the Lord, even the Savior of the world." (*Doctrines of Salvation* 1:186) That is, every man should "become a prophet. . . .," because every man who is a member of the Church "is entitled to the guidance of and inspiration from the Holy Ghost. . . ." (Ibid., p.185) Elder Oaks continued:

> If a servant of the Lord speaks as he is moved upon by the Holy Ghost, his words are "the will of the Lord, . . . the mind of the Lord, . . . the word of the Lord, . . . the word of the Lord, . . . [and] the voice of the Lord' (D&C 68:4). But if the words of a blessing only represent the priesthood holder's own desires and opinions, uninspired by the Holy Ghost, then the blessing is conditioned on whether it [truly] represents the will of the Lord [or not]." (*Ensign,* May 1987, p.37)

But we are obligated by virtue of the Melchizedek Order of the Priesthood to be inspired men in Israel. John Taylor said, "A man cannot speak aright unless he speaks under the inspiration of the Almighty. . . ." (*Journal of Discourses* 21:92) Therefore, what we say should be "scripture" and have the weight of eternity behind it, because it is built upon the rock of revelation. (D&C 68:4) We can only build faith and strengthen Israel if we are willing to pay the price of revelation.

In fact, "what is the priesthood given for?," asked Wilford Woodruff. He answered that it is for revelation, so much so that he asked, "What business have we with this priesthood, if we have not revelation?" He continued: "If we do not have revelation [which is what makes a prophet], it is because we do not live as we should live, because we do not magnify our priesthood as we ought to; if we did we would not be without revelation, none would be barren or unfruitful." (*Journal of Discourses* 21:298) This is so important that "no man should undertake to act in the interests of Zion, unless he lives so as to be guided and directed by revelations from God." (Ibid.)

Great faith is a revealed "assurance" from heaven, a revelation or a gift. (Hebrews 11:1 see footnote b) Therefore, healing the sick or prophesying, or testifying requires that we seek God's intervention, that is, His Spirit, which brings comfort and guidance from above, which creates the utmost confidence (a dynamic and powerful faith) to do or say whatever it is in the mind of God to be done. "Wherefore," declared Jacob, another great prophet of the Western Hemisphere, "we search the prophets, and we have many revelations and the spirit of prophecy; and having all these witnesses we obtain a hope, and our faith becometh unshaken, insomuch that we truly can command in the name of Jesus and the very trees obey us, or the mountains, or the waves of the sea." (Jacob 4:6) The working of miracles is a process of years of seeking the Lord, loving and obeying Him and communing with the Spirit and having experiences with God.

A former bishop and a good friend of mine exemplified power as great as the ancients. He diligently sought all his life to love and obey God and receive revelation, so he could let God reign in his life and bless everyone that he loved. He told me how he took his priests on a high adventure trip to a wilderness area of Wyoming. When they got there, and this was the summertime, they discovered that there was a blizzard. As the boys struggled to get up camp in this high mountain valley, he wondered and prayed about what he should do about this bad weather. The Spirit asked him a question and that was, "What are you going to do about it." He thought to himself, "What do you mean what am I going to do about it?" Then he felt great faith within himself—he knew what God wanted. He climbed up the side of the mountain a little way with one of his sons, a priest. They both raised their arms to the heavens and he commanded the weather to be tempered for their whole time there and for the sun to shine so that the enjoyment and adventure they had planned might be fulfilled. When he finished what was in his heart to say, having spoken by the Spirit in the blessing and feeling love for those boys, and having faith in God, he opened his eyes. He and his son were astonished and amazed to see the whole valley as clear as if there was never a blizzard. It was beautiful—a wonderland. They could see everywhere. The blizzard had been immediately removed and the weather tempered as divinely pronounced. As it turned out that was the only week in that whole Summer without a blizzard in that high mountain valley. A mighty miracle was witnessed and revealed faith or divine "assurance" wrought this wonderful experience.

James O. Mason, a physician, told of a little boy who was getting worse and worse with a bacterial meningitis in his spine. He wrote, "I had serious doubts he would survive." He was asked by the boy's father to give him a blessing and had the following sweet and uplifting experience:

> As we laid our hands upon that little boy, the Spirit whispered to me, "Promise him he will recover. Promise him he'll have no aftereffects from this infection." And so, in the name of Jesus Christ and by the power of the holy Melchizedek Priesthood that I hold, I promised the boy that he would be healed and that he would have no aftereffects.
>
> As I left the room the second time that evening (even though earlier I had had grave doubts), after that manifestation of the Spirit I had an assurance that was much stronger than that of medical science or previous experience. I knew that he would live. And indeed he did. His recovery was uneventful and complete. (*Ensign,* August 1977, p.58)

This man also enjoyed a wonderful prophetic experience as great as those of the ancient prophets. And indeed that is our privilege as well. One friend told how a forest fire was raging out of control and moving quickly toward their homes, and they and their families were in danger of losing their homes and their lives. There was little time left to do anything. So one very faithful man of the Holy Priesthood grabbed my friend, they raised their arms to the square and then commanded the raging fire to halt, harm them not and be contained shortly. My friend then saw with amazement the fire obey immediately and literally stop in its tracks at the word of faith in the priesthood of God. The wind then changed abruptly and the fire quickly moved down the cliffs where it was contained in about two hours. God that day performed a miracle and saved their homes and their lives by virtue of the same power that created universe. The beautiful message is, if we are inspired and faithful, we can exercise the power of the Godhead in behalf of our loved ones.

However, some important promises must be claimed or pursued with vigor or they will simply be lost. Frederick W. Babbel wrote in his book *To Him That Believeth* on pages 98-99 how he was promised by Alma Sonne in the name of the Lord that he would not suffer any serious illnesses or physical problem as a result of his work in Europe. He was called to assist Ezra Taft Benson after World War II in distributing relief to the Saints in Europe, the Near East and South Africa. He lost 40 pounds and a physician confirmed that he had tuberculosis in both lungs. He was dismayed and disheartened at first. Then he decided to claim his lawful right to enjoy what was sealed upon his head. He drove to Palmyra to visit the Sacred Grove. There was deep snow and the weather was blustery and cold. He had to break a trail into the grove as no one was venturing to make any visits in such weather. He recounts:

> After looking around I found a large tree that provided some shelter for me from the swirling snow and harsh wind. Here I knelt and poured out my soul to the Lord. I reminded Him of the blessing which I had been given and informed Him that I had come to this spot to claim that blessing which I desperately desired and needed. How long I spent there I do not recall, but as I left, my soul was at peace. I experience divine assurance as only God can give. (Ibid.)

Six weeks had passed since the first X-rays of his lungs. He was again X-rayed. The doctor thought there was a mix up, but soon discovered that he had the evidence in hand of a miracle. He said incredulously, "Well, I guess you have claimed your blessing. Your lungs appear to be as healthy as when you were born. There is no evidence to indicate that you ever had tuberculosis, so I won't record it in your medical history." (Ibid.)

Brother Babbel concluded that many people are not aware that they must exercise faith and show real intent and determination to receive some blessings. Otherwise, they can be lost and we can suffer needlessly. He taught that we must be happy and anxious to meet any requirements the Lord gives us in a spirit of gratitude and love, or be willing to accept any burden as a blessing to achieve divine ends. We must be patient, keep trying and claim what has been promised to us in the name of the Lord, for "behold, I say unto you that whoso believeth in Christ, doubting nothing, whatsoever he shall ask the Father in the name of Christ it shall be granted him; and this promise is unto all even unto the ends of the earth." (Mormon 9:27)

George Q. Cannon explained, "There is not the seeking for the gift of healing and for the gift to be healed that there ought to be among the Saints and so with other gifts and graces that God has placed in his church for His people. I say to you that it is our duty to avail ourselves of the privileges which God had placed within our reach." And we should "feel after God, and not be satisfied till we have found him. . . . So with all the gifts of the Gospel. . . . Let us seek for these gifts." (*Millennial Star*, April 16, 1894, p.260) If we do, how truly great and wonderful will be the results!

In some cases a second or third blessing is appropriate in exercising our faith. Even the Savior did this. As told by Mark in the New Testament, they brought:

> . . .a blind man unto him to touch him. And he took the blind man by the hand, and led him out of the town; and when he had spit on his eyes, and put his hands upon him, he asked him if he saw ought. And he looked up, and said, I see men as trees, walking. After that he put his hands again upon his eyes, and made him look up: and he was restored, and saw every man clearly. (Mark 8:22-25)

Thomas C. Romney, a very prominent mission president fifty years ago, wrote in his book, foreworded by John A. Widtsoe, the following example:

> Some year ago there lived in a small community of Latter-day Saints in southeastern Utah, a Patriarch who was remarkably endowed with the gift of healing, especially the healing of cancers. A friend of mine with whom I was very intimately associated was afflicted with a malignant rose cancer in his armpit. Everything that medical skill could do for him completely failed in giving him relief or in staying the growth of the cancer, and it appeared that nothing but death could end his terrible suffering. One day, however, he chanced to hear of this Patriarch who had such a miraculous gift.
>
> At once he hitched to a lumber wagon a pair of horses and, accompanied by his mother, they began their tedious journey over the sagebrush plains and hills toward the village in which lived this man of God.
>
> I was thrilled as my friend related to me in considerable detail the result of that visit, for he was entirely healed. The cancer had withered up and there was nothing to show for its one-time presence save a scar where it had been.
>
> My friend related that several times the Patriarch administered to him, first anointing the cancer and then his head with oil and then would follow the most remarkable prayer that he ever listened to. It seemed that the servant of God was actually speaking face to face with his Maker and so

concentrated and intense were his pleadings that when the prayer was finished he was completely exhausted and he would betake himself to the out-of-doors to recover his strength. This experience was repeated several times or until the desired result was achieved.

Many years later I visited the small town where this miracle was wrought and learned from the daughter of the Patriarch that an account had been carefully kept of [this and other cases]. (*World Religions in the Light of Mormonism*, pp.337-338)

Note how the Patriarch pleaded so sincerely. He worked at it and wrestled with the Lord until he succeeded. He did not give up. Determination, fervent prayer and great love characterized his approach. And although he blessed the man repeatedly, he was not guilty of trifling with sacred things. His blessings were divine and beautiful and rich with desire. Many of the greatest blessings flowed out to the ancients chiefly because "they were filled with desire." (3 Nephi 19:24)

Elder Romney told how:

In my father's numerous family there were thirteen of us children down with malaria fever at the same time. I recall how every other day I would come down with a heavy chill to be followed by a raging fever, rendering life almost intolerable. This continued for many weeks, when finally mother came into my room where I was tossing about upon my bed in mortal agony and asked if I would not like my father and President John C. Harper of the Seventy's Quorum to come in and administer to me. Frankly I was indifferent to the suggestion, but to please my mother I consented to them praying for me after anointing me with holy oil.

The faith of my mother and of the elders healed me, for from that day to this I have never had another attack of the malaria fever. I was restored to health immediately. Nothing but the power of God could have wrought such a change in my physical condition. In my own family in recent years I have witnessed similar manifestations of God's power in the restoration to health of some of my own children. (Ibid., p.337)

A high degree of the principle of faith, which is a gift of the Spirit, that is, a divine, positive "assurance" or a manifestation of revealed will—a gift of revelation from on high, plus a strong and determined desire are an unbeatable combination. (Hebrews 11:1, see footnote) Miracles are wrought by such.

For one individual who despaired of her life, a priesthood blessing was a beautiful life saver, because her self-destructive feelings melted away and left her free to enjoy her life again. She said, "They had no sooner lifted their hands from my head than I felt the terrible feelings inside me being removed. It was as though something heavy and most distressing had been gently by firmly taken from me and destroyed. Those feelings have never returned. Yes, a loving Father in Heaven does hear and answer our prayers. I know this, for he has left me no room for doubt." ("No Room for Doubt," *Ensign*, February 1981, p.57)

Harold B. Lee said, "Yes, the Lord can heal sick bodies but the greatest miracle we see is the healing of sick souls." ("Speaking for Himself— President Lee's Stories," *Ensign*, February 1974, p.16) Because this is greater sometimes physical healing is withheld, for "it is better to save a man than raise one from the dead," as stated by the Prophet Joseph Smith. (*The Miracle of Forgiveness*, p.ix) Sometimes, greater good is accomplished when we are healed slowly or not at all, and therefore, have to strive more deeply and solidly for God. In other words, greater growth often takes place in such foreboding soil, because it challenges us to greater spiritual heights. Spencer W. Kimball said, "Is there not wisdom in his giving us trials that we might rise above them, responsibilities that we might achieve, work to harden our muscles, sorrows to try our souls? Are we not exposed to temptations to test our strength, sickness that we might learn patience, death that we might be immortalized and glorified?" (*Faith Precedes the Miracle*, p.97)

Brigham Young said, "It is recorded that Jesus was made perfect through suffering. If he was made perfect through suffering, why should we imagine for one moment that we can be prepared to enter into the kingdom of rest with him and the Father, without passing through similar ordeals?" (*Journal of Discourses* 8:66) President Young explained, "Every trial and experience you have passed through is necessary for your salvation." (Ibid., 8:150) We need to endure well whatever happens and to trust in God implicitly. Howard W. Hunter taught, "We all struggle with health problems occasionally—others do so constantly. Illness and disease are part of the burden of mortality. Have faith and be positive. The power of the priesthood is real, and there is so much that is good in life, even if we struggle physically. . . . We must emphasize our blessings and minimize our disappointments." (*Teachings of Howard W. Hunter*, p.80-81)

President Hunter declared his solemn witness, "I want to say to all within the sound of my voice tonight that you have every reason in this world to be happy and to be optimistic and to be confident . . ." in spite of difficulties. He explained that our illnesses "can be powerful instruments in the hands of God to make us better people. . . ." (Ibid.,p.200) The greatest healings in the

Church and Kingdom of God are not physical, but are spiritual and emotional. Therefore, again, not everyone will be healed, a greater blessing may be offered to help get us out of our comfort zones and get moving in the inner man, in the heart, where the stakes are higher and the rewards are greater. Then when we are really ready, the promised relief comes whether in this life or in the life to come.

Joseph B. Wirthlin, a member of the First Quorum of the Seventy at the time, told about an especially beautiful experience he had at a mission conference with Spencer W. Kimball addressing and inspiring the Saints. He said there was a special sister there who was in a wheelchair:

> Sister Margarete Hellmann had suffered an ailment of the hip since youth. As the years came and went, the affliction brought her an ever-increasing burden of pain. Finally, she could walk only with the aid of a pair of crutches. To facilitate her travel from place to place, and to alleviate the terrible pain she keenly felt with every single step, some of the Saints contributed money and bought her a wheelchair. But this relief was short-lived. Soon, even sitting in her wheelchair was accompanied by almost unbearable pain. Then an inflammation of the nerves on the left side of her face further intensified her suffering. One day she heard the heartening news: the prophet of the Lord was to be in Dresden. She had one all-consuming desire—to attend the conference and touch the prophet.
>
> She had faith and the absolute confidence that the prophet would not even have to take the time to lay his hands upon her head and give her a blessing. She felt assured that it would be with her as it was with a certain woman who, according to St. Mark, had suffered for twelve years and still grew worse. And "when she had heard of Jesus, . . . she said, If I may touch but his clothes, I shall be whole." This she did, and Jesus "said unto her, Daughter, thy faith hath made thee whole; go in peace." (See Mark 5:25-34)
>
> Sister Hellmann had asked her grandson, Frank, to bring her to the service at an early hour and position her wheelchair near the aisle where the prophet was to pass. This statement from her letter tells the rest of the story in her tender words: 'When our prophet came close to me,' she wrote, 'he warmly shook my hand and looked at me in the spirit of love, as did those who were with him. After that, I did not feel any more pain—not then, nor any to this day. That is the greatest testimony of my life!' (*Ensign,* November 1978, p.36)

Elder Wirthlin then said, "It was an unforgettable experience and a powerful testimony of faith and the power of God. . . . And I would pray that each one of us could develop a faith as strong as that of the sister in the wheelchair." (Ibid.) He continued, "It is my testimony that the best way in all the world for us to do this is to serve the Lord and be sure to honor our priesthood." (Ibid.) However, in the words of John Taylor:

> A great many of the Latter-day Saints will fail, a great many of them are not now and never have been living up to their privileges, and magnifying their callings and their Priesthood, and God will have a reckoning with such people, unless they speedily repent. There is a carelessness, a deadness, an apathy, a listlessness that exists to a great extent among the Latter-day Saints. . . . Are the things of God of so small importance, that we can not afford time to spend . . . in attending to the duties of our office. . . . I tell you, ye Elders of Israel, who neglect these things and who shirk your duties, God will remove your candlestick out of its place, and that speedily, unless you repent. And I say so to the Bishops, and I say so to all Israel who hold the Priesthood. We are not here to do our own will, but the will of our Heavenly Father who sent us. . . . He is not going to allow His kingdom to be overthrown, for it will roll forth and spread and increase until the kingdoms of this world shall become the kingdoms of our God and His Christ and he will rule for ever and ever. (*Journal of Discourses* 20:20-21)

Great things are about to happen. We live in exciting times. But "because faith is wanting, the fruits are," declared the Prophet Joseph Smith:

> No man since the world was had faith without having something along with it. The ancients quenched the violence of fire, escaped the edge of the sword, women received their dead, etc. By faith the worlds were made. A man who has none of the gifts has no faith; and he deceives himself, if he supposes he had. Faith has been wanting . . . so that tongues, healings, prophecy, and prophets and apostles, and all the gifts and blessings have been wanting. (*Teachings of the Prophet Joseph Smith*, p.270)

The Lord has counseled us to "ask, and it shall be given you: seek, and ye shall find: knock, and it shall be opened unto you," for the Lord "granteth unto men according to their desire. . . ." (Matthew 7:7 and Alma 29:4) But this desire cannot be a mere wish, it must be a motivating, moving force that compels one to wrestle with the Lord for a blessing. In terms of fulfilling our ordination requirements to be remarkable men, George Q. Cannon asks:

> How many of you are seeking for these gifts that God has promised to bestow? How many of you, when you bow before your Heavenly Father in

your family circle or in your secret places, contend for these gifts to be bestowed upon you? How many of you ask the Father in the name of Jesus to manifest Himself to you through these powers and these gifts? Or do you go along day by day like a door turning on its hinges, without having any feeling upon the subject, without exercising any faith whatever, content to be baptized and be members of the Church and to rest there, thinking that your salvation is secure because you have done this?

I say to you, in the name of the Lord, as one of His servants, that you have need to repent of this. You have need to repent of your hardness of heart, of your indifference and of your carelessness. There is not that diligence, there is not that faith, there is not that seeking for the power of God that there should be. . . . (*Gospel Truth*, pp.154-155)

Brigham Young lamented that, "The Elders of Israel, though the great majority of them are moral men, and as clear of spot and blemish as men well can be, live beneath their privilege; they live continually without enjoying the power of God," which is a tragedy of the heart and of priorities in life. (*Journal of Discourses* 9:289) John Taylor said, "We have indeed a sort of skeleton fixed up; but I think sometimes it needs flesh on the bones and the breath of life, the Spirit of the Living God breathed into it." (*Doctrine and Covenants Commentary*, p.462) We need to be energetic and alive or have a lively, animated connection with the Lord and His Holy Spirit. The choice is ours. Are we willing to devote the time and energy needed?

President Spencer W. Kimball concluded, "You can be a poor priesthood member, or a very wonderful one." (*Teachings of Spencer W. Kimball*, p.501) In other words, you can become very great. He continued, "You can, like your Savior, some day say, 'Peace, be still' (Mark 4:39), and the storm will vanish. You can, like your Savior, some day say,"Bless this blind eye, this unhearing ear, and miracles will happen. Oh, brethren, our miracles are about as strong as we are. The power that you hold is limited only by you and your activities, and your purity of heart. So glory in your priesthood." (*Teachings of Spencer W. Kimball*, p.501) Glory in doing what's right and fulfilling our divine commission for "he that is ordained of God and sent forth [from the deacons to the highest priests of Melchizedek], the same [are] appointed to be the greatest . . . ." (D&C 50:26) That is, the most powerful, the most loving, the most kind, the most loyal and true, the most spiritually gifted even to the point that they are, in every sense of the word, according to Bruce R. McConkie: ". . . prophets in their own right . . . ," for "every person who holds the priesthood is or should be a prophet" of the Lord in the last days to help establish Zion. (*A New Witness for the Articles of Faith*, p.349)

And I would say with Francis M. Lyman, an apostle of Christ, "Thank the Lord that we have Prophets; thank the Lord that this congregation is full of men of prophecy and revelation. . . . The world is enlivened today with men of inspiration from God" in every Ward and Branch of the Church that dearly loves the Lord. (*Conference Report*, October 1899, p.38) May we magnify this calling and shine with the glory that could be ours so beautifully to glorify God and build Zion.

SUMMARY AND CONCLUSION

One old, venerable patriarch said: "Only rarely do we catch the vision of eternity. Our patriarchal blessings are of that order. They transcend the mortal cares that we are so familiar with, and open a vision of eternity. . . ." We live in a day of great and wonderful blessings. Patriarchs are prophets of God. They give inspired blessings that are personal revelations to the Saints. They seal upon people the power and assistance of heaven to achieve the things which God has proposed for their lives. They tell us what God expects of us and what our divine potential is. They are special, encouraging and inspiring. They confirm our status as sons and daughters of Israel or the channel through which the most beautiful of all blessings will flow. They often authoritatively seal us up conditionally to eternal life in glory brighter than the meridian Sun.

Patriarchs are among the most humble, beautiful and inspired men of the Church, but they are human and need our faith and prayers to fulfill their obligation to faithfully prophecy in the midst of the people. The real power behind all the greatest positions in the Church is the Melchizedek Priesthood itself and the great and eternal office of High Priest, which is the highest of all the great offices of the priesthood. And it is probably greater than we will ever know in this life. It is the exalted office of the ancient patriarchs in every dispensation of God's power. Elders also hold a superior, but subordinate, office, but should also stand in the full glory of their callings as lesser priests of Melchizedek to be prophets when they administer after the order of the Son of God the holy ordinances—the comfort and healing blessings of Israel. This is a crowning or awesome privilege. It is a gem or treasure worth more than any other earthy treasure one could consider, for it is to represent the Most High God and be his mouthpiece or spokesman. Therefore, they can give blessings of enormous power and lasting beauty before the heavens. But no one, high or low, can do so without paying the price of inspiration. Faith is a key and we must be good-hearted and obedient inside for the gifts of the Spirit "are given for the benefit of those who love me and keep all my commandments, and him that seeketh so to do . . . ," for the Lord rejoices over those that continually seek after Him with sincerity and real intent. (D&C 46:9 and Matthew 18:13)

Ted E. Brewerton, of the First Quorum of the Seventy, declared:

There is no place in this Church or in any of our families for pessimism or negativism. We should be incurable optimists. Irrespective of the condition of a person, he who is a cynic, a pessimist, or negative has the least progress, happiness, and prosperity. On the other hand, the Lord's way is that the optimist with faith, who is positive, elevating, and edifying, is the individual in or out of the Church who is the most progressive, happy, and prosperous. (*Ensign,* May 1983, p.73, paragraphing changed)

Faith is a very positive quality, attitude or state of mind, and it has dominion over all things. It is a cheerful and happy outlook on life, because it is so connected to the source and fountain of all that is good and beautiful. And we can grow in this wonderful quality. For, as Bruce R. McConkie said, "If we are going to work out our salvation, we must rejoice in the Lord." (*Conference Report,* October 1973, p.48) Joe J. Christensen testified, "How delightful it is to be around people who radiate cheerfulness and enthusiasm! These qualities are contagious. The Spirit comes through with greater power and influence in the presence of those who are of a cheerful disposition than those who aren't cheeful." (*To Grow in Spirit,* p.33) To such, the Lord gives greater faith and divine assurances and they feel the wonder and the glory of God in their lives. For, in the words of George Q. Cannon, "There is nothing on earth, nothing that man can taste or experience that is so sweet . . . so full of delight, as the presence of the Spirit of God. It fills the soul with joy that is inexpressible. (*Gospel Truth,* p.145) We don't get to feel it all the time, but the more we immerse ourselves in every good, wonderful and glorious thing, the greater is the quality of our lives, and it becomes second nature for us to enjoy all things and be very positive, faithful, loyal and true.

Ezra T. Benson, an apostle of our Risen Lord and a progenitor of the late President of the Church, President Ezra Taft Benson, said, "When I feel like blessing my brethren, like lifting them up, and exalting them in my feelings, I feel first-rate myself; but when I feel like dragging them down, I feel contracted in my feelings, my mind does not expand in the principles of 'Mormonism;' but when I feel to bless everybody and do right by night and day, I feel like blessing everybody, and strong like a young lion sallying from his thicket. . . . I feel like blessing those who ought to be blessed, they do not stick anywhere else. [That is, they will not come true, because] God blesses no person, only on condition, neither do His servants. If a man rises up and prophecies great and glorious things on your head it is all on conditions." (*Journal of Discourses* 2:352) In other words, we need to do our part. Joseph F. Smith commenting on this subject declared: "Therefore, if we desire a blessing, let us observe the conditions upon which the blessing is promised, and let us live worthy of that blessing, so that we may be in a position to receive it when it is offered unto us." (*Collected Discourses* 3:239)

Carlos E. Asay, a former member of the Presidency of the Seventy, once told how he was set apart to a calling and received a most remarkable blessing from Alma Sonne, a former general authority, "one that I shall never forget. At the conclusion of the blessing, I thanked Elder Sonne for the beautiful and inspiring words that he had spoken. He graciously accepted my expression of gratitude; however, he placed his hand upon my shoulder, looked intently into my eyes, and said, 'Elder Asay, I had the power and the right to say what I said, but remember, you will write [that is, make] your own blessing by the way you live and serve.' Then he added, 'Go and write [make] the best blessing that has ever been written [or given].' We do, in fact, write [or make] our own blessings by the way we live and serve. Blessings do not come to a person automatically and simply because hands have been placed upon his head and beautiful words spoken. Blessings flow from the divine source and are channeled to mortals when laws are honored and when lives are made to harmonize with the will of Deity." (*The New Era*, October 1981, p.4) A revelation from God states, "And when we obtain any blessing from God, it is by obedience to that law upon which it is predicated." (D&C 130:21) We must do our part. Hence, Harold B. Lee wrote, "If you want the blessing, don't just kneel down and pray about it. Prepare yourself in every conceivable way you can in order to make yourself worthy to receive the blessing you seek." (*The Improvement Era*, October 1966, p.896) Then great and beautiful things will flow into your life.

Spencer W. Kimball said:

> Many times after I have ordained or set apart people I have had the stake president or bishop whisper to me: "You must have been inspired, for you gave that man the very blessing which was most appropriate. It could not have met his particular needs better if you had known him all your life instead of being a total stranger to him."
>
> I have promised life in some cases (though I am generally very conservative); I have promised missionaries and servicemen a safe return; and I have literally trembled in my shoes afterward when I realized what a responsibility I was under, but long ago I have come to the conclusion that I shall speak what I seem inspired to say, having asked the Lord for that inspiration, and any effort on my part to curb the Spirit would be rank folly and unappreciativeness and unresponsiveness to the moving of the Spirit. I have come to realize that . . . his revelations will come about as he explained to Oliver Cowdery." (*Teachings of Spencer W. Kimball*, p.140)

That is, we can have great experiences as well and significantly inspire and build faith in Israel, if we seek diligently to pay the price of preparation. "Laziness and spiritually do not go together," said Joe J. Christensen, "nor do laziness and success. Work is a very important part of the gospel. You cannot be in tune with the Spirit as much as you want to be if you are not digging in and working near your capacity." (*To Grow in Spirit,* p.39)

Oliver Cowdery was told why he had failed in the principle of revelation and it is an important lesson to us all. The Lord said, "Behold, you have not understood; you have supposed that I would give it unto you, when you took no thought save it was to ask me. (D&C 9:7-9) More is required, "you must study it out in your mind, . . . if it is right I will cause [that] . . . you shall feel that it is right; . . . if it be not right, you shall have no such feelings, but you shall have a stupor of thought." (ibid.) This way we will be ready and prepared and miracles will follow as we develop and cultivate the faith and gift to perform them as did the ancients. George Q. Cannon said, "We cannot be the people that God designs we should be, unless we seek after and obtain these spiritual gifts. It should be the constant prayer of all the Latter-day Saints for the Lord to give us those gifts that are suited to our condition . . ." that we might enjoy great things and do great things. (*Millennial Star* 62:354)

Robert D. Hales, of the Quorum of the Twelve Apostles, declared, "My brothers and sisters, I have witnessed the remarkable power of the priesthood to lift and bless, to heal and comfort, to strengthen and empower men, women and children throughout the world. With all the sincerity of my heart, I desire to see the blessings of the priesthood be made accessible to all." (*Ensign,* November 1995, p.34) For as Ezra Taft Benson said, "No greater honor or blessing can come to man than the authority to act in the name of God," which is "to officiate in the most sacred ordinances known to man." (*The Teachings of Ezra Taft Benson,* pp.219, 215) "The honors of men, the wealth of the world, are as nothing by comparison. . . ." (Ibid., p.215) And "no political power or office which may ever come to you will even approach in importance [that] great blessing. . . ." (Ibid., p.688) In fact, "without this priesthood power," declared Spencer W. Kimball, "men are lost." (*Ensign,* June 1975, p.3) May we see and appreciate the crowning privilege and wonder of these things.

Near the end of a beautiful talk on priesthood blessings, James E. Faust declared, "One of the principle reasons for my speaking about this subject is that patriarchal blessings and other blessings testify of the divinity of Christ and the truthfulness of the Church." (*Ensign,* November 1995, p.64)

But equally, they confer upon us extra or additional power to be more successful and effective in life, which is a hidden treasure and wonderful privilege. For to the great Melchizedek Priesthood of God is the right to bless and to bind conditionally on earth and in heaven. (D&C 128:9) Hence, to the Elders and those above them are given the right to receive and the power to interpret manifestations of divine will especially in giving blessings. This requires that we be in tune. This inspiration constitutes the prophetic ability to speak for God. That is, to act as though one were a member of the Godhead in pronouncing blessings. But when done right these blessings are just as eternal and binding upon us, through our own faithfulness, as were the blessings of Abraham, Melchizedek or a blessing from an angel of glory or even from the Great Jehovah, Himself, who is from eternity to all eternity. Because those who receive this conferral, in a very real sense, declared Bruce R. McConkie, "have the hand of God laid upon them." (*Mormon Doctrine,* p.438) Harold B. Lee taught, "Whenever you perform a service by the authority of your priesthood it is as though the Lord were placing his hand on that person. . . ." (*Conference Report,* British Area Conference, August 1971, p.104) For example, to Edward Partridge the Lord said, "I lay my hand upon you by the hand of my servant Sidney Rigdon and you shall receive . . . ," the wonderful blessing of heaven. (D&C 36:2) These heavenly, inspired blessings are ultimately as though the great God of Heaven Himself was there in person. In other words, when we are in tune it is a thrilling experience of joy and love and light and inner glory.

Harold B. Lee after telling about a beautiful priesthood act of healing said, "That miracle didn't come because of me; it didn't come because of the elders; this was because the Lord himself, by my hand and the hands of the elders, put his hands upon the head of that little boy . . . and he received the strength . . . to stand on his feet for the first time since his birth." ("Speaking for Himself—President Lee's Stories," *Ensign,* February 1974, pp.19-20)

Heber C. Kimball had two sons who were called into military action against the Indians in what was called the Black Hawk War of 1866. They were full of fight and eager to smell gunpowder. Elder Kimball, apparently concerned about this attitude, counseled his sons about the great promises God had made to this branch of the house of Israel and blessed them in the name of the Lord, as a high priest of the living God, that they would not even see a single Indian on their campaign. These boys were very disappointed at this promise of the Lord. When they returned three months later, they reported, "'We . . . rode hundreds of miles following the tracks of different bands of hostile Indians, and were close upon them a great many times. They were attacking settlements all around us, killing the settlers and driving off stock.' But the company did not see a single Indian [so great was the power of their father's blessing]. (Orson F. Whitney, *Life of Heber C. Kimball, An Apostle*, 2nd ed., Salt Lake City: Stevens and Wallis, 1945, p.429)." (*Ensign,* May 1987, p.36) John Taylor declared that the elevating effects or fruits of the "gospel in its purity" are that "it shall make prophets of you. . . ." (Samuel W. Taylor and Raymond W. Taylor, *The John Taylor papers* 1:102) That is, men who are inspired give priesthood blessings of great power and inspiration.

Such blessings are a glorious, wonderful privilege. "We should treasure these promises up in our hearts [as given to us in these priesthood blessings]," declared George Q. Cannon, for "they are not idle words, nor idle promises." (*Collected Discourses* 2:76) He taught when we are given the promises of God, "depend upon it, my brethren and sisters. . . ." (Ibid.) For "when the man of God [seals something special upon us] . . . rest assured that will be fulfilled, if you live for it, and not one word will fail. Years may elapse; no matter how many; but if the soul who receives this promise is faithful, every word of it will be fulfilled, because God cannot break His promise." (Ibid.) Priesthood blessings that are truly inspired of heaven have the weight of eternity behind them—the power of the Godhead to assure their fulfillment.

Not only are these blessings eternally important, they also impact one's mortal life, for they are to edify us, make our "hearts glad" and to confer feelings of "joy," to cause us to "taste" of the sweetness, love, beauty and glory of heaven and "rejoice" and to feel the "power of the priesthood," or the testimony of Christ. Through such we are deeply strengthened and fortified. (B. H. Roberts, *Comprehensive History of the Church* 4:117, *Times and Seasons* 6:905, Elisa R. Snow, John Lyon, "Sacred to the Memory of John Smith, Patriarch" a poem) Such privileges are a priceless gift, never to be forgotten, if we are filled with the life giving glory of the Priesthood. That is, in the words of LeGrand Richards, "They [these blessings if they are as great as they could be] are to give us the [needed] inspiration that will enable us to make good here in mortality, that we will be worthy of the great call that came to us before the foundation of the world." ("Patriarchal Blessings," May 27, 1953, address at Brigham Young University, p.6)

Lorenzo Snow declared, "It is true that once in a great while there is a man who can break out from the common track of doing things [and be filled with the glory and power of God], and such a man will increase in influence, in the knowledge of God, and in the riches of eternity." (*Journal of Discourses* 5:66) We can grow and advance step by step in love with all that

God is and does. And it is more important than any other thing in life. And it is a matter of the heart, the affections of all our inward parts or inner being.

Brigham Young declared, "If I do not enjoy all I anticipated, if my happiness is not as complete as I anticipated, if the light of the Holy Spirit is not in my heart to that degree which I expected it would be . . . , the cause is in myself. . . . It is a mistaken idea to suppose that others can prevent me from enjoying the light of God in my [own] soul." In fact, "All hell cannot hinder me from enjoying Zion in my own heart, if my individual will yields obedience to the requirements and mandates of my heavenly Master." (*Journal of Discourses* 1:311) And if I do, "then what have you got? You have got heaven in your own bosoms, you have got Zion in your hearts, you have obtained all the glory, all the peace, all the joy, all the comfort, and all the light you anticipated. . . ." (Ibid.) This is the greatest of all wealth. No one could be richer. We must forge ahead valiantly whatever our circumstances "leaving others to do as they please, determined to do right, though all mankind besides should take the opposite course." (Ibid., p.312)

And as we were ordained to be great and remarkable men after the order of the Son of God, may we rise and shine and bless with the full glory and power of the ancient prophets. If we do, we will become the happiest people who ever lived on the earth. And Zion will flower, manifest exquisite beauty in her midst and become the glory of all the earth. It is worth it. It is important. And it is rewarding, beyond measure, for "My Spirit," saith the Lord, "shall fill your soul with joy" and consolation, and "the spirit giveth life" in thrilling abundance. (D&C 11:13 and 2 Corinthians 3:6) In fact, "there is no blessing ever offered to the ancients that is not ours to obtain" and enjoy, declared Elder Bruce R. McConkie. (*A New Witness for the Articles of Faith*, p.40)

But the sobering reality is, if we value other things more than the treasures of heaven, we will set our hearts on the wrong things. That is, whatever taps our deepest loyalties or engenders our greatest enthusiasm is literally the god we worship. If we truly worship the God of Israel, we will seek His gifts and graces with faith, energy and determination. We will literally adore the privilege and invitation of our everlasting commission to minister as inspired men and prophets in Israel. May we realize our good fortune and immerse ourselves in the things of God, for that is our highest destiny, that is, it is "[our greatest] work and [our] glory" to be messengers of the covenant and help "to bring to pass the immortality and eternal life of man." (Moses 1:39) (See Appendix A and B for how many times we are exhorted to pray always and continually for help to do this. That is, that we might grow in our love for God.)

PRAY ALWAYS

"...learn to fear the Lord thy God always." (Deuteronomy 14:23)

"Be ye mindful always of his covenant; the word which he commanded to a thousand generations. . . ." (1 Chronicles 16:15)

"And he spake a parable unto them to this end, that men ought always to pray, and not to faint. . . ." (Luke 18:1)

"Watch ye therefore, and pray always, that ye may be accounted worthy to escape. . . ." (Luke 21:36)

". . . pray always with all power and supplication in the spirit. . . ." (Ephesians 6:18)

"Rejoice in the Lord always: and again I say, Rejoice." (Philippians 4:4)

". . . ye must pray always, and faint not. . . ." (2 Nephi 32:9)

". . . always retain in remembrance, the greatness of God. . . . And behold, I say unto you that if ye do this ye shall always rejoice, and be filled with the love of God. . . ." (Mosiah 4:11-12)

". . . remember to retain the name [of the Son of God] written always in your hearts. . . ." (Mosiah 6:12)

". . . I would that ye should be steadfast and immoveable, always abounding in good works. . . ." (Mosiah 6:15)

". . . always returning thanks unto God. . . ." (Alma 7:23)

". . . having the love of God always in your hearts, that ye may be lifted up at the last day and enter into his rest." (Alma 13:29)

"And if ye do always remember me ye shall have my Spirit to be with you." (3 Nephi 18:7)

"And if ye shall always do these things blessed are ye, for ye are built upon my rock." (3 Nephi 18:12)

"Verily, verily, I say unto you, ye must watch and pray always, lest ye be tempted by the devil, and ye be led away captive by him." (3 Nephi 18:15)

"Therefore ye must always pray unto the Father in my name." (3 Nephi 18:19)

". . . and always remember him . . . that ye may always have his Spirit to be with them." (Moroni 4:3)

"Pray always, that you may come off conqueror; yea that ye may conquer Satan . . . and . . . the servants of Satan. . . ." (D&C 10:5)

"Pray always, and I will pour out my Spirit upon you, and great shall be your blessing—yea, even more than if you should obtain treasures of the earth and corruptibleness to the extent thereof." (D&C 19:38)

"Therefore, let the church take heed and pray always, lest they fall into temptation." (D&C 20:33)

"Pray always, lest you enter into temptation and lose your reward." (D&C 31:12)

"Wherefore, be faithful, praying always having your lamps trimmed and burning, and oil with you, that you may be ready at the coming of the Bridegroom." (D&C 33:17)

". . . seek earnestly the best gifts, always remembering for what they are given." (D&C 46:8)

"Pray always that you enter not into temptation, that you may abide the day of his coming. . . ." (D&C 61:39)

"Praying always that they faint not; and inasmuch as they do this, I will be with them. . . ." (D&C 75:11)

". . . in prayer always, vocally and in thy heart . . . proclaiming the gospel. . . ." (D&C 81:3)

"Pray always, that ye may not faint. . . ." (D&C 88:126)

"Search diligently, pray always, and be believing, and all things shall work together for your good. . . ." (D&C 90:24)

"What I say unto one I say unto all; pray always lest that wicked one have power in you, and remove you out of your place." (D&C 93:49)

". . . and pray always, or they shall be removed out of their place." (D&C 93:50)

"And seek the face of the Lord always, that in patience ye may possess your souls, and ye shall have eternal life." (D&C 101:38)

". . . for men ought always to pray and not to faint. . . ." (D&C 101:81)

PRAY CONTINUALLY

"Seek the Lord and his strength, seek his face continually." (1 Chronicles 16:11)

"Bind them continually upon thine heart. . . ." (Proverbs 6:21)

"Therefore turn thou to thy God . . . and wait on thy God continually." (Hosea 12:6)

"By him therefore let us offer the sacrifice of praise to God continually, that is, the fruit of our lips giving thanks to his name." (Hebrews 13:15)

". . .and they did press their way forward, continually holding fast to the rod of iron. . . ." (1 Nephi 8:30)

"Behold, my soul delighteth in the things of the Lord; and my heart pondereth continually upon the things which I have seen and heard." (2 Nephi 4:16)

". . .pray unto him continually by day, and give thanks. . . ." (2 Nephi 9:52)

"For I pray continually for them by day, and mine eyes water my pillow by night, because of them; and I cry unto my God in faith, and I know that he will hear my cry." (2 Nephi 33:3)

". . .the Spirit of the Lord Omnipotent, which has wrought a mighty change in us, or in our hearts, that we have no more disposition to do evil, but to do good continually." (Mosiah 5:2)

". . .watch and pray continually, that ye may not be tempted above that which ye can bear, and thus be led by the Holy Spirit, becoming humble, meek, submissive, patient, full of love and all long-suffering." (Alma 13:28)

". . .watching and praying continually, that they might be delivered from Satan, and from death, and from destruction." (Alma 15:17)

"Yea, he that repenteth and exerciseth faith, and bringing forth good works, and prayeth continually without ceasing—unto such it is given to know the mysteries of God. . . ." (Alma 26:22)

"Yea, and when you do not cry unto the Lord, let your hearts be full, drawn out in prayer unto him continually for your welfare, and also for the welfare of those who are around you." (Alma 34:39)

"Yea, and I also exhort you, my brethren, that ye be watchful unto prayer continually, that ye may not be led away by the temptation of the devil, that he may not overpower you, that ye may not become his subjects. . . ." (Alma 34:39)

". . .they do put their trust in God continually." (Alma 57:27)

". . .they do observe to keep his statutes, and his judgements, and his commandments continually; and their faith is strong. . . ." (Alma 58:40)

"And they did pray unto the Lord their God continually, insomuch that the Lord did bless them, according to his word. . . ." (Alma 62:51)

"Keep my commandments continually, and a crown of righteousness thou shalt receive. And except thou do this, where I am you cannot come." (D&C 25:5)

"And you must practice virtue and lowliness before me continually. Even so. Amen." (D&C 46:33)

". . .treasure up in your minds continually the words of life. . . ." (D&C 84:85)

AN AFFIRMATION FOR POSITIVE AFFECT

I am strong, confident and determined. I am beautiful and special inside. I adore people. I love life. Everything is interesting, enjoyable and fascinating. Every moment is precious and filled with gladness and delight. I look forward to all the adventures and opportunities in store for me. I learn from everything that I do. I will manifest the greatness and beauty within me by making healthy, intelligent and constructive choices in life. I love truth. I am honest, tender-hearted, loyal, loving and true. I am clean and sober and prayerful and straight-forward in all that I do. I look ahead, think ahead and plan ahead. I will make my future brighter and happier. I will show all the nobility and beauty of my real or true self and shine or be aglow with all the magnificent good within me. I'm getting better and better and better everyday.

If this feels good to you, and you are not suffering from a psychiatric or psychological disorder, merely read the above or other positive statements five times everyday to help reprogram yourself into being a more positive and optimistic person. To do any good it must be used in this way for several months, perhaps even for a full year. This is, of course, not to replace the treasuring of the beauty in deep and loving prayer. It is a suggestion only, providing a tool that has been useful to many.

BIBLIOGRAPHY

SCRIPTURES:

The Book of Mormon: Another Testament of Jesus Christ. Translated by Joseph Smith. Salt Lake City, Utah: The Church of Jesus Christ of Latter-day Saints, 1989.

The Doctrine and Covenants of the Church of Jesus Christ of Latter-day Saints. Salt Lake City, Utah: The Church of Jesus Christ of Latter-day Saints, 1989.

The Holy Bible containing the Old and New Testaments. Authorized King James Version. Salt Lake City, Utah: The Church of Jesus Christ of Latter-day Saints, 1989.

The Pearl of Great Price. Salt Lake City, Utah: The Church of Jesus Christ of Latter-day Saints, 1989.

BOOKS:

1980 Devotional Speeches of the Year. Provo, Utah: Brigham Young University Press, 1981.

1995-1996 Church Almanac. Salt Lake City, Utah: Deseret News, 1994.

Allen, James, *As A Man Thinketh*. (Lithographed by Publishers Press in Salt Lake City, Utah) Salt Lake City, Utah: Bookcraft, Inc.

A New Concordance of the Holy Bible, King James Version. New York, New York: American Bible Society, 1960.

Andrus, Hyrum, *Principles of Perfection*. Vol. 2. Salt Lake City, Utah: Bookcraft, Inc., 1970.

Babbel, Frederick W., *To Him That Believeth*. Salt Lake City, Utah: Bookcraft, Inc., 1982.

Bachman, Milton V., Jr., *The Heavens Resound: A History of the Latter-day Saints in Ohio 1830-1838*. Salt Lake City, Utah: Deseret Book Company, 1983.

Ballard, Melvin J., *Three Degrees of Glory,* a discourse printed as a pamphlet or booklet delivered in the Ogden Tabernacle September 22, 1922. Salt Lake City, Utah: Magazine Printing Company.

Barron, Howard H., *Orson Hyde: Missionary, Apostle, Colonizer.* Bountiful, Utah: Horizon Publishers, 1977.

Bates, Irene M. and E. Gary Smith, *Lost Legacy: The Mormon Office of Presiding Patriarch.* Urbana and Chicago, Illinois: University of Illinois, 1996.

Beecher, Maureen Ursenbach (comp.), *The Personal Writings of Eliza Roxey Snow.* Salt Lake City, Utah: University of Utah Press, 1995.

Bennett, Wallace F., *Why I Am A Mormon.* New York, New York: Thomas Nelson & Sons, 1958.

Bennion, Lowell L., *An Introduction to the Gospel.* Salt Lake City, Utah: Deseret Sunday School Union Board, 1955.

Bennion, Lowell L., *The Religion of the Latter-day Saints.* Salt Lake City, Utah: L.D.S. Department of Education, 1940.

Benson, Ezra Taft, *God, Family, Country: Our Three Great Loyalties.* Salt Lake City, Utah: Deseret Book Company, 1974.

Benson, Ezra Taft, *The Teachings of Ezra Taft Benson.* Salt Lake City, Utah: Bookcraft, Inc., 1988.

Bergera, Gary James (comp.), *The Autobiography of B. H. Roberts.* Salt Lake City, Utah: Signature Books, 1990.

Brooks, Juanita, *John Doyle Lee: Zealot—Pioneer Builder—Scapegoat.* Glendale, California: The Arthur H. Clark Company, 1973.

Burgess, Alan K. and Max H. Molgard, *Stories That Teach Gospel Principles.* Salt Lake City, Utah: Bookcraft, Inc., 1989.

Burton, Rulon T., *We Believe: Doctrines and Principles of the Church of Jesus Christ of Latter-day Saints.* Salt Lake City, Utah: Tabernacle Book, 1994.

Burton, Theodore M., *God's Greatest Gift.* Salt Lake City, Utah: Deseret Book Company, 1976.

Calhoun, Margie, *Stories of Insight and Inspiration.* Salt Lake City, Utah: Bountiful Press, 1993.

Calhoun, Margie, *When Faith Writes the Story.* Salt Lake City, Utah: Bountiful Press, 1993.

Cannon, Donald Q. and Lyndon W. Cook (comp.), *Far West Record: Minutes of The Church of Jesus Christ of Latter-day Saints, 1830-1844.* Salt Lake City, Utah: Deseret Book Company, 1983.

Cannon, George Q., *Gems For The Young Folks.* Salt Lake City, Utah: Juvenile Instructor Office, 1881.

Christensen, Joe J., *To Grow in Spirit: A ten-point plan for becoming more spiritual.* Salt Lake City, Utah: Deseret Book Company, 1983.

Christ's Ideals for Living. Salt Lake City, Utah: Deseret Sunday School Union Board, 1955.

Clark, James R. (comp.), *Messages of the First Presidency.* 5 vols. Salt Lake City, Utah: Bookcraft, Inc., 1965.

Collier, Fred C. (comp.), *The Teachings of President Brigham Young.* Vol. 3. Salt Lake City, Utah: Colliers Publishing Company, 1987.

Conference Report. Salt Lake City, Utah: The Church of Jesus Christ of Latter-day Saints. (talks given at Semi-annual General Conferences of the Church).

Cook, Lyndon W., *Revelations of the Prophet Joseph Smith.* Provo, Utah: Seventy's Book Store, 1981.

Cowley, Matthew, *Matthew Cowley Speaks.* Salt Lake City, Utah: Deseret Book Company, 1960.

Crowther, Duane S., *Gifts of the Spirit.* Salt Lake City, Utah: Bookcraft, Inc., 1965.

Dew, Sheri L., *Ezra Taft Benson: A Biography.* Salt Lake City, Utah: Deseret Book Company, 1987.

Dew, Sheri L., *Go Forward with Faith: The Biography of Gordon B. Hinckley.* Salt Lake City, Utah: Deseret Book Company, 1996.

Durham, G. Homer (comp.), *Evidences and Reconciliations. by John A. Widtsoe.* Salt Lake City, Utah: Bookcraft, Inc., 1970.

Durham, G. Homer (comp.), *Gospel Standards: Selected from the Sermons and Writings of Heber J. Grant.* Salt Lake City, Utah: Improvement Era Publication, Deseret News Press, 1941.

Durham, G. Homer, *N. Eldon Tanner: His Life and Service.* Salt Lake City, Utah: Deseret Book Company, 1982.

Durham, G. Homer (comp.), *The Discourses of Wilford Woodruff.* Salt Lake City, Utah: Bookcraft, Inc., 1946.

Durham, G. Homer (comp.), *The Gospel Kingdom: Selections from the Writings and Discourses of John Taylor.* Salt Lake City, Utah: Bookcraft, Inc., 1987.

Duties and Blessings of the Priesthood. 2 vols. (Part A and Part B). Salt Lake City, Utah: The Church of Jesus Christ of Latter-day Saints, 1984 and 1993.

Ehat, Andrew F. and Lydon W. Cook, *The Words of Joseph Smith.* Salt Lake City, Utah: Bookcraft, Inc., 1980.

Evans, Richard L., Jr., *Richard L. Evans—The Man and the Message.* Salt Lake City, Utah: Bookcraft, Inc., 1973.

Featherstone, Vaughn J., *Charity Never Faileth.* Salt Lake City, Utah: Deseret Book Company, 1980.

Featherstone, Vaughn J., *Do-It-Yourself Destiny.* Salt Lake City, Utah: Bookcraft, Inc., 1977.

Firmage, Edwin B. (comp.), *The Memoirs of Hugh B. Brown.* Salt Lake City, Utah: Signature Books, 1988.

Fish, Errol R., *Promptings of the Spirit.* Mesa, Arizona: Cogent Publishing, 1990.

Gibbons, Francis M., *Heber J. Grant: Man of Steel, Prophet of God.* Salt Lake City, Utah: Deseret Book Company, 1979.

Goates, L. Brent, *Harold B. Lee: Prophet and Seer.* Salt Lake City, Utah: Bookcraft, Inc., 1985.

Goates, L. Brent, *He Changed My Life:* Personal Experiences of Harold B. Lee. Salt Lake City, Utah: Bookcraft, Inc., 1988.

Green, Forace (comp.), *Cowley & Whitney on Doctrine.* Salt Lake City, Utah: Bookcraft, Inc., 1963.

Groberg, John H., *In the Eye of the Storm.* Salt Lake City, Utah: Bookcraft, Inc., 1993.

Hartshorn, Leon R., *Classic Stories from the Lives of our Prophets.* Salt Lake City, Utah: Deseret Book Company, 1971.

Hartshorn, Leon R., *Outstanding Stories by General Authorities.* Salt Lake City, Utah: Deseret Book Company, 1970.

Hatch, Orrin G., *Higher Laws: Understanding the Doctrines of Christ.* Salt Lake City, Utah: Deseret Book Company, 1995.

Heinerman, Joseph, *Manifestations of Faith.* Magazine Printing and Publishing, 1979.

Heslop, J. M. and Dell R. Van Order, *Joseph Fielding Smith—A Prophet Among the People.* Salt Lake City, Utah: Deseret Book Company, 1971.

Hinckley, Bryant S., *The Faith of Our Pioneer Fathers.* Salt Lake City, Utah: Deseret Book Company, 1959.

Jessee, Dean C. (comp.), *The Papers of Joseph Smith.* 2 vols. Salt Lake City, Utah: Deseret Book Company, 1992.

Journal of Discourses. 26 vols. Los Angeles, California: General Printing and Lithograph Company, 1961. (photo lithographic reprint of originals: Liverpool, England: F. D. Richards and Sons, 1855-1886.)

Kimball, Edward L. (comp.), *Teachings of Spencer W. Kimball.* Salt Lake City, Utah: Bookcraft, Inc., 1982.

Kimball, Spencer W., *Faith Precedes the Miracle.* Salt Lake City, Utah: Deseret Book Company, 1979.

Kimball, Spencer W., *The Miracle of Forgiveness.* Salt Lake City, Utah: Bookcraft, Inc., 1969.

Kimball, Solomon F., *Life of David P. Kimball and Other Sketches*. Salt Lake City, Deseret News Press, 1918.

Knowles, Eleanor, *Teachings of Howard W. Hunter*. Salt Lake City, Utah: Deseret Book Company, 1994.

Kraut, Ogden, *The Gift of Tongues*. Salt Lake City, Utah: Ogden Kraut.

Larsen, Stan (comp.), *A Ministry of Meetings: The Apostolic Diaries of Rudger Clawson*. Salt Lake City, Utah: Signature Books, 1993.

Lee, Harold B., *Stand Ye in Holy Places*. Salt Lake City, Utah: Deseret Book Company, 1976.

Ludlow, Daniel H., *A Companion to Your Study of the Doctrine and Covenants*. Salt Lake City, Utah: Bookcraft, Inc., 1978.

Ludlow, Daniel H. (comp.), *Encyclopedia of Mormonism*. 4 vols. New York, New York: Macmillan Publishing Company, 1992.

Ludlow, Victor L., *Principles and Practices of the Restored Gospel*. Salt Lake City, Utah: Deseret Book Company, 1992.

Lund, Gerald N., *The Coming of the Lord*. Salt Lake City, Utah: Bookcraft, Inc., 1971.

Lundwall, Nels Benjamin (comp.), *Discourses on the Holy Ghost*. Salt Lake City, Utah: Bookcraft, Inc., 1959.

Lundwall, Nels Benjamin, *Temples of the Most High God*. Salt Lake City, Utah: Bookcraft, Inc., 1968.

Madsen, Truman G., *Joseph Smith, the Prophet*. Salt Lake City, Utah: Bookcraft, Inc., 1989.

Marston, Keith, *Missionary Pal: Reference Guide for Missionaries & Teachers*. 1968 ed. Salt Lake City, Utah: Publishers Press, 1959.

Matthews, Robert J. (contributor), *Thy People Shall Be My People and Thy God My God: the 1993 Sperry Symposium on the Old Testament*. Salt Lake City, Utah: Deseret Book Company, 1994.

Maxwell, Neal A., *Even As I Am*. Salt Lake City, Utah: Deseret Book Company, 1982.

Maxwell, Neal A., *Wherefore, Ye Must Press Forward.* Salt Lake City, Utah: Deseret Book Company, 1977.

McConkie, Bruce R., *A New Witness for the Articles of Faith.* Salt Lake City, Utah: Deseret Book Company, 1985.

McConkie, Bruce R., *Doctrinal New Testament Commentary.* 3 vols. Salt Lake City, Utah: Bookcraft, Inc., 1973.

McConkie, Bruce R. (comp.), *Doctrines of Salvation: Sermons and Writings of Joseph Fielding Smith.* 3 vols. Salt Lake City, Utah: Bookcraft, Inc., 1972.

McConkie, Bruce R., *Mormon Doctrine.* 2nd ed. Salt Lake City, Utah: Bookcraft, Inc., 1975.

McConkie, Bruce R., "Only An Elder," (talk given at a Regional Rep. Seminar on October 3, 1974 printed as a pamphlet). Salt Lake City, Utah: The Church of Jesus Christ of Latter-day Saints, 1981.

McConkie, Bruce R., *The Millennial Messiah.* Salt Lake City, Utah: Deseret Book Company, 1982.

McConkie, Bruce R., *The Mortal Messiah.* 3 vols. Salt Lake City, Utah: Deseret Book Company, 1980.

McConkie, Bruce R., *The Promised Messiah.* Salt Lake City, Utah: Deseret Book Company, 1978.

McConkie, Joseph Fielding, *Prophet & Prophesy.* Salt Lake City, Utah: Bookcraft, Inc., 1988.

McConkie, Joseph Fielding, *The Spirit of Revelation.* Salt Lake City, Utah: Deseret Book Company, 1984.

McConkie, Joseph Fielding and Robert L. Millet, *The Holy Ghost.* Salt Lake City, Utah: Bookcraft, Inc., 1989.

McConkie, Mark L., *Doctrines of the Restoration.* Salt Lake City, Utah: Bookcraft, Inc., 1989.

McConkie, Mark L., *The Father of the Prophet.* Salt Lake City, Utah: Bookcraft, Inc., 1993.

McKay, David O., *True to the Faith.* Salt Lake City, Utah: Bookcraft, Inc., 1966.

Millennial Star. Numerous vols. Manchester and Liverpool, England: The Church of Jesus Christ of Latter-day Saints, 1840-1970.

Millet, Robert L. and Joseph Fielding McConkie, *Our Destiny: The Call and Election of the House of Israel.* Salt Lake City, Utah: Deseret Book Company, 1982.

Millet, Robert L., *When a Child Wanders.* Salt Lake City, Utah: Deseret Book Company, 1996.

Monson, Thomas S., *Live the Good Life.* Salt Lake City, Utah: Deseret Book Company, 1988.

Newquist, Jerreld L. (comp.), *Gospel Truth: Discourses and Writings of George Q. Cannon.* Salt Lake City, Utah: Deseret Book Company, 1987.

New Webster's Dictionary and Thesaurus of the English Language. Danbury, Connecticut: Lexicon Publications, Inc., 1992.

Nixon, Loretta D. and L. Douglas Smoot, *Abraham Owen Smoot: A Testament of His Life.* Provo, Utah: Brigham Young University Press, 1994.

Oaks, Dallin H., *The Lord's Way.* Salt Lake City, Utah: Deseret Book Company, 1991.

On Earth and In Heaven: A Course of Study for the Melchizedek Priesthood Quorums of the Church of Jesus Christ of Latter-day Saints. Salt Lake City, Utah: Deseret News Press, 1966.

Pace, Glenn L., *Spiritual Plateaus.* Salt Lake City, Utah: Deseret Book Company, 1991.

Packer, Boyd K., *That All May Be Edified.* Salt Lake City, Utah: Bookcraft, Inc., 1982.

Peterson, Mark E., *Children of Promise: The Lamanites: Yesterday and Today.* Salt Lake City, Utah: Bookcraft, Inc., 1981.

Peterson, Mark E., *Joseph of Egypt.* Salt Lake City, Utah: Deseret Book Company, 1981.

Pratt, Orson, *Orson Pratt's Works*. Salt Lake City, Utah: Deseret News Press, 1945.

Pratt, Parley P., Jr., *Autobiography of Parley P. Pratt*. Salt Lake City, Utah: Deseret Book Company, 1938, 1985.

Prince, Gregory A., *Power From On High: The Development of Mormon Priesthood*. Salt Lake City, Utah: Signature Books, 1995.

Rector, Hartman and Connie, *No More Strangers*. Vol. 3. Salt Lake City, Utah: Bookcraft, Inc., 1976.

Rich, Ben E., *Scrapbooks of Mormon Literature: Religious Tracts*. 2 vols. Chicago, Illinois: Press of Henry C. Etten & Co.

Richards, G. LaMont (comp.), *LeGrand Richards Speaks*. Salt Lake City, Utah: Deseret Book Company, 1972.

Richards, LeGrand, *Just to Illustrate*. Salt Lake City, Utah: Bookcraft, Inc., 1961.

Roberts, Brigham H., *Comprehensive History of the Church of Jesus Christ of Latter-day Saints*. 6 vols. Provo, Utah: Brigham Young University Press, 1975.

Roberts, Brigham H., *New Witness for God. Vol. 2*. Salt Lake City, Utah: Deseret Book Company, 1926.

Roberts, Brigham H., *Outlines of Ecclesiastical History. 6th ed.* Salt Lake City, Utah: The Church of Jesus Christ of Latter-day Saints, 1950.

Roberts, Brigham H., *The Seventy's Course in Theology*. First Year, Salt Lake City, Utah: Deseret Book Company, 1931.

Rodale, J. I., *The Synonym Finder*. Emmaus, Pennsylvania: Rodale Press, Inc., 1978.

Roget's International Thesaurus. 3rd ed. New York, New York: Thomas Y. Crowell, 1962.

Romney, Thomas C., *World Religions in the Light of Mormonism*. Independence, Missouri: Zion's Printing and Publishing Company, 1946.

Shapiro, R. Gary, *An Exhaustive Concordance of the Book of Mormon, Doctrine and Covenants and Pearl of Great Price.* Salt Lake City, Utah: Hawkes Publishing, Inc., 1977.

Sill, Sterling W., *The Nine Lives of Sterling W. Sill: An Autobiography.* Bountiful, Utah: Horizon Publishers and Distributors, 1979.

Skousen, Max B, *How to Pray and Stay Awake.* Salt Lake City, Utah: Bookcraft, Inc., Max B. Skousen, 1949.

Snow, Eliza R., *Bibliography and Family Record of Lorenzo Snow.* Salt Lake City, Utah: Deseret News Company, 1884.

Sonne, Conway B., *A Man Named Alma: The World of Alma Sonne.* Bountiful, Utah: Horizon Publishers, 1988.

Smith, Henry A., *Matthew Cowley, Man of Faith.* Salt Lake City, Utah: Bookcraft, Inc., 1984.

Smith, Hyrum M. and Janne M. Sjodahl, *Doctrine and Covenants Commentary.* Salt Lake City, Deseret Book Company, 1968.

Smith, Joseph (comp.), *Lectures on Faith.* (Delivered in 1835 in Kirtland, Ohio) Salt Lake City, Utah: Deseret Book Company, 1985.

Smith, Joseph F., *Gospel Doctrine.* 5th ed. Salt Lake City, Utah: Deseret Book Company, 1939.

Smith, Joseph Fielding, *Answers to Gospel Questions.* 3 vols. Salt Lake City, Utah: Deseret Book Company, 1966.

Smith, Joseph Fielding, *Church History and Modern Revelation, Being a Course of Study for the Melchizedek Priesthood Quorums for the Years 1947-1950.* 2 vols. Salt Lake City, Utah: The Council of the Twelve Apostles of The Church of Jesus Christ of Latter-day Saints, 1946-1950.

Smith, Joseph Fielding (comp.), *Teachings of the Prophet Joseph Smith.* Salt Lake City, Utah: Deseret Book Company, 1965.

Smith, Joseph Fielding, *The Restoration of All Things.* Salt Lake City, Utah: Deseret Book Company, 1944.

Smith, Joseph Fielding, *The Way to Perfection*. Salt Lake City, Utah: Genealogical Society of The Church of Jesus Christ of Latter-day Saints, 1953.

Smith, Joseph, Jr., *History of the Church of Jesus Christ of Latter-day Saints,* ed. B. H. Roberts. 7 vols. Salt Lake City, Utah: Deseret Book Company, 1974.

Smith, Lucy Mack, *History of Joseph Smith by His Mother,* Preston Nibley (comp.), Salt Lake City, Utah: Bookcraft, Inc., 1958.

Staker, Susan, *Waiting for the World's End: The Diaries of Wilford Woodruff.* Salt Lake City, Utah: Signature Books, 1993.

Stuy, Brian H. (comp.), *Collected Discourses.* 5 vols. Burbank, California: B. H. S. Publishing, 1991.

Talmage, James E., *Jesus the Christ: A Study of the Messiah according to Holy Scriptures both Ancient and Modern.* Salt Lake City, Utah: Deseret Book Company, 1915, 1990.

Talmage, James E., *The Articles of Faith.* Salt Lake City, Utah: The Church of Jesus Christ of Latter-day Saints, 1987.

Tate, Lucile C., *Boyd K. Packer: A Watchman on the Tower.* Salt Lake City, Utah: Bookcraft, Inc., 1995.

Tate, Lucile C., *David B. Haight: The Life Story of A Disciple.* Salt Lake City, Utah: Bookcraft, Inc., 1987.

Tate, Lucile C., *LeGrand Richards, Beloved Apostle.* Salt Lake City, Utah: Bookcraft, Inc., 1982.

Taylor, John, *Mediation and Atonement.* Salt Lake City, Utah: Deseret News Company, 1964.

Taylor, Samuel W. and Raymond W. Taylor (comp.), *The John Taylor papers.* 2 vols. Redwood City, California: Taylor Trust Publishers, 1985.

The American Heritage College Dictionary. Boston, Massachusetts: Houghton Mifflin Company, 1993.

The Evening and the Morning Star. 2 vols. Kirtland, Ohio and Independence, Missouri: The Church of Jesus Christ of Latter-day Saints, 1832-1836.

The LDS Speaker's Source Book. Salt Lake City, Utah: Aspen Books, 1991.

The Priesthood and You: A Course of Study for the Melchizedek Priesthood of The Church of Jesus Christ of Latter-day Saints. Salt Lake City, Utah: The First Presidency, 1966.

Times and Seasons. 5 vols. Salt Lake City, Utah: Modern Microfilm Company (Photo mechanical Reprint of Original Edition), 1839-1846.

Von Harrison, Grant, *Drawing on the Powers of Heaven.* Provo, Utah: The Ensign Publishing Company, 1979.

Ward, John L., *Is There a Patriarch in the Home?.* Bountiful, Utah: Horizon Publishers, 1984.

Webster's Ninth New Collegiate Dictionary. Springfield, Massachusetts: Merriam-Webster Inc., 1988.

Wells, Robert E., *We Are Christians Because. . . .* Salt Lake City, Utah: Deseret Book Company, 1985.

White, Arnold Dee, *J. Golden Kimball's Golden Moments.* Orem, Utah: Cedar Fort, Inc., 1994.

Whitney, Orson F., *Gospel Themes.* Salt Lake City, Utah: The Church of Jesus Christ of Latter-day Saints, 1914.

Widtsoe, John A., *Discourses of Brigham Young.* Salt Lake City, Utah: Deseret Book Company, 1978.

Widtsoe, John A., *Priesthood and Church Government.* Salt Lake City, Utah: Deseret Book Company, 1939.

Williams, Clyde J. (comp.), *The Teachings of Harold B. Lee.* Salt Lake City, Utah: Bookcraft, Inc., 1996.

Williams, Clyde J. (comp.), *The Teachings of Howard W. Hunter.* Salt Lake City, Utah: Bookcraft, Inc., 1997.

Yorgason, Blaine and Brenton, *Spiritual Survival in the Last Days.* Salt Lake City, Utah: Deseret Book Company, 1990.

PERIODICALS:

"A Blessing from President Kimball," *Ensign* (February 1977), pp.4-6.

"Anglo-American Miracle," *The Plain Truth* (October/November 1970), pp.3-8.

Asay, Carlos E., "Write Your Own Blessing," *The New Era* (October 1981), pp.4-6.

Baker, Harry E., "What Can a High Priest Do?," *The Improvement Era* (September 1910), pp.1031-1035.

Ballard, Melvin R., "A Promise and Its Fulfillment," *The Instructor* (November 1965), pp.458-460.

"Being Patriarch is a Humbling Call," *Church News* (November 30, 1974), pp.10, 12.

Benson, Ezra Taft, "The American Challenge," *Speeches of the Year*. Brigham Young University (April 21, 1970), pp.1-10.

Benson, Ezra Taft, "Seek the Spirit of the Lord," *Ensign* (April 1988), pp.2-5.

Benson, Ezra Taft, "Your Charge to Increase in Wisdom and Favor with God and Man," *The New Era* (September 1979), pp.40-45.

Buehner, Carl W., "Blessings We Receive Through Membership in the Church," *Speeches of the Year*. Brigham Young University (October 19, 1960), pp.1-8.

Cannon, George Q., "Topics of the Times," *Juvenile Instructor* (October 15, 1891), pp.620-623.

Cullimore, James A., "Gifts of the Spirit," *Ensign* (November 1974), pp.27-28.

Curtis, Lindsay R., "Healing: Call The Elders or The Doctor?," *Church News* (March 25, 1967), p.7.

Deseret News Weekly (December 27, 1851) Vol.2, No. 4, p.14.

Dunn, Paul H., "By Faith and Hope, All Things are Fulfilled," *Ensign* (May 1987), pp.73-75.

"Fall of infamous wall means modern miracle for this German family," written by Gerry Avant, *Church News* (October 17, 1992), pp.6, 10.

Faust, James E., "Gratitude As a Saving Principle," *Ensign* (May 1990), pp.85-87.

Faust, James E., "Priesthood Blessings," *Ensign* (November 1995), pp.62-64.

Featherstone, Vaughn J., "A Self-Inflicted Purging," *Ensign* (May 1975), pp.66-68.

Foy, Connie LaVall, "How Could He Have Known?," *Ensign* (October 1991), p.27.

Goaslind, Jack H., "Look to the Future with Optimism," *Ensign* (April 1997), pp.22-27.

"Good News for the Average Man," *The Plain Truth* (May 1980), pp.39, 45.

Gourdin, Leon W., "Woman Healed Through Faith, Prayer, Power of Priesthood," *The Improvement Era* (July 1966), p.646.

Hales, Robert D., "Blessings of the Priesthood," *Ensign* (November 1995), pp.32-34.

Hansen, Ron, "Terminate the Pregnancy!," *Ensign* (February 1988), pp.56-57.

Heslop, J. M., "Stake Patriarch, 92, Loves Church Job Over Any Other Duty," *Church News* (March 16, 1974), p.13.

Hillman, Robert K., "I Know It Wasn't Luck," *Ensign* (September 1995), pp.62-63.

Hinckley, Gordon B., "Excerpts from Recent Addresses of President Gordon B. Hinckley," *Ensign* (October 1996), p.73.

Ireland, Jackie, "Is There Any Reason You Can't Come to Church," *Ensign* (July 1992), p.22.

Ivins, Antoine R., "Blessings are Predicated," *The Improvement Era* (December 1961), pp.936-937.

Jeppsen, Malcome S., "A Divine Prescription for Spiritual Healing," *Ensign* (May 1994), pp.17-19.

Kimball, Spencer W., "Pray Always," *Ensign* (October 1981), pp.3-6.

Kimball, Spencer W., "Pres. Kimball: Convert World," David Croft, comp., *Church News* (March 22, 1975), p.5.

Kimball, Spencer W., "President Kimball Speaks Out On Administrations to the Sick," *The New Era* (October 1981), pp.45-50.

Kimball, Spencer W., "The Example of Abraham," *Ensign* (June 1975), pp.3-7.

Kimball, Spencer W., "The False Gods We Worship," *Ensign* (June 1976), pp.3-6.

Kimball, Spencer W., "The Foundations of Righteousness," *Ensign* (November 1977), pp.4-6.

Lee, Harold B., "Divine Revelation," *Speeches of the Year*. Brigham Young University (October 15, 1952), pp.179-183.

Lee, Harold B., "How to Receive a Blessing from God," *The Improvement Era* (October 1966), pp.862-863, 896-898.

Lee, Harold B., "To the Defenders of the Faith," *The Improvement Era* (June 1970), pp.63-65.

Lee, Harold B., "Understanding Who We Are Brings Self-Respect," *Ensign* (January 1974), pp.2-6.

Llewwllyn, Ian, "Fear and a Priesthood Blessing," *Ensign* (September 1990), p.54.

Ludlow, Daniel H., "Of the House of Israel," *Ensign* (January 1991), pp.51-55.

Lundberg, Joy Saunders, "The Priesthood: God's Gift of Love," *Ensign* (February 1993), 15-19.

"Man Who Knew: firm gospel witness," *Church News* (September 9, 1984), p.6.

Mason, James O., "As a Doctor, I Doubted," *Ensign* (August 1977), p.58.

McConkie, Bruce R., "Think on These Things," *Ensign* (January 1974), p.45-48.

McKay, David O., "The True End of Life," *The Instructor* (January 1964), pp.1-2.

Melchin, Gerald E., "Thy Sins Are Forgiven," *Ensign* (January 1995), pp.19-21.

Merrill, Joseph F., as quoted in "Prophet receives revelation for Church," *Church News* (February 20, 1993), p.14.

Monson, Thomas S., "Preparation Precedes Performance," *Ensign* (September 1993), pp.70-73.

Monson, Thomas S., "Your Patriarchal Blessing: A Liahona of Light," *Ensign* (November 1986), pp.65-67.

Mowbray, John, "Credo," *Scouting* (October 1979), pp.41-42,81.

"No Hands, No Eyes—But No 'Handicaps,'" *Ensign* (July 1979), p.13.

"No Room for Doubt," *Ensign* (February 1981), p.57.

Oaks, Dallin H., "Priesthood Blessings," *Ensign* (May 1987), pp.36-39.

Packer, Boyd K., "Personal Revelation: The Gift, The Test, and The Promise," *Ensign* (November 1994), pp.59-62.

Packer, Boyd K., "Prayers and Answers," *Ensign* (November 1979), pp.19-21.

Packer, Boyd K., "The Candle of the Lord," *Ensign* (January 1983), pp.51-56.

Packham, Lynn, "Testimony from a nonexperience," *Ensign* (August 1974), pp.65-66.

Parberry, Janet Gundersen, "One Sunday Afternoon," *Ensign* (January 1982), p.65.

Peterson, H. Burke, "Adversity and Prayer," *Ensign* (January 1974), pp.18-19.

Porter, L. Aldin, "The Spirit of Prophecy," *Ensign* (November 1996), pp.9-11.

Principe, Louis, "Your Son Has a Brain Tumor," *Ensign* (July 1990), p.61.

"Questions and Answers," *The New Era* (March 1992), pp.17-19.

"Report of the 165th Annual General Conference of The Church of Jesus Christ of Latter-day Saints," *Ensign* (May 1995), p.1.

Richards, LeGrand, "Patriarchal Blessings," *Miscellaneous Speeches*. Brigham Young University (May 27, 1953), pp.1-10.

Richards, LeGrand, "Patriarchal Blessings," *The New Era* (February 1977), pp.4-7.

Ricks, Kellene, "A rich life among a people he loves," *Church News* (July 14, 1990), p.4.

Riddle, Chauncey C., "What A Privilege To Believe," *Sunstone* (May 1988), pp.8-11.

Romney, Marion G., "Q and A," *The New Era* (October 1975), pp.34-35.

Rose, Rebecca, "My Miracle," *The New Era* (June 1995), p.54.

Russell, Mart, "In the Days of Boats and Trains," *The New Era* (August 1973), pp.47-49.

Scott, Richard G., "Obtaining Help from the Lord," *Ensign* (November 1990), pp.84-86.

Sill, Sterling W., "We Believe in God," *The Improvement Era* (February 1955), pp.438,440.

Smart, William B., "Lorenzo Snow: Mighty Man of God," *The Instructor* (June 1967), pp.220-222.

Smith, Eldred G., "Calling of Patriarch is To Bless Fellowman," *Church News* (May 29, 1976), p.6.

Smith, Eldred G., "What Is a Patriarchal Blessing," *The Instructor* (February 1962), pp.42-43.

Smith, Joseph Fielding, "Latter-day Prophets Receive Revelation," *The Instructor* (November 1963), pp.382-383.

Smith, Joseph Fielding, "The Twelve Apostles," *The Improvement Era* (April 1935), pp.208-212.

Smith, Joseph Fielding, "We Are Here to Be Tried, Tested, Proved," *Speeches of the Year*. Brigham Young University (October 25, 1961), pp.1-5.

Sonne, Alma, "The Power of Little Things," *Speeches of the Year*. Brigham Young University (October 27, 1964), pp.1-6.

"Speaking for Himself—President Lee's Stories," *Ensign* (February 1974), pp.15-21.

Talmage, James E., "The Honor and Dignity of Priesthood," *The Improvement Era* (March 1914), pp.407-411.

"We couldn't bear to lose the little boy," *Church News* (July 21, 1990), p.10.

Williams, Fenton L., Sr., "The Spirit's Voice," *Ensign* (February 1974), pp.27-28.

Wirthlin, Joseph B., "Let Your Light So Shine," *Ensign* (November 1978), pp.36-37.

RECORDINGS:

Christensen, Bernell, "After the Trial of Your Faith," Covenant Communications, Inc., 1989.

Dunn, Paul H., "Seek and Ye Shall Find," Covenant Recordings, Inc., 1985.

UNPUBLISHED:

Bates, Irene M., "Transformation of Charisma in the Mormon Church: A History of the Office of Presiding Patriarch, 1833-1979," a dissertation for the University of California, Los Angeles, 1991.

"Digest of the Minutes of a Meeting of Patriarchs with General Authorities," Salt Lake City, Utah: Salt Lake City, Utah: The Church of Jesus Christ of Latter-day Saints, Church Historian's Office (October 11, 1958, photocopy in possession of author), pp.1-8.

Extra—a Utah Salt Lake City South Mission monthly notice. Vol. 1, No. 28, (February 27, 1987) V. Dallas Merrell, president at the time (photocopy in possession of author)

Gonzalez, F. S., "The Patriarchal Order of the Priesthood," (photocopy in possession of author), pp.1-8.

"Handbook for Stake Patriarchs," Salt Lake City, Utah: The Church of Jesus Christ of Latter-day Saints, Church Historian's Office (photocopy in possession of author), pp.1-12.

Journal History of the Church of Jesus Christ of Latter-day Saints, Salt Lake City, Utah: The Church of Jesus Christ of Latter-day Saints, Church Historian's Office.

Lee, Harold B., "From the Valley of Despair to the Mountain Peaks of Hope," (Memorial Services Address delivered May 30, 1971 as quoted in *LDS Collectors Library '97*, Infobases, Inc., 1996.

Lee, Jennie May Woodbury, "Patriarch Charles R. Woodbury," Provo, Utah: Brigham Young University Archives.

McConkie, Bruce R., "Personal Revelation," address given to Salt Lake Institute of Religion (January 22, 1971)

Patriarchal Blessing of Joseph F. Smith given by John Smith on June 25, 1852, Provo, Utah: Brigham Young University Archives (photocopy in possession of author), pp.1-2.

Rich, Sarah DeArmon Pea, "Journal of Sarah DeArmon Pea Rich," Provo, Utah: Brigham Young University Archives.

Smith, Eldred G., An address given at Brigham Young University (November 8, 1966, photocopy in possession of author), pp.1-12.

Smith, Eldred G., "Patriarchal Blessings," Salt Lake City, Utah: The Church of Jesus Christ of Latter-day Saints, Church Historian's Office (talk given on January 17, 1963, photocopy in possession of author), pp.1-8.

Smith, Joseph Fielding, "Address of President Joseph Fielding Smith," address given at Brigham Young University (June 15, 1956), pp.1-8.

Young, Emily Dow Partridge, "Diary of Emily Dow Partridge Young," Provo, Utah: Brigham Young University Archives.

NAME AND AUTHOR INDEX

SUBJECT INDEX

ABOUT THE AUTHOR

Donald Edward Goff, Ph.D. was raised in Park Ridge, Illinois. He was converted and joined the Church at the age of sixteen. He served a mission in Michigan and Indiana from 1968 to 1970. He graduated from Brigham Young University with a Bachelor of Science degree; received a Master of Arts degree from the University of Illinois (Springfield) and more recently a Doctor of Philosophy degree in psychology from the Union Institute in Cincinnati, Ohio. He greatly values the office of High Priest, however, far above any of these educational accomplishments. Careerwise, he received honors as a District Scout Executive for the Boy Scouts of America, as a United States Naval Officer and as an administrator of Mental Health. Wanting to be a practitioner, Dr. Goff, now counsels troubled youth in an adolescent hospital. He has held numerous Church positions including that of High Councilor, and wrote the book *Priests of the Most High God* on the office of High Priest. He is married to the former Susan Joan Brown and has five children. He considers his Temple marriage to be the greatest thing that has ever happened to him in his life.